THE
FIGHT
ABROAD AND THE
FEAR BACK HOME

THE
FIGHT
ABROAD AND THE
FEAR BACK HOME

ITALIANS OF THE CALIFORNIA COAST DURING WORLD WAR II

J. MICHAEL NIOTTA, PH.D.

AMERICA
THROUGH TIME®
ADDING COLOR TO AMERICAN HISTORY

For Anthony and Dick, and in memory of
Stevie, Frankie, Anna, Lucy, Toni, Phyllis, George,
and all the others who played such an important part.

America Through Time is an imprint of Fonthill Media LLC
www.through-time.com
office@through-time.com

Published by Arcadia Publishing by arrangement with Fonthill Media LLC
For all general information, please contact Arcadia Publishing:
Telephone: 843-853-2070
Fax: 843-853-0044
E-mail: sales@arcadiapublishing.com
For customer service and orders:
Toll-Free 1-888-313-2665

www.arcadiapublishing.com

First published 2019

Copyright © J. Michael Niotta, Ph.D. 2019

ISBN 978-1-63499-187-2

Typeset in 10pt on 13pt Sabon
Printed and bound in England

Foreword

Roughly a quarter of Italy's population left home before the start of World War I. Seeking opportunity, many of these individuals made the long voyage to America. When the United States entered World War II, well over a million of them had naturalized, but another 600,000 never completed the process. Aside for the ability to vote and to serve on a jury, the Constitution afforded these resident aliens the same rights as citizens. By the start of the war, Italians made up the largest ethnic group residing in America, and after the U.S. military joined the fight, Italians represented the largest ethnic group to serve, offering a force of some 500,000 strong. Figures showed that every division in the U.S. Army contained about 500 soldiers who could trace their heritage back to Italy. These men served bravely at sea, in air, on land, and on the home front as well.

Although Italy was an Axis Power, America's Italians were clearly helping Uncle Sam win the war. They had so many young men serving that in just one California town alone, "the government saluted nine Italian mothers, each of whom had four sons in the U.S. armed forces." Not surprisingly, seven of those nine proud women never naturalized. Unfortunately, the new travel restrictions impacting Italians, Germans, and Japanese forbade these mothers from visiting their boys before they shipped out to war.

Somehow, the contribution of half a million sons and fathers was not enough of a sacrifice to prove the allegiance of America's Italians. So, while sailors, soldiers, and airmen of Italian descent served abroad, many of their family members and friends stateside faced great injustices. Presidential and military directives, proclamations, and executive orders turned mothers, fathers, sisters, aunts, cousins, and grandparents into the enemy. President Franklin D. Roosevelt's orders, carried out by J. Edgar Hoover's Federal Bureau of Investigation (F.B.I.), the Department of Justice (D.O.J.), the U.S. Army, and various other governmental agencies, brought on random home searches, property seizure, curfew and travel restrictions, suppression of native language and customs, forced relocation, and even suicide and internment.

Not long after the attack on Pearl Harbor, what can only be described as martial law swept over the nation, giving all Italian, German, and Japanese resident aliens a new name. They were now known as "enemy aliens." This is the story of honorable men who served their country bravely—on land, in air, and at sea. But so much more than just the fight abroad is conveyed. This is also the story of the fear back home, and the treatment of Italians living along the California coast. The secrets, the shame, and the injustices can no longer remain hidden.

Acknowledgments

I would like to acknowledge everyone who contributed to the completion of this project, and extend respect to those who have served and to those who continue to do so. I completed the final edits for this book while deployed to an undisclosed overseas location. My appreciation to those who agreed to be interviewed—Anthony J. Amador, Richard "Dick" Williams, Frannie Niotta-LaRussa, Jack Niotta, Sr., John and Barbara Guarnieri, Jeanne and George Niotta (R.I.P.), Nickie Bushor, Florence Poli-Quinn, Tony Poli, Bill Grinnell, Christine Campagna-Ziemantz, MSgt Steven Sandoval, Anna Dragna-Niotta (R.I.P.), and Frank Paul Dragna (R.I.P.). You made this story what it is. Many thanks to Jay Slater, Alan Sutton, Kena Longabaugh, Jamie Hardwick, and the rest of the staff at Fonthill Media; and thanks to the Galardo, Amador, Guarnieri, LaRussa, Poli, Rizzotto, Bovi, Campagna, Cacioppo, and Niotta families, along with all their wonderful extensions—we just keep growing!

I would also like to mention Jenessa Warren and Laurie Williams-Warren, Catlin Meininger, Mike Rizzotto, Jason Vanantwerp, Tina Schneider, Frankie Cascioppo, the staff at Lestat's Coffee on Adams, the 147th Combat Communications Squadron, Meyer Lansky II, Nolan Apostle, Larry Henry, Christian W. Cipollini, Richard N. Warner, Warren R. Hull, plus Casey McBride, Craig Timmins, and the rest of the folks at National Crime Syndicate. Immense gratitude to whoever invented the TapeACall app, and, lastly, an extra special credit goes out to my wife, Jessy, and son, Dylan, for putting up with my madness and for all the moments of family time robbed by research and writing.

Author's Note

It is important to note that highlighting the hardships suffered by Italian and German citizens living in the United States during World War II, and comparing their treatment to that of the Japanese, does not—in any way—belittle or take away from the struggle that those of Japanese descent endured. Rightly so, the tragedy they faced has been outlined in detail. The plight of other ethnic groups who were wronged during this time, however, still remains largely unknown, hence this effort to educate and alter the annals of history.

As books often do, this one grew out of research and interviews conducted for another—my first non-fiction title, *The Los Angeles Sugar Ring*. Initially, *The Fight Abroad* was slated to focus on The Lucky Bastards Club, the elite group my grandfather, Stephen G. Niotta, Sr., belonged to. But I soon came to find that several books had already tackled the subject. Inadvertently, Stevie's daughter, my Aunt Frannie, put me in contact with a family friend, in the hopes that he could help fill in some of the gaps with my grandfather's story. I had the privilege of speaking with Mr. Williams—Dick—about the war on many occasions, and soon came to realize that I did not need to write a book about the club. What I needed to do was to give a voice to the men in my family that served so proudly.

I remain grateful for the opportunity to work with my Great Uncle Anthony J. Amador on the project as well. I would not have been able to tell this tale so fully or so well without his insight, or without the additional material he offered. After the war, he joined an *alumni* group of veterans. These men circulated memoirs and journals about their experiences. In addition to his own accounts, and the thirty-page *War History of the U.S.S. Mississippi* that ship members were given in 1945, Tony Amador also supplied two unpublished manuscripts that filled in many of the finer details concerning his time abroad. These sources are *Aboard the U.S.S. Mississippi BB41: A Day by Day Account* by John Yakushik and *World War II from a Battleship's Bridge* by Paul M. Barnes.

Mr. Yakushik, who served as a ship repairer on the *Mississippi*, went into furniture sales after the war, a line of work he stayed in until retirement. He passed in Arkansas, on March 16, 2007, at the age of eighty-two. Though his manuscript has yet to be published, his detailed accounts have been with the Boone County Heritage Museum in Harrison, Arkansas, since a few years after his death. Mr. Barnes, who began work with a law firm just prior to the start of the war, picked back up with his practice after returning home, and even became a partner. He served as a naval officer aboard the *Mississippi* and passed away on December 29, 2012.

Anthony Amador commented that not only were these sources not published, but that it was "against regulations to keep logs on the ship, and if they caught you doing it, you were subject to get thrown in the brig." Despite the warning, many men in the fight did keep journals or took notes. Thankfully, some of these fine gentlemen even published their stories. My great uncle informed me that instead of keeping a journal, he saved pictures: "I had a photo album that I kept, and on the bottom, I would just put down there, 'Pearl Harbor' or 'Gilbert Islands'—day to day where we were going."

In regards to the material on enemy aliens, despite the eventual declassification of pertinent F.B.I. files that had been locked away for over half a century, and despite the 2001 release of *A Review of the Restrictions on Persons of Italian Ancestry during World War II*, sadly, the truth is still not being taught in the classroom or accurately represented in the current literature. In October, Californians celebrate Italian-American heritage month, but few can explain why. In our talks about life during the war, my grandmother, Anna Dragna-Niotta, mentioned "the fear" that impacted Italians. It was not until after her passing that I learned just how warranted those fears actually were. It truly was a near miss for California's Italians. There is a danger in ignoring the past. It is far too easy to repeat mistakes, especially the ones we did not know were made.

Contents

Part I
The Fear

It is possible for a nation like the United States, proud of its traditions of democracy, individual liberty and fair play to come near to losing its soul in a time of crisis, even during a "good war."

Dr. Stephen Fox, from *UnCivil Liberties*

1

After the Attack

According to Jerre Mangione, "unlike the mass internment program of the West Coast Japanese and Japanese Americans, which was simultaneously operated by the War Relocation Authority," this other program "was not made known to the general public." Mangione, Director of the Immigration and Naturalization Service, added that although a secret, "the media were aware of its existence."

Finding Out

"I was working on a model airplane. It was Sunday. That's when I heard about Pearl Harbor. I remember very well." Richard "Dick" Williams was just sixteen; the oldest of eight and the only boy in a fatherless family residing in a small Nebraskan town. Although television would not be around for another decade, this did not keep word from catching a whirlwind. Like a shotgun's blast, news of the dreadful occurrence fanned out, hitting everyone. Newspapers and radio announcements flooded reports over and over. The world seemed to know almost instantly. America had just been attacked and the Japanese were responsible. "I remember going to school the next day and the teacher saying, 'Oh, this is nothing. What can a little island do to a great nation like ours?' Very naïve." Mocking his teacher's words, Dick mouthed, "Oh what can those folks do? Little island like that."

Back in Hawaii, the trauma continued. Below deck on the U.S.S. *West Virginia* at the time of the attack, small-town Blackwater, Oklahoma, boy Orville Edmiston barely managed to survive. The aerial torpedo strike hit his ship first. Early as it was, Orville and his fellow shipmates were far from fit for duty. In fact, he was still in his underwear. Like many other sailors, Orville stayed up late for the semi-finals of the battle of the bands. The competition was nearly over. A horn-player himself, Orville had even partaken in the performance. He was a regular with the

West Virginia's band and a sit-in for the *Arizona* group. After such a fun night of music, dancing, and festivities, no one was ready for what came.

According to the story Orville Edmiston told his grandson, Steven Sandoval, a master sergeant (MSgt.) in the Air Force National Guard, the sailors were pretty far below deck when the torpedo struck: "The cabin started flooding and they couldn't get the hatch open. It took five or six guys to get the door open because the metal was bent and out of place." Thankfully, Orville and his shipmates made it topside, but the *West Virginia* was already sinking. Seeing a neighboring ship docked close, they made their play.

"They were able to shimmy across the ropes to a sister ship then got to shore. And that's when the *Arizona* famously got hit." The blast flung Orville to the ground. Following protocol, he and many of the other survivors ran for the designated rendezvous, a nearby arena. The attack eventually stopped, but for Orville and the others, it was far from over. Over the course of the next few days, he sailed through the wreckage, his craft but one of many small boats circling the harbor, pulling corpses from the water. In all, 2,403 military personnel perished.

Far off on the coast, in the Boyle Heights section of Los Angeles, another sixteen-year-old learned of the tragedy. Neighborhood Italian Anthony "Tony" J. Amador was hustling on the football field when he and his pals found out: "We had a touch football game on—my brother and cousin and other guys from the neighborhood—we went up against another team. That's when we got the news." Just a year older than Dick and Tony was a popular senior at L.A.'s Dorsey High, Frank Paul Dragna. Folks always seemed to notice Frankie. He dressed well, played football well, moved with confidence, and exuded a hell of a lot of moxie. In line with his family's plan, Frankie had already been accepted to the University of Southern California (U.S.C.) and was slated to begin law school as a Trojan that spring. Like most, he and his younger sister, Anna, heard of the devastation through a radio speaker.

Although longtime Boyle Heights residents as well, the Niotta family had since relocated, settling into another Italian section of the city. The Sicilian population of Lincoln Heights had skyrocketed so much since the coming of the roaring twenties that the spot now wore a new name: "Little Sicily," which nestled in right beside L.A.'s official Little Italy, forming an even larger pocket of Italians. A go-getter, Stevenson "Stevie" George Niotta began hustling among the working class at a very young age. Gifted with his father's entrepreneurial gene, the kid solidly knew how to earn a few dollars. At the time that was certainly something; newsmen were already referring to the bleak curtain the economy hid under as "the depression." After graduating from Manual Arts High, Stevie gave up slinging papers at the *L.A. Daily* for more promising work. He went into business with his father, Big George. Stevie was twenty when the Japanese hit Pearl Harbor. Either he heard about the tragic event from the headlines or from someone down at the *Daily*; his older brother, Michael, still worked there.

Despite the saddened, angered, and fearful uproar tearing through the country, on the morning after the destruction, fifteen-year-old Anna Rosalia Dragna headed into Susan Miller Dorsey High ready for class. "The day after it happened," she recalled, "the next day at school … all of the students were called into the quad." Assuming the voice and tone sounding early that morning while she rallied with the other children, Anna pulled her shoulders back, stood a little taller, and then spoke: "We are proud to say all of our Japanese students are here today, except for one, who has been confirmed ill." Although the administration never officially divulged why this announcement was made, Anna eventually understood. Clarifying, she explained that "it assured people that the kids in their classes with them weren't spies"—a threat many did not take lightly. A very real fear festered among her fellow classmates. What remained a secret to Anna and countless others were the actions that took place throughout the night.

The Roundup

Death on American soil flipped a switch, signaling a green light for federal action. Long rehearsed, the moves came quickly. Mere hours after the attack, the president gave federal operatives all the authority they needed. But according to author-historian Dr. Stephen Fox, the Feds got started even earlier. "Even before President Roosevelt had a chance to sign" the proclamations drafted by the D.O.J., "the FBI, under orders from Attorney General [Francis] Biddle, began to arrest and detain several thousand aliens." Door to door they moved, rounding up suspects. From the start, it was very clear that the Japanese were not the only target. Agents snatched Doris Giuliotta's father and shipped him off to an internment camp. They came after Anita Perata's husband, too, and as they marched him off to a detention facility, her home was "ransacked by the FBI." The day that will "live on in infamy" had definitely made a new enemy out of "the old country."

Those picked up and hauled in soon found themselves detained in facilities like L.A.'s Terminal Island and New York's Ellis Island. There they waited to be questioned and judged. None were charged with a crime. They were not even told why they were being taken. The only explanation offered was that a presidential warrant required them to leave immediately. Filippo Molinari wrote about his experience in a letter he sent from an internment camp in Montana: "At 11 p.m., three policemen came to the front door and two to the back. They told me that, by order of President Roosevelt, I must go with them. They didn't even give me time to go to my room and put on my shoes."

Wearing slippers, Filippo Molinari rode a train from California to Montana through snow and temperatures of 17 degrees and below. They refused to let him grab his coat. The confused passengers aboard these trains were never told their destination, and those in charge took steps to ensure their new prisoners remained in the dark. All the windows aboard the train were blacked out. For the children and spouses who had just witnessed a father or husband being taken away by government officials in the middle of the night, the anxious fear would not soon be sated. Those left behind were not filled in on the whereabouts of their loved ones until sometime after they had settled into their new surroundings. Arrests like this took place all over.

Just two days after the attack, a report in the *Bakersfield Californian* indicated that "nearly 400 Germans and Italians were taken into custody during the night" and that "nearly 900 Japanese nationals" were "seized in the last 48 hours." The attorney general made an announcement the following day, stating the toll claimed another thousand, reaching 2,303. But the roundups did not cease there.

The Los Angeles Times, December 10, 1941
"F.B.I. Rounds Up 'Alien Enemies'"

Italian and Germans Included with Japanese in Wholesale Arrests

Calling Germans and Italians "alien enemies" along with Japanese, the government clamped rigid wartime restrictions on 1,100,000 such persons in this country, and its possessions today, while Federal agents conducted a nationwide roundup of those considered dangerous. All those being seized are being turned over to the Immigration Service for temporary detention. Attorney General Biddle repeated his request that all matters pertaining to alien seizures be handled only through the F.B.I.

Making an already frightful and heartbreaking situation even more horrible, in many cases, it was the family breadwinner hauled away. Unemployed housewives were left with no means to generate income, to pay the bills, or to support their children. The government even put a hold on their savings. "Families who had witnessed the arrests were confounded by the unfolding events as to the fate of their spouses, and particularly their own financial solvency, since detainees' assets had been frozen."

Italian Fears

For a young girl, Anna Dragna understood the situation fairly well—perhaps even better than most. She knew that her family was not exempt, and even if they never came for her, there were others she loved who wore a target—those who had not yet naturalized. For more than forty years, Grandma Rizzotto had lived in America—first New York then Los Angeles—yet in all that time she never learned more than a few words of English. Much more likely in their cross-hares though, as she rightly decided, was her father, Jack; if they came for anyone, they would definitely come for him. A few years earlier, authorities nabbed him over his gambling operations. Although he managed to escape jail time and deportation, Jack Dragna's involvement in city vice, and his previous bootlegging activities during prohibition, provided enough ammo to shoot down his citizenship application. They denied him on moral grounds. Yes, her father had been lucky. But how long would luck last with Italy now among the Axis Powers?

The threat of subversive acts proved to be a source of fear for both citizen and alien. The potential for another attack on U.S. soil did more than just put citizens on edge. It also stirred the prospect of reprisal against aliens. And many of them feared such retribution. Smartly, those making the decisions gave ample thought and consideration to the idea of vigilantism.

La Grande Observer, March 2, 1942
"Mob Violence In State Is Feared"

Seattle—Attorney General Smith Troy told the Tolan congressional committee investigating enemy alien problems today that state officials fear only a spark may be needed to start mob violence against Japanese, Germans or Italians in Washington.

Another Attorney General keeping the bigger picture in mind was Francis Biddle. He weighed the issue of discrimination and the probability of foreigners being lynched by angry mob. Although his stance on the subject proved somewhat unpopular, it did not keep newsmen from continually conveying—or even criticizing—his message. As the *L.A. Times* noted: "Biddle said tonight the government is taking every precaution to guard against espionage, sabotage, or other fifth column activities and warned emphatically against the persecution of alien enemies." The attorney general preached "the persecution of aliens—economic or social"—was a "two-edged sword." It could "easily drive people now loyal" off to the opposing side. Severely hampering efforts to keep the peace were fears of another attack.

Worry over a follow-on act of terrorism sprouted early. Americans believed this second attack would take place on the mainland, somewhere on the West Coast. This tension made it much more difficult to dissuade citizens from taking out their fears and frustrations on aliens. For many, this anxiety eventually subsided, but for some, the tension only intensified. Lingering, it bit inside like a secret that could never be uttered. An odd air hovered throughout the country. But for those living along the coastline out West, and especially in California, the mixture of clashing thoughts and responses hit far heavier. Paranoia over the unknown-enemy mingled with a strong sense of patriotism. A desire to fight the evil definitely existed, but who exactly the bad ones were and whether or not they were already living among good American citizens quickly came into question. Are our neighbors plotting? Are they spies? And no doubt also an uncomfortable situation to address, two major coastal cities with exceedingly large Italian populations had an Italian-American as mayor. Angelo Rossi held office in San Francisco and Fiorello LaGuardia in New York.

Anna Dragna stayed abreast of the media coverage. The avid reader would go on to become editor of her school paper, *The Sky Writer*, then later major in journalism at U.S.C. As the country prepared to enter the fight, she followed the articles and radio broadcasts, keeping her thoughts fixed on the madness on the home front. The fear inside quietly gnawed. When would it come to a head? In the weeks following the tragedy, the newspapers circulating and the stories whispered all continued to grow more and more troubling. Naïvely, many believed the measures being taken came about as a direct response to the Japanese strike on a U.S. territory.

2

Preemptive Efforts

The Alien Registration Act

Far from a whim, the immediate response following the devastation at Pearl Harbor had long been organized. For more than a year prior, citizens of Japan, Italy, and Germany living within the U.S. were unknowingly under surveillance. But the president was mindful of a potential issue before that. In May 1938, he even issued a warning; the *Richmond Item* printed, "aliens in this country are warned by President Roosevelt against any efforts to undermine the institutions of this democracy." So, when the attack on December 7, 1941, drove America out of neutrality, the country was far from unprepared. Precautions began more than two years earlier.

Italy's attack on France in that first summer of the new decade was a move President Roosevelt did not take kindly to. Likely in response, the U.S. draft began shortly after. But the draft was not the only mandatory registration held in 1940. Another of equally immense proportions preceded it. Italy's alliance with the Axis Powers spurred the president to take a greater interest in resident aliens. Anyone born outside the country that was living within U.S. borders fell under a lens. Just two weeks after Mussolini invaded France, Congress passed the Smith Act. It came to be known as the Alien Registration Act of 1940.

Fox explained that "Like no other event before Pearl Harbor, the collapse of France in June 1940, catalyzed the American government to act against potential domestic enemies." Francis Biddle and Jerre Mangione of the Immigration and Naturalization Service (I.N.S.) agreed with this assessment, adding that Congress was "moved to a point of hysteria by the rapid conquests of the Nazi armies." Mangione even labeled the "hurried" Smith Act a "neurotic reflection of congressional fears."

The new act required all non-citizens, aged fourteen and older, who were residing in the United States to register with the I.N.S. The initial plan involved a mass registration of resident aliens within police stations throughout the country, but some foresaw issues with this approach. The newly appointed head of the I.N.S. program, Attorney General Francis Biddle, along with his assistant, Earl Harrison, decided the atmosphere would deter participation. Instead, they opted for a more familiar and less menacing setting. "To minimize the unfriendly implications of mandatory fingerprinting," post offices would be used. This was but one of many efforts made by Biddle and his group to help soothe the anxiety of resident aliens. Tact and diplomacy, in their shared opinion, were paramount in assuring non-citizens that the new act was not an outward expression of hostility.

Even before the Japanese hit Pearl Harbor, with the war brewing overseas, an "anti-alien sentiment remained" strong in "many sections of the country." Now singled out by the Smith Act, non-citizens faced newer problems. While the announcement struck fear in some, in others it spurred something far worse. Leaching on to make an easy buck, many corrupt lawyers capitalized by offering overpriced and unnecessary services. Issues arose in the workplace as well. Appealing to an "American sense of fairness" via radio and newspapers did not keep employers from "overreacting to the potential danger of a fifth column," or from "firing employees who were not citizens."

To combat such issues, Francis Biddle and Earl Harrison put together a small but ethnically diverse team to head up its public relations campaign. In addition

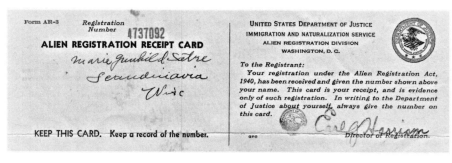

Above: Alien Registration Act identification card (front), 1940. (*Author's personal collection*)

Below: Alien Registration Act identification card (back), 1940. (*Author's personal collection*)

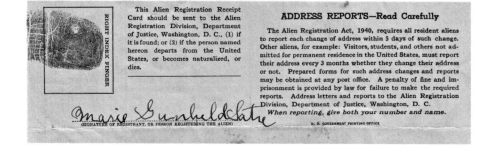

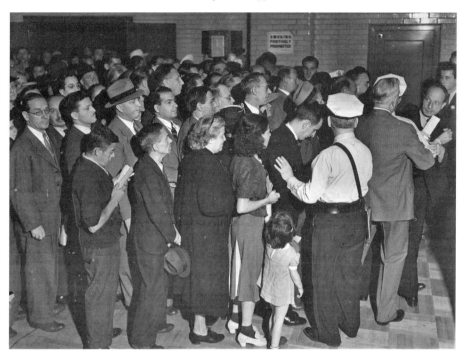

Post office registration for aliens, New York City, August 26, 1940. (*Author's personal collection*)

to a Jewish and a Yugoslavian selection, Brooklyn-born Sicilian-American Jerre Mangione was also handpicked. In regard to why, Mangione expressed, "to what extent his choice was motivated by my Italian background I would never know, but it may well have been a primary consideration since the number of Italian aliens in the country far surpassed that of any other immigrant group." Harrison believed that as an ethnic writer, Mangione could deliver their message with the empathy others could not. The primary concern of this new collective was made evident in the speeches they wrote for top officials: "… to assure the public once again that the government considered the vast majority of the foreign-born population to be loyal and law-abiding, regardless of where they were born." Everyone in this department, from the attorney general down, understood the importance of "continued amity" between citizens and resident aliens. They hoped to avoid a repeat of the violent discrimination toward German aliens living in America during World War I.

As director of the I.N.S. public relations program, Mangione implemented the mandatory registration campaign with "news releases, question-and-answer pamphlets, and other information materials that would tell the aliens what to do." Yet, despite a variety of efforts, "it was impossible to convince many of the aliens that registration would not get them into trouble." Fearful of the consequences for entering the country illegally, a large number of those required to register saw it as a precursor to deportation. "Others simply refused to believe they would not be placing themselves in jeopardy by identifying themselves as aliens." Some found their fears warranted.

The San Bernardino Sun, April 23, 1941
"$25,000 Bond Set in Alien Registration"

LOS ANGELES, April 22—Bertram W. Zenzinger, 36, a German, was held on $25,000 bail today on charges of failing to register as an alien. Federal bureau of investigation officers declined to discuss the arrest nor could they explain the unusually high bail. Zenzinger was believed to have come here from South America about a year ago.

When the Alien Registration Act of 1940 went into effect, America had no active intentions of entering the war. The mass registration came merely as a precaution intended to highlight who of interest resided within U.S. borders. Those of age among the 600,000 Italian citizens living stateside were required to register and many of them did. This included members of the Amador, Niotta, and Dragna families. The Amadors came from Corleone, Sicily, and from Torino, in the northern part of Italy. The Dragnas and their Rizzotto cousins also came from Corleone, and the Niotta family from nearby Piana dei Greci. Members of each household married Americans. Born in the states, their children became citizens.

In all, more than a million resident aliens responded to the mandate. By then, large Japanese and German populations had established themselves in the country. But far greater in size, and greater than any other ethnic group present during that decade, was the Italian community. They had been migrating to the U.S. in vast numbers since the late 1800s. They fought in World War I, helped establish and build many of America's cities, and soon they would fight in the new war as well. Unfortunately, the fact that the Japanese attack took the lives of forty-five Italian-American service members was completely overlooked.

The Draft

In September 1940, a former selective service initiative returned. The draft made its debut during the Civil War and resurfaced in 1917 after enlistment for World War I proved slow. Not yet involved in the battles raging in Europe and the Pacific, Congress met with resistance when they attempted to bring the draft back. In fact, institution of the first ever peacetime draft in U.S. history only narrowly passed. It came at an awkward time for the president, with the election only a couple months off. Roosevelt proved successful and was reelected for a third term that

November. Shortly before the vote, he signed the Selective Training and Service Act, kicking off the first of several rounds of the draft.

The first call singled out males aged twenty-one to thirty-six and was not limited to Americans. Non-citizens living in the country were also expected to register and serve. While eighteen has long been viewed as the age of adulthood in the U.S., this was not the case during the war. Anyone under twenty-one was legally considered a minor. Parents remained legally responsible for all the expensive little misdeeds of their children until they ripened to the knowledgeable age of majority. This fact seems funny, especially considering the number of families started by teenagers during this and earlier decades. Even more confusing, the law stipulated that a young lady automatically became an adult after marrying; yet, the same rule did not apply to young men, and so, during World War II, a twenty-year-old male who had just headed off to war and was prepared to die for his country was still considered a minor. Odder still, if he had a sixteen-year-old bride at home, the law recognized her as an adult. Legislators failed to iron out this quirk until roughly the mid-'70s. The *Journal of Political Economy* blamed the pull to reduce the age of majority on the demand for easier access to birth control. "State laws providing family planning services to young women were altered after 1969," and "the age of majority was lowered in almost all states between 1969 and 1974."

Nine months after the first round of the draft came the call for a second batch of draftees. Pearl Harbor still had not been hit. This group of registrars locked in those who were not yet twenty-one the first time around, which now included Stevie Niotta. He reached draft age that June. Students remained exempt regardless of their age, but Stevie was not a student. His school days were behind him. He was working for his father at the Wolf Music Company and at a newer family-owned venture, a neighborhood bar called Gerries. Of age as well, Stevie's older brothers, Michael and George, Jr., filled out the necessary paperwork. A tad younger, Dick, Tony, and Frankie still remained beneath the age marker.

Just after Valentine's Day 1942—seven and a half months after the second registration—a third draft was held. The U.S. had officially entered the war and with a legitimate need for bodies, some of the former exemption clauses began to lift. The new draft broadened its reach, going older (to forty-four) and younger (to include eighteen-year-old minors). With the upcoming fourth generation of the draft, the term "older" went even further. The "Old Man's Draft" is what many labeled it, as it called for those forty-five to sixty-four—men the young ones around the household called "Grandpa" and sometimes even "Great Grand Dad!" Frankie's fathers registered, and so did Stevie's. Unable to read or write, Big George had his youngest son fill out the document then penned his own signature on the bottom. Each father listed himself as self-employed; Jack as a rancher and George as the owner of a barbecue café.

Despite the growing need, not everyone of age who registered was taken. Some were excused for medical reasons, problems with their vision or for having flat feet.

Others remained stateside because they possessed skills vital to the war effort on the home front. "When the war broke out and the United States started drafting, I was one of the first guys called in," explained Italian-American Ratzi Trezza, who told the draft board he was essential as a commercial fisherman. Trezza did more than just fish locally, though, he voyaged far out to Alaska for salmon. Fish being a vital food source for those overseas, and fish oil a necessity for factory production stateside, the board deferred Trezza from service, but they refused to let up after only one try. Every six months, a new notification indicated that he had been classified as 1-A again. This signaled Trezza to return before the board to be reviewed all over. His two brothers left for the fight, but the Pittsburg, California, resident fished stateside for the duration.

During the fifth generation of the draft registration, in June '42, service again requested the commitment of young men aged eighteen to twenty. By their reckoning, they had already nabbed everyone they were going to get except those too young to slide into a uniform. But efforts to lock these individuals in once they ripened continued. The year ended with a sixth installment—men who reached eighteen after June 30, 1942—and a year later, a final, or "Extra Registration," went into effect. They really reached with this last effort. The registration sought males aged eighteen to forty-four who were living abroad. This accounted for expats, permanent vacationers, and draft dodgers.

In all, some 45 million men registered to serve in World War II. From this, more than 10 million citizens and legal residents found themselves drafted and called upon to serve. This figure fails to include the large number of those who willingly enlisted though: men like Stevie, who signed up during October 1942; Dick, who joined the Army straight out of high school; or Tony, who dropped out his senior year to enlist in the Navy. The statistic did, however, include Frankie Dragna.

Women's Vote, Women's Repatriation

The call for an alien registration just prior to the draft, stirred an older, far more confounded issue. This involved American-born women who, through marriage, had lost their U.S. citizenship. Jeanne Niotta recalled this happening to her grandmother. Although Christian Ernst Breunle came to America back in 1917, by the time of the Second World War he still had not naturalized. Many could say the same. Although he married a citizen—his wife, Nellie Augusta Willard, was born in Leominster, Massachusetts—her citizenship was renounced the moment she said "I do." "When my grandmother married my, I guess you'd say 'illegal' grandfather—who came from Germany—she lost her citizenship." The same legislation impacted Frankie and Anna Dragna's mother, Frances. First-generation American Francesca Rizzotto-Dragna was born in New York City on September 1, 1901. At the age of twenty, she married an alien, and in doing so, she forfeited her native-born right to citizenship. The issue began shortly after the turn of the century.

In the summer of 1906, the House of Representatives attempted to resolve a current issue regarding citizenship. "The primary purpose," according to the *Los Angeles Herald*, was to "devise means of checking the abuses of American naturalization by persons who take out papers with the deliberate purpose of returning immediately to their native countries." Allegedly, these new Americans were giving "much trouble" to the State Department, "by claiming immunity from all the obligations of the natives of their own government." This was causing discontent abroad and "much diplomatic correspondence." As a result, reports of reformation in the passport system—primarily in regards to citizenship—began to hit the papers later that same year. On December 21, 1906, *The Los Angeles Times* hinted these changes might affect "the status of American women marrying foreigners," minors, and U.S. citizens living abroad.

Come late February of the next year, Congress passed the Expatriation Bill—also known as the Expatriation Act of 1907. The bill claimed to "fix" the "status of American women who marry foreigners and of foreign women who marry Americans." But the new "fix" stirred all kinds of problems. Widows living abroad had issues with collecting inheritance. Financial burdens struck women stateside too. By marrying a foreigner, they expatriated themselves and, in essence, became a "foreigner" as well. John Watkins of the Washington publication *The Evening Star* explained in late November 1907: "Regarded as foreigners, they have been deprived of their property rights in those of our states forbidding foreigners to hold property." The one reprieve these women did receive during the fiasco came rather backhanded; if her alien husband were to die, "her American citizenship will be restored to her when she becomes widowed."

Things did not change for the better until September 22, 1922, with the introduction of the Cable Act.

The Philadelphia Inquirer, October 12, 1922
"Woman's Equality in Citizenship"

One more grievance of woman against man-made laws has been removed by Congress. The Cable act, just signed by the President, provides that an American woman who marries an alien does not lose her citizenship in consequence. In other words, her national allegiance is her own, and not her husband's. Ordinarily this may make no great difference; the wife makes her husband's home her own. But during the late war a considerable number of American-born women became automatically enemy aliens, with disastrous results to their property interests in America. By the same act, however, the alien wife does not become an American citizen when her husband does; she must take out her own papers.

Just two years after earning the right to vote, this came as another triumph for women. But as the papers highlighted, "this law is not retrospective."

Unfortunately, the new act did not assist American women whose citizenship had already been stripped. Those who married within the 1907 and 1922 perimeters remained affected. Frances Dragna, Nellie Breunle, and a great number of others fell into this category. In the case of Frankie and Anna's mother, she just missed the mark. If Frances Rizzotto had waited another five months to marry Jack Dragna, she would have retained her birthright.

The Washington Times, October 2, 1922
"Isadora Duncan to Land Today at Ellis Island"

Dancer Married Alien Too Late to Benefit Under Recently Adopted Cable Act.

Isadora Duncan, born in California, but regarded officially as an alien because she married Serge Essenine, a Russian poet, will be landed at Ellis Island today from the steamship Paris and given the usual examination provided for aliens, according to immigration officials at the Department of Labor.

A week after Congress approved the Cable Act, the papers announced that "women married to aliens will not be permitted to register as voters," barring them from participating in the November election. Such nuances of the act confused women for years. Many wondered whether or not the act applied to them and whether or not they were legally still a citizen. Another backhanded escape for these women surfaced in 1936. A newer act granted repatriation, but only if they divorced their alien husbands.

When exactly Frances Dragna found out that she lost her citizenship remains unknown. Once she discovered the situation and learned of a helpful clause though, she likely urged her husband to naturalize. A caveat stipulated that "if a (former) American woman's alien husband became a naturalized U.S. citizen after the marriage, she would regain her citizenship through the very husband with whom she had lost it." Jack Dragna declared intent shortly after the Christmas of 1937, while his older brother, Tom, took out papers earlier that same year. Although Tom was successful, Jack ran into problems.

According to Meg Hacker, The Archives Director at The National Archive, the 1907 act "tethered" a wife "to her husband through his political or legal standing." Basically, "if the United States, for whatever reason, would not grant him citizenship, it would not extend any repatriation opportunities to his wife." For the Dragna family, this proved to be a hardship. In the summer of '40, when officials turned down Jack Dragna's petition, he tried appealing, and after half a dozen years of red tape, the family patriarch finally received a decision.

Nevada State Journal, June 30, 1944
"Deny Citizenship to Jack Dragna"

Los Angeles, June, 29—Jack I. Dragna, prominent figure in the prohibition era, today was denied U.S. citizenship on the grounds he had failed to prove good character. Dragna, who has a $559,000 tax lien pending against him based on his asserted profits from operating a Nevada still while the Volstead act was in force, had received his first papers and asked for final naturalization.

The *L.A. Times* reported on the incident in greater detail. Under lengthy interrogation about gambling interests, Jack Dragna admitted that "he had a part interest in the gambling ship S.S. *Monfalcone*, which was anchored off the coast of California in 1930, and that later he operated a poker club in Hawthorne." Despite such forthright responses, Judge Beaumont did not arrive at a favorable conclusion. "I have found the petitioner has a fine family" and "this speaks volumes in his behalf. If he continues his present law-abiding way of life, I sincerely hope that sometime in the future he can become an American citizen."

The high level of uncertainty over citizenship status spurred a lot of confusion and letters. Craving answers, puzzled husbands and wives wrote immigration offices and newspaper editors begging for clarification. Letters started to trickle in right after the 1907 bill took hold. The topic infrequently saw print, and on occasion, an editor would even include a desperate note scrawled by a nervous housewife. Many feared they were no longer Americans. The frequency of these requests picked up heavily with the coming of the new decade. A war was now raging overseas and matters had not gone well for alien women during the last one. But far more than the war overseas stirred their efforts; serving as catalyst, another act had passed.

The Fresno Bee, June 23, 1940
"Congress Aids Women to Regain Citizenship"

Washington, June 22—Congress approved legislation today to facilitate repatriation of American women who lost their citizenship by marrying aliens. The measure sent to the White House provides that a woman now married to an alien, but who has resided in the United States continuously since the date of marriage may apply to a federal court for restoration of citizenship, paying a fee of $1 when repatriation is granted.

President Roosevelt made it official with the Repatriation Bill. Opting for a patriotic flair, he signed the document on the Fourth of July. In addition to benefiting married women, the new act also assisted alien children. "The President also approved a bill permitting aliens who enter the United States under the age of 16 to become naturalized after they are 21 without making a formal declaration of intention."

At the age of forty, Frances Dragna filled out paperwork for an oath of allegiance to the country of her own birth. Line (8) of the document indicates, "I lost, or believe that I lost, United States citizenship solely by reason of my marriage on April 30, 1922 to Jack Ignatius Dragna, then an alien, a citizen or subject of Italy, and my marital status with such person is not terminated." Line (10) reads: "I hereby apply to take the oath of renunciation and allegiance as prescribed in Section 335(b) of the Nationality Act of 1940 to become repatriated and obtain the rights of a citizen of the United States." The paperwork was signed and dated just over two weeks before the attack on Pearl Harbor. Unfortunately, Jeanne Niotta's grandparents, the Breunles, were not yet citizens when America joined the fight. As a result, the pair faced difficulties associated with a series of new proclamations impacting resident aliens.

Proclamations, Camps, and Taking Residents

In addition to the draft and the alien registration—two exceedingly large-scale efforts—the president took even earlier measures to secure national security. Sensing the country might eventually enter the conflict, Roosevelt charged F.B.I. Director J. Edgar Hoover with gathering intelligence. This may have even prompted the Alien Registration Act. Efforts went under way in the summer of 1939, not long before Italy's French invasion. President Roosevelt requested a list of anyone who might do harm to the U.S.; individuals to arrest, question, and intern upon the onset of war. Tasked federal agents dug into the history and current activities of the nation's resident aliens. The Bureau devised a system of categorizing these individuals, placing them into groups "A," "B," or "C," depending on their determined level of threat.

According to Mangione, the D.O.J. was also busy: "In the Attorney General's office, unbeknownst to the general public, procedures were being established for arresting aliens and setting up civilian boards to give them hearings." The department also drafted several proclamations. Once signed by the president, these documents would grant officials the power to arrest, detain, and intern citizens of any country the U.S. had declared war on. President Roosevelt signed proclamation 2525 mere hours after the attack, putting a target on anyone of Japanese descent. In the morning, he signed two more. Proclamation 2526 added Germans to the list, and 2527, Italians.

This authority to intern came from an age-old piece of legislation, the Enemy Alien Act of 1789. Sadly, in addition to citizens of Axis Power countries, the decision also impacted "thousands of men and women who had been victimized by the Nazi and Fascist regimes." German-born Jews and an assortment of other refugee groups lucky enough to escape Hitler's grasp and land within American borders soon found themselves interned.

Preparations did not cease there. Pressing forward, all Italian consulates in the U.S. were shut down, and more than five months before the attack, Attorney General Francis Biddle instructed Edward J. Ennis, head of the D.O.J.'s Alien Enemy Control Unit, to put together and ready more detainment facilities.

F.B.I. Chief J. Edgar Hoover (left), Mail Censorship Advisor Byron Price (center), and Attorney General Francis Biddle (right) confer before Biddle takes the stand during a Senate Judiciary Committee hearing, Washington, December 14, 1942. (*Author's personal collection*)

Oakland Tribune, November 18, 1941
"Alien Detention Camps to Be Expanded Three-Fold by U.S."

One Million Aliens

Alien registration figures show there are approximately 1,000,000 Italian, German and Japanese Nationals in the United States, but about 40 per cent of these have applied for citizenship. Attorney General Biddle said at a recent press conference that there would be no mass arrests of foreigners in event of war. In event of hostilities, the War Department probably would operate the detention camps, as it did in the last war, and the Justice Department would determine whom should be held. The Army recently completed a detention camp on Long Island, presumably as a preparedness step.

One of these facilities readied by the D.O.J. was Montana-based Fort Missoula. Not much time passed before the spot, and others took on residents. On March 31, 1941, authorities seized every Italian and German ship within U.S. waters. In all, twenty-eight Italian vessels were taken. Though predominately fishing boats, this figure did also include the pleasure liner *Il Conte Biancamano*. Roughly 1,000 Italian fishermen and performers employed by the *Il Conte* found themselves interned in Montana. Pearl Harbor was still intact.

At Fort Missoula, the newly detained Italians joined 114 Italian nationals already imprisoned—visitors of the World's Fair and seventy waiters brought from Italy to work the Italian pavilion in New York. Soon other Italians would be sent in by train; some of them fathers of American service members. The majority of these individuals remained in internment for three years. According to Jerre Mangione, whose duties with the D.O.J. brought him to a variety of internment camps throughout the country, Fort Missoula "quartered an equal number of Italians, Germans, and Japanese."

Conversely, the detention camp—now a museum—indicates another figure. www.fortmissoulamuseum.org states that between the years 1941 and 1944, the Department of Justice used the facilities to house "1,200 non-military Italian men, 1,000 Japanese resident aliens, 23 German resident aliens, and 123 Japanese Latin and South Americans." Describing the changes made to the facilities in order to house these new detainees, the museum explained that "a 10-foot fence topped with barbed wire" surrounded the grounds and a 40-foot guard tower perched at each corner. Those maintaining order were equipped with billy clubs and gasmasks for their 37-mm tear gas guns.

Fort Missoula Alien Detention Camp, Missoula, Montana, 1941. (*Author's personal collection*)

3

The Life of an Enemy Alien

Hearing Boards and Internment

On Christmas Eve 1941, *The Los Angeles Times* reported that "when the big roundup took place a couple of weeks ago, the FBI didn't run into any fireworks." Those being hauled in rarely tried to escape or resist their captors. L.A.'s F.B.I. head, Richard Hood, commented "some did a lot of protesting innocence," but most took the arrests complacently. Cultural norms may have moved Italians to conform to and obey these governmental directives. Several theories have been posed. Coming from a land of far greater economic and political struggles—and a place of fewer freedoms—Italians had already come to expect and accept ill treatment from public officials and those in uniform. This viewpoint accounts for what Americans took for a docile response. Not only were many Italians distrusting of the military and law enforcement, they feared the consequences of refusing to get in line.

Some have theorized differently, though, suggesting that Italian citizens felt as if they had done something wrong, felt shame, and that they obeyed quietly so as not to draw any further attention. This too might have been the case. A third hypothesis is conveyed in the *Pace International Law Review*. Although the homeland of Italian aliens was now at war with their new home, Paula Branca-Santos exclaimed that "they were in America, the land of opportunity, and freedom," and for this reason, "it is doubtful that many of them imagined that their freedom would be significantly limited." Simply put, they put faith in American justice and believed they would not be punished for something they did not do. Sadly, the events did not play out in this fashion.

Although resident aliens from Italy were not citizens on paper, a vast number of them still considered themselves American; many had viewed themselves in this light for most of their lives. Immigrating to the United States as children, they were raised in Italian boroughs. Because they remained huddled in these neighborhoods among their own, they still spoke their native tongue, and yet a large portion of this population had little or no memories at all of what life was like back in Italy: they married Americans, their children were born citizens, and a good number of them were now military service members. Per Mangione's estimation, by the time of the attack on Pearl Harbor, roughly 10 percent of Italian resident aliens had "husbands or sons in the American armed forces," and this number rose steadily during the course of the war.

Although a large portion of the older Italian citizens who had been living in America for a number of years never learned to read or write in English, many of these same individuals could not perform the task in Italian either. With the dire need to enter the workforce in order to provide for themselves and their families, few of these individuals found time to study or to attend the classes that most needed in order to pass the citizenship exam. Mangione explained: "… their failure to become citizens could be ascribed to their difficulty with the English language and to the traditional prejudice of Americans toward immigrants from Southern and Eastern European nations." Despite this fact, in their hearts and minds, they truly believed themselves to be American, Italian-American.

Whatever the reason for the overwhelming compliance that federal agents encountered when they came knocking on Italian doors, before the year's end, the papers announced that nearly 3,000 individuals had been arrested. Those not immediately shipped off to an internment camp now faced the clock. When their review before the board finally arrived, their character and allegiances came into question. Civilian panels had been quickly put together by the D.O.J., specifically for this purpose. These judges were tasked with deciding if the accused posed a threat, and whether or not they might side against the United States.

Unfortunately, the cases being presented before the boards lacked specific details. Panel members received little if any information as to why the accused had been deemed a potential threat. Considering an unfavorable decision meant internment for the duration of the war, serving on a board came as a heavy responsibility. Making the already tense ordeal an even greater hardship, none of the accused were permitted legal counsel. Civil rights, without question, were being violated. Although these resident aliens were not American citizens, the 14th Amendment did still afford them many of the same rights. Non-citizens are not permitted to vote, work for the government, or sit on a jury, but the Constitution does extend them the rights of due process of law and equal protection. This seems only fair, considering they were subject to the draft and a large number of them had served America bravely in World War I.

While Jerre Mangione did attempt to downplay the power of these governing bodies, intimating that all they really did was make a recommendation to the attorney general, he did admit that "the boards were not bound by any courtroom rules for establishing evidence" and that "hearsay information carried far more weight than it should have." As one journalist from an Italian paper in America commented from Fort Missoula, "So what if I did write in a newspaper that I thought Mussolini was doing a good job? Does that make me a Fascist?" Driving his point, he exclaimed: "I was finished with that son of a bitch as soon as he teamed up with that other son of a bitch in Germany, but I can't get that through the skulls of those people in the Attorney General's office."

The Long Beach Independent, December 21, 1941
"U.S. District Attorney Starts Hearings Tomorrow for 445 Enemy Aliens"

Federal agents have some 445 enemy aliens in custody in Los Angeles, and beginning tomorrow, hearings for the Japanese, Italian, and German nationals will be held. The hearings will be conducted by United States District Attorney William Fleet Palmer and his assistant, Leo V. Silverstein. Studies are being made by Palmer and his associates, pending the appointment of a five-man civilian board to hear the cases. Now being detained at the county jail, the federal prison on Terminal Island, and the immigration station at Los Angeles harbor, the aliens will either be released or placed in internment camps as "dangerous to the public peace or safety of the United States."

F.B.I. records, which remained classified until 2001, suggest that affiliations such as membership or employment of various groups forced specific Italians to be targeted, questioned, and even interned. This list included instructors who taught at Italian-language schools sponsored by the Italian consulate, those with ties to Italian newspapers and radio printed and broadcasted in the U.S., or anyone that the rumor mill deemed a Fascist or Fascist sympathizer. Also included on this list of those to question and potentially intern were Italian veterans of World War I. Those who joined Italian veteran associations such as the *Ex Combattenti* fell under heavy scrutiny. Groups like this still donated to programs that supported widows back in Italy. Although Italy fought alongside the U.S. during World War I, ties to the old country and especially acts of charity were viewed as sympathetic to, and in aid of, the enemy.

Just over a week after the F.B.I. began grabbing non-citizens, some 200 enemy aliens arrived in a camp near Tujunga, in the eastern end of Los Angeles. The camp, a Civilian Conservation Corps (C.C.C.), earlier served as a relief home for out-of-work laborers who suffered from the joblessness of the Great Depression. "Housed today behind a barbed wire fence are 200 enemy aliens who were arrested last week by the FBI," reported *The Long Beach Independent*. Although the camp, "consisting chiefly of two bunkhouses," was "taken over by the Immigration and Naturalization Service," the "guards are said to be FBI men."

In late December, many of the West Coast Italians that were deemed a threat were shipped from temporary detainment facilities in California, such as the federal jail at Terminal Island, to camps further inland. Those that arrived at Fort Missoula joined the nest of Italians—seamen, waiters, entertainers, and World's Fair guests—who had been held captive for roughly nine months. The day after Christmas, *The Los Angeles Times* reported that another "group of 23 Italian, Japanese, and German aliens" was heading for the "Missoula (Mont.) internment camp," and that "about 100 local aliens previously had been sent to Montana," plus "several carloads of Southern California aliens were scheduled to be placed aboard the same train at Sacramento." On the other end of the country, East Coast Italians held at Ellis Island—ironically where many of them first entered the country—were moved further inland as well. In the U.S. territory of Hawaii, a camp of tents in Honolulu's harbor was used to house enemy aliens. The facility was called San Island.

After settling into a camp, internees were permitted to telephone their loved ones and briefly tell them they were alright. They could not, however, divulge their location. At this early stage, they still may not have even known where they were being held. Prior to their arrival, many detainees were questioned by a board. Sometime later, the Department of Justice and the War Department came to see the flaws in the system they had put together. Far too often, rumors, fear, racist beliefs, and witch hunt tactics influenced the outcome, causing unnecessary over-internment. Aside for the extra cost of feeding, guarding, and housing these individuals, the biggest drawback for the War Department—and the real reason for reevaluations—is that over-internment stood to hinder the war effort stateside. It deprived key industries of essential workers. Although fish remained a vital product throughout the war, the vast majority of Northern California's fishermen were of Italian descent, and at least half of them were not citizens. As the papers noted, "Fishermen on San Francisco and Monterey bays, two affected areas, are predominantly Italian, and more than 50 per cent are aliens, although long-time residents of the United States." For reasons such as this, on August 21, 1942, Attorney General Francis Biddle "issued a circular to assure a rehearing to those interned, as abuses and misconduct had been perpetrated by the boards."

A second hearing meant that some detainees would finally get a chance to plead their case. Making this a difficult goal to achieve, they still had not been informed of the charges against them. While perhaps less bias, the newer proceedings were still far from adequate. Civilian boards rather than judiciary representatives were again employed. Once more, the accused could not seek legal counsel. These were, after all, not truly legal proceedings. An upside to the new hearings was the inclusion of family members. Fathers, mothers, spouses, and siblings were permitted to appear on the behalf of the accused. Traveling on their own expense, they helped plead the case of their loved ones. The burden of proving innocence, trustworthiness, and allegiance to the United States still fell entirely upon the internee. They remained guilty despite a lack of proof or evidence, and they would remain that way unless they proved convincing before the board. As a result of these hearings, some enemy aliens did receive parole. Back at home, they remained under surveillance and faced a number of new restrictions.

During imprisonment, internees were permitted to write letters. In fact, much of what is known about these camps has been gathered from such correspondence. Although allowed to write, caveats stipulated restrictions such as only one postcard and two letters a week. Naturally, all internee mail went through a rigorous inspection process, receiving "sanitization." Anything thought to be cryptic, or to elicit a negative emotion in the internee, received a thick black redacting line. Also blotted out were abbreviations, drawings, initials, profanity, anything thought to be a code, and all mention of the war and Italy. Additionally, for whatever reason, rules forbade internees from corresponding with other internees. This proved difficult for internees with spouses or relatives housed in a different camp.

Letters explain that some detainees were rotated often between camps. Based on Dr. Stephen Fox's interviews with internees and their family members, Italians were housed mainly at Camp McAlester in Oklahoma, Fort George Meade in Maryland, Fort Missoula in Montana, Dodd Army Airfield at Fort Sam Houston in San Antonio, Texas, and Camp Forrest in Tennessee. According to author Jan Jarboe Russell, of the five internment camps in Texas, El Paso's Fort Bliss also housed German and Italian men. Fox expressed that in most instances enemy aliens remained segregated. Other reports run somewhat contrary though, suggesting that conditions and regulations depended chiefly on the location of the internment camp, the nationality of those detained, and the agency running the installation; the D.O.J. was not in charge of every facility.

Making the rounds of internment facilities in his work for the D.O.J., Jerre Mangione found that women and children were also interned in these camps. Although they were initially kept separate from the men, shortly after Mangione's facility tour began, a shift in policy strategically steered away from "women only" camps. Approval of a general population atmosphere allowed for married couples to finally be reunited. The presence of women and children in these internment camps contradicts the scant coverage newspapers offered the public. But the reports that reached the American public were largely provided by the Associated Press. Like internee letters, these articles adhered to strict censorship, conveying a very specific message.

While Dr. Stephen Fox's research indicated the presence of ethnically segregated camps, this may have been socially enacted rather than governmentally mandated. Mangione specified that in situations of shared facilities, internees gravitated toward their own of natural accord. Dining differed camp to camp as well. In some installations each group had its own dining hall with a separate menu that catered—as best it could—to ethnic tastes. In other locations, the internees themselves produced the bulk of what they ate, growing crops right there on the grounds. Working internment conditions definitely existed, and those that labored received a small wage for their services. Thankfully, much consideration went to Geneva Convention protocol. American troops captured overseas, after all, were to be treated in a reciprocal manner. Another factor that kept the conditions manageable in these facilities were the random inspections conducted by the International Red Cross. For these reasons, some installations made greater efforts. Some camps even offered libraries, flower gardens, access to gym and athletic equipment, and various other leisure amenities.

Those Not Taken

From the start, it was very evident that federal agents were not only after the Japanese. Italians were being targeted and taken. This, Anna Dragna could not ignore, nor could she escape the truth—those remaining were not in the clear. Surveillance of the Italian enclaves continued. Agents turned up at all hours of the night. Reading the papers, Anna discovered the trouble Italians were facing reached far passed her home in California. The other coast was affected too. *The New York Times* reported policemen had begun "a check-up of 256,000 aliens of enemy nations in" the New York area and that "similar action" would "be started by police departments in other cities, towns, and villages throughout the United States." Allowing government operatives "to put their fingers on any alien in any community at almost any time" appeared to be the intent.

Confiscation of Italian-owned boats along the coast by the Navy and Coast Guard commenced as early as mid-December. Later that month, enemy aliens got word they needed to turn in what was being called contraband.

The San Bernardino County Sun, December 28, 1941
"Aliens To Lose Radio, Cameras"

December 27—Attorney General Francis Biddle today ordered Japanese, German, and Italian aliens living in seven western states to surrender all short wave radio sets and cameras in their possession to local police authorities by 11 p.m. Monday. The order resulted from Army reports that unauthorized radio messages were being received and sent on the west coast. It was said that a similar order would be issued for the rest of the nation next week. Willful failure to surrender the radios and cameras, Biddle said, will result in forfeiture of the equipment and arrest and internment in an Army concentration camp for the duration of the war of the alien involved.

In a time before television, when households received their music, entertainment, and news from a speaker, word that the family radio had to be turned in came as a heavy hit. Chet Campanella remembered his father hiding theirs in the chicken coop out back. In addition to radios and cameras, the order also included binoculars, flashlights, and, of course, guns and ammunition. Maps and photographs of installations soon made the list as well. Although some items appeared harmless, proximity to the ocean was taken into account. Flashlights for instance, according to the Army, could be used to signal an enemy boat. So, before the close of the year, "thousands of expensive pieces of photographic and radio equipment had been turned in to police stations." In California, the numbers reached great heights. Roughly 1,250 items were received in Oakland and more than 3,000 in San Francisco.

Authorities had been dropping into homes in Los Angeles unannounced ever since the night of the attack, but the frequency picked up shortly after the New Year. Naturally, these surprise visits stirred a whole range of emotions. For Tony Amador, these activities hit especially close to home. Returning from school one afternoon, he heard that authorities had paid a visit to his next-door neighbor. "In the two-block stretch where we lived, we were mostly Italian," Tony conveyed, referring to his family's area of Boyle Heights. "We lived right next door to my grandparents," which is who the agents came to see. Tony explained that his mother's father was not a citizen: "I was at school when it happened, but my mother told me about it later." After searching the premises, "they took

S.F.P.D. Officer Edward Quast looking over weapons turned in by enemy aliens, 1942. (*Author's personal collection*)

something out of his radio so he couldn't transmit during the war." Tony just could not picture his grandfather as a threat. He was so advanced in age that he passed away shortly after the war.

Many of the surrounding families in this and other neighborhoods received similar attention. Some encountered far worse. What spurred the surge of inspections was likely a bit of quality control following the deadline on Biddle's contraband turn-in order. The decision to hold the mass turn-in not only gave non-citizens little time to comply, it also overwhelmed the local authorities tasked with accepting these items. Police officials lacked sufficient guidance on how to receive, document, and store the large influx of property. Ultimately, this oversight resulted in the loss of personal property. In many instances, prized family heirlooms never made it back to their rightful owners.

In addition to the loss of property, a variety of Italian-dominated trades and Italian-owned businesses suffered. After getting word from the military that a bar run by an alien could "impair military efficiency" and serve as "nests for treasonous activities," Monterey's mayor barred enemy aliens from selling alcohol. However, more than just bar and liquor store owners felt the sting. Restrictions on commercial fishing soon called for all-American crews, putting a vast number of Italian fishermen out of work, and those Italian citizens well-off enough to own their own fishing boats and to hire on crews were forced to make lay-offs and tie their vessels to the docks. Despite the new restrictions, organizations such as the Crab Fisherman's Protective Association attempted to find a way to allow loyal non-citizens to continue fishing. None were successful.

Although the Japanese dominated the fishing trade in the Los Angeles area, the demographics differed greatly further north in cities like San Francisco, Monterey, and Santa Cruz, where the bulk of the crews were manned by Italians. It is surprising that the restrictions on alien fishermen did not commence sooner; the president was aware of the potential for trouble years before the attack on Pearl Harbor. In fact, on New Year's Day 1938, *The San Bernardino Daily Sun* indicated that President Roosevelt was "seeking new legislation which eventually would terminate Japanese and other alien fishing operations in American waters."

Despite being forced from the ocean, some enemy aliens managed to remain close to the industry; a number of Italian fishermen took up work in the fishing canneries just outside of the restricted lines, but soon, higher powers severed this job market as well. Bringing still further hardship, an order forced all state-licensed canneries to bar enemy aliens from operating food sterilization machinery. Soon, any non-citizen who regularly conducted business with the government, the state, or any of its counties ran into some measure of trouble. Alameda County refused to pay an Italian car dealer from Oakland $5,309.50 owed for five vehicles the county purchased a few days after the attack on Pearl Harbor. Their excuse for refusing to pay their bill was that federal law barred

Italian fisherman Salvatore Di Grande looking out over Fisherman's Wharf and all the Italian ships that have been docked for weeks due to new restrictions, San Francisco, January 30, 1942. (*Author's personal collection*)

trading with the enemy. They did not return the cars. Sadly, the incident was not isolated. In a report to the Governor's Council in late January 1942, Governor Olson indicated his intent to instruct state governmental heads to revoke all business and professional licenses held by enemy aliens in California. Fired or let go, Italians sought employment elsewhere. But who in their right mind was going to hire an enemy? Leaders within the country's Italian-American communities reached out to the White House for assistance.

The New York Times, January 11, 1942
"U.S. Italians Make Plea to Roosevelt"

Ask Him to Lift 'Intolerable Stigma of Being Branded as Enemy Aliens'

Representatives of 200,000 Italian-American trade unionists appealed to President Roosevelt yesterday to remove "the intolerable stigma of being branded as enemy aliens" from Italian and German nationals who had formally declared their intention of becoming American citizens by taking out first papers before America's entry into the war.

The President was told that the present indiscriminate classification of Italian and German nationals as enemy aliens was "not only a humiliating blow to their honor, long-cherished ideals and self-respect, but also a detriment to our own interests as Americans, since it deprives our country of the valuable services these people could render in the all-out fight against the fascist dictators."

That same month, a second call to filter into the post offices was made. It had been more than a year since all non-citizens living in the country registered with the I.N.S. This time, only enemy aliens specifically were pinpointed—some 1.1 million. Again came the threat of internment until the war's end for non-compliance. I.N.S. public relations figure Jerre Mangione was tasked with heading up publicity for the program, which kicked off in mid-January '42 with Presidential Order 2537. Attorney General Biddle announced the government's dual objective—"strengthening our internal safety and protecting the loyal alien, even if he has become technically an alien enemy." The Western Command's 135,843 German, Italian, and Japanese aliens—residents of California, Oregon, Washington, Arizona, Nevada, Utah, Idaho, and Montana—were slotted to process through their local post offices during the first week of February.

The newspapers explained "the alien must submit a photograph of themselves and answer questions concerning their relatives here and abroad, and their activities and occupations since the original registration of all non-citizens in 1940." This time, participants received a booklet complete with a picture, fingerprint, and signature. The booklet—which came to be called the "pink book"—was required on their person whenever they left home.

The large number of aliens who required registration and the mass call for local photographers to snap and print pictures proved hectic and chaotic. In Los Angeles alone, 36,000 needed to be processed. On February 4, the *L.A. Times* boasted that during the first two days of the second registry, the "block-line," which formed at San Pedro and 22nd Street, held roughly 6,800 Japanese, Italian, and German aliens. The numbers proved staggering on the other coast as well. "Postmaster Albert Goldman announced that 7,887 enemy aliens registered in New York City," which brought the "total in the city to 76,230."

Shortly after the New Year, word of yet another difficult directive arrived. The new order constrained travel and instituted a curfew. Initially, the area of impact fell shy of Los Angeles, halting just 50 miles outside county limits. But newer zones continued to be designated, and soon the restriction pushed straight into L.A. Beginning on February 24, all enemy alien travel required permission and approval. Travel by plane, regardless of the situation, would not be granted.

The San Bernardino Daily Sun, February 5, 1942
"Curfew Restrictions Provided as Meanderings of Aliens Curtailed"

Feb. 4—Attorney General Francis Biddle today designated a large area of California in which enemy aliens will be subjected to a curfew, and be permitted to travel only between their homes and jobs, after Feb. 24. The prescribed area, about 500 miles long and varying from 30 to 150 miles in width, extends from the Oregon border along the coast line to a point about 50 miles north of Los Angeles. Biddle explained that the restricted area does not extend south to the Mexican border because no recommendations for such actions in southern sections of California had been received yet from the war department.

The new restriction stipulated that "between the hours of 9 p.m. and 6 a.m. all enemy aliens shall be within the place of residence indicated on their identification certificates." When not at work, they were required to either be in their registered residence, "going between those two places," or not more than 5 miles from home. Biddle was soon overridden on this point though. Far less lenient and unmoved by the human condition of the enemy alien situation, Lieutenant General John L. DeWitt disagreed with how Attorney General Francis Biddle was handling matters. The head of the Western Defense Command took a far more pragmatic approach and challenged Biddle on even the tiniest matters. When Biddle advocated for a 9 p.m. curfew, DeWitt demanded it be lowered to 8 p.m. and won, causing enemy aliens to be in their homes at night an hour earlier.

The curfew, regardless of its 8 or 9 p.m. timeframe, did not go over well with the country's Italians. Many found themselves arrested for merely going to work.

Department of Justice Alien Registration "Pink Book," Italian alien, Brooklyn, NY, February 21, 1942. (*Author's personal collection*)

Geyserville Press, October 9, 1942
"Eight Italian Alien Workers Under Arrest"

Charge Is Violating Curfew Laws by Not Having Proper Permits

Eight Italian enemy aliens, all employees of the Italian-Swiss Colony winery at Asti, were this Friday arrested on charges of violating the curfew regulations applicable to enemy aliens. So far as can be learned, there is no suspicion of disloyalty against any of the aliens. Rather it is the result of a dispute over red tape. The management of the winery, which, like all other business institutions is short of laborers, had applied for a blanket permit to work aliens at night.

During the dispute over the establishment's permit, the Italian workers in question were held in a cell in a Santa Rosa jail. The feds had every intention of sending them "to the United States marshal at San Francisco" to have their fate decided—internment for the duration of the war or a hefty fine. This story was not uncommon. In fact, by June 1942 alone, some 1,500 Italians had already been arrested for breaking curfew, for having contraband in their possession, or for violating travel restrictions. Assistant Special F.B.I. Agent H. C. Van Pelt, indicated that of the 195 violators arrested in his area of Northern California, 131 were Italian and sixty-four German.

Among the population affected by the new travel and curfew restrictions was Giuseppe DiMaggio. The DiMaggios, like Stevie Niotta's family, came from the mountains of Sicily in the city of Piana dei Greci. The new restriction barred Giuseppe and Rosalia DiMaggio from entering their restaurant in Fisherman's Wharf. It also kept them from visiting their son, the famed baseballer, Joe DiMaggio. Struck by a similarly devastating blow were many U.S. military members who had just completed their pre-deployment training. Following graduation, soldiers, sailors, and airmen often enjoyed a short window of time during which their loved ones could visit. In grim instances, this became the last time they saw their parents or a girlfriend. Countless lives were lost; sons and fathers who never returned from battle. Sadly, this privilege was denied service members with enemy alien mothers, fathers, grandparents, siblings, and significant others—travel restrictions strictly forbade it.

Forced Relocation

While residents within restricted areas remained subject to curfew and travel restrictions, residents of other zones encountered something far more shocking. "Specified districts which enemy aliens may not enter" at all were also announced that February. Under direction of the Army, they were labeled military zones. Any enemy alien dwelling there needed to evacuate quickly. Business owners with shops beyond these borders faced a difficult call as well—either hire a citizen to look after their interests or close up till the war's end. Al Bronzini indicated that although their home was not in one of these zones, their family's fruit market was: "My father received a notice that his beloved Banana Depot was off limits."

The Los Angeles Times, February 11, 1942
"Alien Enemy Control Unified Efforts Sought"

No Choice Given

Even if an alien has lived in a forbidden zone for 50 years he must still move. He is an alien even if he has first papers or his sons are in the United States armed forces. An alien cannot move elsewhere and keep his job in a forbidden zone. He does not have to move if he lives in a curfew zone.

By early February, eighty-six forbidden zones had been established in California. But the areas to evacuate were far from limited to the Golden State, or even to the coastline out West. Forbidden zones included perimeters around various utility buildings, water sources, production factories, airports, and many other installations all over the country. Other restricted zones within the neighboring states in the defense command were expected to be announced as well. This included Oregon, Washington, Idaho, Montana, Utah, Nevada, and Arizona.

A handful of L.A. destinations were "among the territories to be cleared by Feb. 15." This included the "Los Angeles and Vernon manufacturing districts, Long Beach, West Hollywood, Southwest Los Angeles, Downey, Huntington Park, North Hollywood, East Los Angeles, and three sections of Burbank." The second deadline—February 24—was slated for "the 40-square-mile district bounded by Western Ave., Manchester Blvd., the Pacific Ocean, Sepulveda Blvd., and Rosecrans Ave." The military did not target Boyle Heights for evacuation. In fact, they even set up an alien information center on South Boyle Avenue, mere blocks from Tony Amador's home. Closer to the boundary, and just shy of the cut off, were Frankie and Anna Dragna, who lived with their parents, Jack and Frances, at 3927 Hubert in Leimert Park. They had only lived there for about a year before the zones began to be announced. Builders completed construction of their Spanish-style home in early 1941.

Long before the war overseas brewed, going as far back as she could remember, Anna's parents instructed her to "speak American" and fit in. This had been, as she understood, largely due to the discrimination her parents suffered in their younger years, first in New York then later out West. With the curfew now in effect, federal agents taking Italians away, and the announcement of forced relocations, the message her parents conveyed seemed to apply more so than ever.

A little more than 300 miles north of Anna Dragna lived Vitina Spadaro, a grade school student in Monterey. Coming home from class, her mother and father explained they would have to move. Their residence sat too close to the ocean. Vitina's father, Giuseppe, came to America from Sicily in 1920, and although he naturalized, Vitina's mother had not completed the process. For this reason, their family had to make a choice: they could send their mother away and remain at home or they could all leave together. Many faced a similar dilemma, though in most cases, the lone non-citizen was a husband or a grandparent well into their eighties. Because few could afford the luxury of renting a second home, and because the breadwinner of the family was oftentimes the enemy alien forced to relocate, the only viable option for most was to leave their home and seek out a place they were all permitted to stay in.

Vitina Spadaro remembered having a difficult time finding a new place to live. As soon as "the owners found out we were aliens, we were turned down." Although the process proved lengthy and disparaging, the Spadaros eventually settled in Salinas. Shortly after the move, however, they heard about the large-scale plan for the Japanese. Like other families that had been branded enemies and forced to relocate, the Spadaros feared that moving further inland would not be enough to appease the government. They feared they, too, would be taken. Heightening their anxiety, "word got around that they were going to do the same thing to the Italians" directly after, and the word that spread was anything but rumor.

Perhaps for the sake of simplicity, or to save time and money, the government abandoned the formal approach of handing out the bad news. Those designated for removal did not greet a messenger bearing a telegram, and no letter dropped in their box either. The official order of forced relocation from forbidden zones up and down the coast was not sent by mail or divulged over the telephone. Enemy aliens discovered they would have to leave their own homes via word of mouth, through radio broadcasts and newspaper reports, and by the mass of signs now littering their neighborhoods. "Placards giving notice that enemy aliens are completely barred" were posted in a number of counties and in at least "97 defense areas in California." In some areas, the Boy Scouts were recruited to tack up relocation notices—posters written in German, Japanese, and Italian. The harsh decision hit some 10,000 coastal residents. All of them would be forced some place further inland.

Pressed by wartime urgency, none received sufficient time to prepare or hunt out a new destination. Some had less than two weeks to pack everything they owned and get out. The first batch was set to evacuate by the February 15 deadline; the second had to be gone by February 24. To those impacted, complying with this directive under the constraints, wartime restrictions, and social-ills appeared impossible. There was not enough time. Even without the stigma of being Italian—an enemy alien—finding housing was exceedingly challenging.

Desperately in need of assistance, Italians flooded their local law enforcement and information offices. They bombarded the attorney general's office with pleas for help as well. They needed to find new jobs and a place to live immediately. "They asked scores of questions pertaining to the eviction proceedings" and outlined their hardships and troubles. Definite patterns emerged. "Irritated by reports of discrimination and unwarranted discharges from jobs on 'vague suspicion,' Biddle reminded the nation that dangerous aliens have [already] been apprehended." The attorney general also "asked private industry to avoid discrimination against aliens who are employed or seeking employment." Despite the effort, few citizens or business owners heeded the request, and despite the circumstances, special hearings or considerations for those facing relocation were never granted. "No hearing boards ever functioned in California for those who had been relocated."

A week and a half after the need to evacuate hit the papers, the first ousting occurred, and officials definitely shaved leniency from their objective: "Washington dispatches indicated no exceptions will be permitted in evacuation of Japanese, Germans, and Italian nationals from the 86 designated zones in California." The elderly and sick were not given consideration; they could not remain with their naturalized or American-born relatives. Joe Aiello, an Italian citizen and U.S. resident for fifty-six years, was carted out of his home in a wheelchair, and they carried ninety-seven-year-old Placido Abono from his on a stretcher.

The Bakersfield Californian, February 16, 1942
"First Evacuation of Axis Aliens Completed"

San Francisco—Hundreds of enemy aliens, the vanguard of many thousands yet to be removed, were cleared from California's key military and industrial areas over the week end. They were residents of 69 restricted zones for which the government had set an evacuation deadline of last midnight. Even as the first exodus was being completed, government men looked to Washington for guidance in carrying out further orders for the removal of thousands of other aliens from prohibited zones in California by February 24.

With the second evacuation, a bit of confusion set in—were they to be out by midnight on February 23 or did they have until the close of the following day? "After eleventh hour confusion over the evacuation deadline," Tom C. Clark, the Western Defense's alien coordinator, intervened with an answer from Washington that quelled the impending arrests. "Earlier, enforcement agencies insisted that the deadline was midnight tonight and said that enemy nationals still in their homes in prohibited areas tomorrow faced arrest."

Although Anna Dragna saw her Japanese friends on the Dorsey campus the morning after the attack, by March, all of them were gone. As a student at the much more ethnically diverse Theodore Roosevelt High, Tony Amador certainly noticed the empty seats. "In the high school that I went to," Tony explained, "we had Russians, Mexicans, Italians, Armenians, Japanese, Chinese, Jews, and we had some black students in school too." Though the bulk of Los Angeles still remained predominately segregated—and white—Boyle Heights presented a very different picture. Tony recalled that "a Japanese family that lived nearby was taken away to one of those camps." He never gave a moment's thought to them being any sort of a threat. Like his girlfriend Lucy Niotta's family, they ran a local grocery. Making the connection, he wondered what made one more dangerous than the other. After all, other than the way they looked—the features of their face, their almond-slivered eyes, and the shade of their skin—he failed to see any real difference. For Tony, the answer would continue to evade. After all, he was only sixteen.

Anna remained more in tune with the directives affecting her people. Even in her eighties, what came to pass would stick in her mind. Anna spoke of a fear so great, it touched whole communities—a people—and she spoke of a very near miss. "Many Italians," she firmly noted, "worried they would suffer the same fate as the Japanese." The Japanese had just been taken and the military and the papers all promised that the Italians would soon follow. Reading what reporters penned and hearing the rumored word, Anna just assumed that one day the agents would come knocking; that they would find her a threat, just as they had her Japanese schoolmates and neighbors. They would herd her and her family up then ship them off to God knows where. Smartly, she had made the connection between the announcement in the quad and the administration's intent. They tried calming the fear; to severe it before it egged on into fists of hatred. But knowing was no kind of a blessing. Knowing peeled away the bliss. For this young and inquisitive girl, it only raised the red flag further. More so than it did for Tony, the actions taking place pressed the question—what separated us from them? Certainly Anna looked more American, but was that really enough to keep her and her family safe?

Interviews that Dr. Stephen Fox conducted with victims and their family members years after the ordeal had ended spotlight a common theme—uncertainty. "We were so in the dark," some indicated, explaining "we didn't know how long this was going to last." Others referenced the media coverage, stating "every day the paper would say something different." In Vitina Spadaro's case, the rumors were true; her family had already been forced to move from their home in Monterey and now the Japanese were heading to Manzanar. What assurances did Vitina or anyone else have that the Italians would not soon follow? Unfortunately, the threat struck Vitina's mother especially hard. "My mother always lived in fear that the Italians were going to be put away."

These fears were not isolated to the fragile minds of startled women, or reserved to teenage girls like Anna Dragna and Vitina Spadaro. Italians branded as enemy aliens had already felt the repercussions—stripped of their possessions, barred from their jobs and businesses, removed from their schools and classmates, forced to leave their homes, and even placed in internment. Although Tony Amador's family managed to escape relocation, another family that would eventually marry into the Niotta clan was not so lucky. Proclamation 2526 affected the future wife of Stevie's young nephew, George.

"I remember that happening," admitted George's wife, Jeanne Niotta, in regards to the forced relocation of her grandparents, the Breunles. "When World War II broke out, they lived in Englewood." Although the pair were attending night school to become citizens—her grandfather for the first time and her grandmother to repatriate after marrying a non-citizen—they "had to move from the ocean. That's why they moved from Englewood to Alhambra."

Perhaps the only real "safe" zones near the water for enemy aliens were those situated on the other side of the country, but East Coast Italians were by no means unmolested. Back East, they suffered contraband, curfew, and travel restrictions as well, and orders banned Italian fishermen from the seaports, too. Italian boats were either moored or confiscated. A very big difference between these two coasts existed, though. Although large Italian populations existed in cities like New York and Boston, as they also did in San Francisco and Los Angeles, no mass relocation occurred back East, namely because the bulk of the country's Japanese resided out West, in California. Another reason why the Pacific Coast suffered harsher treatment were the predictions of the next attack.

West Coast Attacks and Fifth Column Activity

Not long after the attack on Pearl Harbor, rumors began to spread about the West Coast being the next target. Mayhem and devastation were prophesized somewhere along the waters of California, but Bill Grinnell, a sophomore at Dorsey High when Pearl Harbor was hit, recalled much more than mere rumor: "There was an attack on a little refinery north of Los Angeles, on the coast—between Los Angeles and Santa Barbara." He explained that a "submarine came in and fired." Another incident came to mind as well, one which occurred in Redondo Beach: "I think it was Thanksgiving. A couple Navy planes came in and dropped depths charges in the bay right off Redondo Beach, because there was a one or two-man submarine." Clarifying, he added "they verified that after the war."

Grinnell's contentions were accurate. On the evening of February 23, 1942, after hearing a "whistling noise and a thump," the Hollister family scrambled out the front door of their coastal home in Winchester Canyon, in Santa Barbara County. Outside they spotted "bright flashes" of light "near an oil field on the shore." The Hollisters were not the only ones that noticed. According to *The Los*

Angeles Times, "In an adjacent canyon on this rural stretch of coastline about 100 miles northwest of Los Angeles, Ruth Pratt was tending to her garden." Ruth heard the explosions as well: "I thought something was going wrong at the refinery. Then there was something like a whizzing sound coming right at me." That next morning, a radio broadcast cleared up their questions. "A Japanese submarine had shelled the Ellwood oil field, the first enemy attack on the U.S. mainland since the War of 1812."

A submarine hitting a refinery within 100 miles of his home and then the sighting of a small enemy sub even closer—right off Redondo Beach—left Bill Grinnell feeling a very positive threat existed. Some measure of action, therefore, was certainly in order: "We were very afraid that our ships would be silhouetted against the light glow from Los Angeles, so we felt very vulnerable that there would be an attack. Everybody prepared for it." While Grinnell had no recollections about any local actions against non-citizens, he was "aware that some nationals, or non-citizens—the Japanese, and Germans, and so forth" were under investigation. The term "fifth column" did not escape him either.

Fifth Columnists were the hidden threat lying dormant; enemy alien spies who lived among us and waited for orders from the Axis Powers to strike against America. J. Edgar Hoover described them as "the naturalized citizen whose cloak of citizenship is a sham, and is dangerous to the nation's security." The papers wrote about them, the rumors abounded, and laws were enacted in order to protect citizens from the impending threat. Fears such as this, regardless of likelihood, drastically took hold. During the onset of the alien program, the civilian populous agreed the military should handle the issue. Pearl Harbor largely influenced this frame of mind, with fear and rumor shaping many decisions to come. Like no other event before it, the attack highlighted America's lack of immunity from being hit at home, and the more recent actions along the waters of Los Angeles and Santa Barbara Counties only intensified this sentiment.

Hardship, Guilt, and Stigma

The new restrictions on resident aliens created a variety of hardships. Limited to a 5-mile radius from their homes, many of these individuals were unable to visit relatives, to tend to the ill, or to be present during the funerals and weddings of loved ones and friends. The stigma that came along with being labeled an enemy in one's own neighborhood weighed heavy as well. Proclamations and executive orders helped bring about the negative stereotype that resident aliens born from Axis countries were not only untrustworthy, they were traitors. Sadly, for some, coping proved too difficult.

The shame and feelings of betrayal associated with being branded an enemy coupled with the anxiety of being physically forced from their homes.

Compounded, it became too much for some. At least a half dozen Italian suicides have been connected to the events that occurred early in 1942. Each of these men took their own lives within a five-day period in February after learning they had to relocate. In Marin County, fifty-five-year-old Paul Grell shot himself in the head. The *San Anselmo Herald* reported that he was "said to be despondent over the fact that he could not obtain work because he was an alien and that he was also afraid of being moved inland away from the sea where he had worked for many years." In Stockton, sixty-nine-year-old Italian landscape gardener Giovanni Tassano hung himself.

News of suicide as a direct result of military directives did not remain a secret to those calling the shots. During a series of hearings held before Congress in San Francisco during late February, at least three instances of Italian suicide were relayed—self-inflicted deaths linked to relocation orders, and to being branded an enemy. When the stock market tanked in 1929 and much of the population lost everything, some responded drastically by jumping off bridges and diving out office windows. Their world had ended. For a number of Italians living along the California coast during this traumatic ordeal, this was their market crashing. Like Mr. Tassano, Giovanni Sanguenetti also hung himself. For Martini Battistessa, throwing himself in front of a passing train was the only answer. Giuseppe Michele opted instead to slit his throat with a butcher knife. Stefano Terranova left a suicide note. He wrote: "I believe myself to be good, but find myself deceived" then leapt from a three-story building. According to Rose Scudero, an American citizen who, at the age of twelve, was forced to relocate with her enemy alien mother, "They didn't fully explain to these people why they did this. They felt they had done something wrong. They felt so guilty."

Because blacklisted areas coincided with larger Italian populations up north, those residing in the upper half of the state suffered a greater number of hardships. The cities of Monterey and Pittsburg are full of tragic stories. Monterey resident Rosina Trovato received word she had to relocate on the very same day she learned that her son and nephew had both died at Pearl Harbor. Nancy Mangiapane, another Monterey resident, had three small children and another child on the way when the family got word they had to leave. The fact that Nancy had two brothers already serving in the military held no bearing whatsoever. Nor did it matter that her husband, Albert, had been going to school to earn his citizenship for quite some time. Although his job as a fisherman dragged out the process, the need to balance the two did not deter him. In order to attend, he broke up his time at sea. After catching classes from 2–4 p.m., he headed back to the waters to fish from 7–9 p.m. Despite the effort, Albert still had not received his second papers by the coming of the new order, so he had to go. Nancy and the children were citizens, so they were legally permitted to stay, but they would not have been able to support themselves alone. The family moved to San Jose instead, taking along Nancy's mother and father. Although the elderly couple in their eighties had lived in America since 1916, neither had naturalized, and so they, too, became the enemy.

Italians had long been heavily involved in California's fruit and vegetable trades and in a variety of other integral industries spread throughout the state. For this reason, California's Italians definitely felt the sting of the new order. Those situated further north took a harsher brunt of these effects, chiefly because such large populations of Italian fishermen resided in cities like San Francisco, Santa Cruz, and Monterey. Yet the Italians in the northern end of the state tasted greater hardship for another reason as well. The Army designated Pittsburg, California's Camp Stoneman as an arrival and staging area. Every enemy alien there had to get out. Of the 2,500–3,000 Italians forced to vacate the Bay Area "peninsula" due to military operations, close to 2,000 of them were from the city of Pittsburg.

Oakland Tribune, February 5, 1942
"Pittsburg Italians Hard Hit by Alien Rule"

Attorney General Francis Biddle's order barring enemy aliens from specified areas of California struck this community like a bolt of lightning. The bulk of its 10,000 population is Italian or of Italian descent. Most of its Italian colony has lived here nearly all their lives. They don't know where they will go or what they will do. A pitifully bewildered group, they are flocking to their parish priests, to the corner policeman, to anyone who can tell them what is to come. Probably no community in the entire United States has been hit as hard by the ruling as Pittsburg. Hardly one family in every thousand will escape the evacuation order. There are 1,742 registered aliens in the community. But it would be virtually impossible to count the relatives with Italian blood, all of whom are affected directly or indirectly by the evacuation order.

Addressing the issue, the *Oakland Tribune* hit on a recurring theme: "The common complaint against the ruling is that many of these people would have been citizens had they been able." The journalist highlighted that the bulk of these individuals came to America as teenagers and were unable to write or read even in their native language. They needed schooling if they hoped to pass the citizenship exam, but night schools were not available in prior years. Also, these resident aliens worked long hours to support themselves and to provide for their families. "As the years passed," the residents of Pittsburg "accepted themselves as Americans—though without voting privileges, and raised their children as American citizens. They built the community and they helped build America." They offered up their sons to World War I as well, and the American Legion in that city was even named after the son of Italian immigrants who gave his life heroically. By the close of the year, Francis Biddle would give such points deeper consideration.

For some, living in a "safe" zone failed to minimize the worry. The papers continued to announce newer prohibited areas—areas that, for many, seemed to move closer and closer to their doorstep. The reach of this anti-Italian net spread, moving further out from the waters of the California coast. Although the relocation order did not strike Southern California quite the way it did the north, Angeleno aliens were definitely impacted. Like Pittsburg, the climate in L.A. soon got very militarized as well; likely to ensure the evacuation of forbidden zones took place peacefully and efficiently, armed military guards began patrolling areas of Los Angeles. Residents received word of these intended activities back in early February, when *The Los Angeles Times* printed the list of L.A.'s forbidden zones and announced that "Army sources admitted some of the 13 territories in the Los Angeles area are patrolled." Bill Grinnell remembered the events well. Several thousand troops took up residence in a large park near his high school.

Grinnell expressed that soldiers set up tents right there in the park and stayed for at least the remainder of his time at Dorsey. He recalled the presence of anti-aircraft guns as well, which the military strategically placed throughout Southern California. One of these weapons sat in nearby Baldwin Hills. Martial law, it seemed, had seeped into the California way of life.

Santa Ana Register, August 22, 1942
"Martial Rule in Effect on Coast"

Los Angeles—Call it anything you wish, a retired Army colonel told a conference of mayors last night, the entire Pacific coast is now under martial rule. "We have been living under martial rule since Feb. 19, when the President promulgated his order authorizing removal of enemy aliens and American citizens of Axis-power descent from designated zones," Col. William A. Graham told 15 Pacific coast mayors.

Italians and Germans expected to be hauled off in mass and imprisoned just like the Japanese, but this was not the only "relocation" they feared. Also heavy on many minds was the possibility of being shipped back to their former homes. Heightening this fear, Italy and Germany were now places of all-out war. For most Italians who had been living stateside for a number of years, Italy existed only in memories. For these Italians, America truly did serve as the only home they recognized.

Management Problems, Opposing Viewpoints, and the Executive Order

Without fail, difficulties arise whenever multiple agencies are required to come together. Understanding this, no one expected that collaborating on a project as large scale as the "enemy alien problem" would be easy—and it was not; disagreements occurred, and fear and competition took a toll on order. From very early on, the human aspect of the endeavor suffered. Making it all worse were the issues of inconsistency and overlapping duties. Policies established one day were contradicted or overruled the next, which not only elevated tensions and confusion among enemy aliens, it spurred an even wider gap among governmental agencies. The apparent lack of order must have raised questions among the American public as well. Who was running the show? Did they have any clue what they were doing?

Sentiments varied. The fear resonating during the early part of the war certainly brought on a heightened sense of apprehension. It also fostered outright distrust of anyone even thought to be a foreigner. While many shared this view and stood behind the Army and its military directives, others saw these actions as excessive, unjust, and unconstitutional. Some felt resident aliens were being singled out and discriminated against; their civil rights were being violated. Those of this opinion sincerely believed individual consideration should be given. Others argued concessions like that could not be made during a wartime posture. Yet another group voiced a completely different complaint, egging on about the leniency of the Department of Justice.

Out in San Francisco, in late February 1942, amid the first two scheduled purges of enemy aliens from the coast, National Defense Migration Hearings were held before the House of Representatives. Key advocates met with board members on February 21 and 23. Similar hearings were also scheduled for later that month out in Portland, Seattle, and Los Angeles, and still more hearings were set to take place in March. The State Personnel Board had already met and discussed the decision to oust all enemy aliens from civil service positions. Appearing before that board was American Civil Liberties Union (A.C.L.U.) representative Ernest Besig, who "called for equal treatment for all citizens and expressed fear that enforcement of the plan would be injurious to the democratic process." In addition to this, the A.C.L.U. also approached Attorney General Earl Warren over "constitutionality of the board's policy." Responding to these efforts, E. H. Christian, a board member from Hayward, insisted his mind would not be changed: "If you are more interested in protecting the rights of Japanese, Italians, and Germans in this country than in winning the war, go ahead."

Los Angeles County's Civilian Defense Council strongly posed that the Army and Navy should continue to handle the situation and even recommended that all "comings and goings" of enemy aliens within the combat zones of the Pacific Coast "be regulated by the two military services" with "the hope of averting widespread sabotage of vital war and defense facilities." The committee pushed for "working internment" camps, too, and for all enemy language schools to be shut down. Going further, mandates stipulated that enemy aliens could not gather in groups larger than twenty-five unless granted government permission. Pushing the limits, alien use of telephones and automotive equipment went under scrutiny. The Defense Council felt all such activity should be done only under government supervision, which raised a new question: should all home phones and personal vehicles be confiscated from enemy aliens as well?

Amid all the anti-alien sentiment, some did publicly voice opposition to the actions being taken. When Japanese–American civil service employees (U.S. citizens) were removed from their government positions, the Los Angeles Industrial Union Council went on record to say they opposed city and state policies because they felt they promoted "disunity and intolerance at a time when unity and understanding are needed." They anchored their argument on the fact that all civil service employees are U.S. citizens and State employees are even required to take an oath of loyalty to the United States. Expressing their belief and concern, the board urged the State to halt any additional activities geared toward American citizens of Italian and German heritage.

Indecision and arguments led President Roosevelt to defer to the War Department again and again, even when the Department of Justice raised pressing concerns over what was turning out to be an unrealistic, ineffective, discriminating, and exceedingly costly military agenda. Despite mixed emotions about how best to handle the situation, efforts to safeguard the state and to protect against potential threats continued. Unfortunately, it came at the expense of thousands. Although Proclamations 2525, 2526, and 2527 already placed a variety of restrictions on enemy aliens, efforts really got going on February 19, 1942. The first of the initial relocations had just occurred and the second was slated in another five days. In between evacuations, President Roosevelt signed Executive Order 9066. The new order not only forced state and federal agencies to get on board with the military's objectives, it also gave the War Department authority over Attorney General Francis Biddle.

The directive stirred a wide range of opinions. Again in opposition stood the A.C.L.U., who even protested.

The San Bernardino County Sun, February 23, 1942
"A.C.L.U. Protests"

New York, Feb. 22—The American Civil Liberties union today protested as "unprecedented and founded on no specific evidence of need" President Roosevelt's executive order establishing military areas from which citizens or aliens may be removed. The objection was voiced in a telegram by Roger N. Baldwin, A.C.L.U. president, to A.C.L.U. offices in San Francisco and Los Angeles, instructing them to "assist in protecting the civil rights of Japanese-American citizens" affected by the order.

Although Italians wrote the organization for assistance, in addition to writing the President for help, the A.C.L.U. chose to focus on the Japanese situation.

Their harsher treatment made it apparent that differences between the three enemy alien groups existed. Noting this, Japanese supporters lobbied for a lesser punishment—one more on par with the treatment of their Axis contemporaries. *The San Bernardino County Sun* reported that during the San Francisco hearings held late that February, "Pacific coast Japanese marshaled their friends and leaders before a congressional committee" to "plead for treatment as considerate as that accorded Germans and Italians in the evacuation they regard as inevitable." *The Sun* even paralleled the mass evacuation of Japanese with "the Nazi government's treatment of Jews" and warned these efforts would only "invite reprisals."

Compared to the Japanese, the Italians and Germans were granted a level of leniency. Newspapers commented with headlines like "Local Italians Favored in New Alien Evacuation." The large number of service members with Italian citizens as parents may have garnered such concessions. That aside, the military agenda still slated Italian and German citizens for mass removal following the Japanese exodus. As the *Santa Cruz Sentinel* reported in March '42, shortly after the Japanese had been moved out, "the same evacuation will be requested for Italian and German aliens." General DeWitt would not forget. His intentions and feelings remained far from secret. "Evacuate enemy aliens in large groups at the earliest possible date," he expressed to a fellow officer, adding that "sentiment is being given too much importance."

Although adamant about not granting any special treatment for enemy aliens, General DeWitt ultimately gave in to a list of caveats that the papers referred to as "certain exceptions." These clauses were intended to save the elderly, those aged seventy or older, along with the families "of Germans and Italians in the armed forces." This included their children, wives, parents, sisters, and brothers.

Troubling to some, Executive Order 9066 also granted military leaders the power to target U.S. citizens. Pasquale DeCicco naturalized in 1909, and Mario Valdastri earned his citizenship by serving in the U.S. armed forces during World War I. Despite being American citizens, both men still found themselves interned. The War Department, now wielding the power of 9066, superseded Constitutional rights. They were fully sanctioned to arrest and detain American citizens without charge, explanation, or legal representation. They could intern prisoners in a military guarded camp for as long as they felt necessary.

Mario Valdastri explained that although targeting and interning U.S. citizens not of Japanese descent was not a standard practice, he was not alone in being singled out. San Francisco businessman Nino Guttaradauro was another naturalized American citizen who received exclusion orders that forced him to leave the coast. Lawyers, public officials, and newspaper editors made the list, too, and when it came time to oust these citizens, the military did not rely on signs tacked up by the Boy Scouts, they sent in federal agents.

The San Bernardino Sun, October 11, 1942
"Army Expels Five Italians"

SAN FRANCISCO, Oct. 10—The army disclosed tonight five Italians, included three leading members of the San Francisco Italian community, have been ordered expelled from the territory of the western defense command. Col. Karl R. Bendetsen, chief of the wartime civilian control administration, said the following men had been ordered out of the Pacific coast military zone: Sylvester Andriano, former San Francisco city supervisor and chairman of local draft board 100. Ettore Patrizi, editor and publisher of daily L'Italia and Voce Del Popolo, Italian language newspapers. Renzel Turko, attorney, and Sam Fusco and Remo Bosia. All five are American citizens.

A report from the Roberts Commission, released in late January 1942, is often faulted for prompting the various orders directed at non-citizens of Axis countries, and for raising suspicion of U.S. citizens. Though never substantiated, the report alleged that Japanese-Americans in Oahu had aided in the attack, leaving those stateside even more apprehensive and fearful of anyone not a citizen. If it happened once, it could happen again, became popular sentiment. Not wanting to take any chances, President Roosevelt handed over authority to the U.S. Army.

Presidential proclamations and the executive order affected more than just the civilian populous. Service members were harmed as well. Steve Ghio, an Italian-American serving in the U.S. Navy, returned home on leave during the spring of 1942 only to find his house boarded up. Many of the surrounding homes appeared empty as well. No idea where his family could be, Ghio went to the police for assistance. Describing how the wartime orders impacted her family, Gloria Sylvernale indicated that her brother left for the war shortly after their father returned from six months in a detention camp out in Texas. The treatment their father endured no doubt weighed heavily on the mind of that new service member. Unfortunately, instances such as these—instances that brought harm to the families of American military members overseas in the fight—were far from rare.

Going global, directives against citizens of Axis countries were not limited to America's land borders and territories. All over the world, citizens of Axis countries met with discrimination, questioning, arrest, detainment, and even internment. Detention facilities and internment camps waited. In Australia, the authorities rounded up and arrested hundreds of Italian sugar field workers. America's neighbors, Canada and Mexico, also got involved. General DeWitt even paid a personal visit to Mexico to ensure buy in on a very questionable upcoming maneuver. Conferring with the country's former president, Lazaro Cardenas—now a military general like DeWitt—the pair came to a mutual arrangement.

The Long Beach Independent, March 10, 1942
"Mexico Clears Sonora of All Enemy Aliens"

Nogales, March 9—the government took further action today against enemy aliens in the state of Sonora. German, Italian, and Japanese nationals in Sonora were ordered to leave within a week. Naturalized citizens of German or Italian birth were told to report to a concentration center at Guadalajara.

The Department of Justice got involved in the matter as well, and in compliance with requests from the D.O.J., the governments of more than a dozen Latin American countries seized Japanese, German, and Italian citizens—upward of 6,500 individuals. Technically, the United States had no legal right, or grounds, to request a foreign government to turn over citizens of Axis countries. American officials had a plan for these individuals, though, so they made the effort regardless of legalities. The plan was to use these "imported" enemy aliens as a means of trade; a potential bargaining chip for retrieving prisoners of war (P.O.W.s). In a shady attempt to legalize the tactic—the internment of large numbers of non-citizens not even residing on American soil—the I.N.S. waited until after foreign officials escorted their detainees over the U.S. border. After that, Immigration charged them with illegal entry and locked them up. Jerre Mangione referred to the play as an "international form of kidnapping" and expressed that one commander of an Immigration Services camp stated "only in wartime could we get away with such fancy skullduggery."

Former President of Mexico General Lazaro Cardenas confers with Lt. Gen. John DeWitt, Agua Caliente, Mexico, 1942. (*Author's personal collection*)

Pushing Further

By the close of February 1942, most of California's coast had been declared a military zone. Forced relocations triggered by the proclamations and the new executive order continued to bring hardships upon immigrant families and to test the loyalty of non-citizens who had come to call America their home. Enemy aliens were no longer near the ocean or utility facilities and anyone else thought to be an immediate threat now sat in custody. Despite the level of control, General DeWitt was still not satisfied. It appeared obvious to some he intended to push further—and he did. Wielding the power of the new order, the commander of the western division moved quickly.

On March 2, General DeWitt issued Proclamation Number 1 and instituted a nest of new zones. The red line for enemy aliens now ran the coastline from Canada to Mexico, trailing along the southern border of Arizona. Announcing the update, DeWitt remarked to the press that "he considered American-Japanese potentially more dangerous to the nation's welfare than German and Italian aliens." Shortly after that, the Japanese—citizen and not—were taken.

The Oregon Statesman Journal, March 4, 1942
"Army to Evacuate Aliens"

Restricted Areas Set on Coast
Zones Outlined in Order; All Enemy Aliens to Move

San Francisco, March 3—Evacuation of enemy aliens and American-born Japanese from all the coastal area and much of the fertile inland valleys of the pacific coast was promised Tuesday in a sweeping army order setting up new prohibited and restricted areas. Lieut. General J. L. Dewitt, commanding general of the western defense command, marked off half of the states of Washington, Oregon, California and Arizona as military area one, from which enemy aliens will be excluded by future order. He hinted this exodus would start soon.

Sadly, the president submitted to the whims of the Army and its general, agreeing to the mass internment. Jerre Mangione explained that Attorney General Francis Biddle "fought it tooth and nail, insisting the evacuation was unnecessary." Instead, he urged a continuation of the D.O.J.'s policy of selective internment. This mandated detaining "only those aliens of Japanese birth who by their activities, affiliations, or relationship in Japan might be considered potentially dangerous." Unfortunately, Biddle was not successful.

Going further, under General DeWitt's new proclamation, any place within the western division not labeled military area one would serve as military area two. There, an additional ninety-seven smaller forbidden zones were now located.

DeWitt's plan, it seemed, was to declare the entire coast a warzone, and to intern every enemy alien within its borders. Combatting this, Biddle continued to press the civil rights angle, and to point out the repercussions of pushing loyal non-citizens over to the Axis Powers. Sadly, he took a beating from the press for it. Going against the systemic grain, Biddle met with opposition from his contemporaries as well—from military leaders, various elected officials, and law enforcement. Mostly their complaints centered upon on what they considered leniency.

The Los Angeles Times, March 12, 1942
"Many Declared to Be Escaping Internment; Biddle Leniency Flayed"

Mar. 11—Fear was expressed here today that the program of the Army for evicting dangerous enemy aliens from strategic areas in the Pacific Coast may be impaired seriously by an excessively lenient attitude of the Dept. of Justice. Through the machinery of appeals boards operating under the authority of Attorney General Biddle, it was asserted, more than half of the enemy nationals rounded up by the Federal Bureau of Investigation agents are escaping internment.

Apparently, Biddle's "catch and release" record heightened fears. "Of the total cases heard,"—over 1,600 of them—"766 brought orders for internment." But "after showing of evidence, 270 aliens were released outright." *The L.A. Times* further highlighted that "statistics made available by Biddle" showed roughly a third of the 1,632 individual pleas made before alien hearing boards, resulted in placement "under parole to citizen sponsors." A sponsor vouched for the "continued good behavior" of the alien and kept in contact with the individual. Parolees reported regularly and remained under close watch. They received similar—and at times even more stringent—treatment than Italian soldiers held stateside as P.O.W.s.

Floyd Gonella claimed that, during the war, his parents occasionally drove to a detention facility in San Francisco to pick up a man they knew from their hometown. He was not an enemy alien, he was an Italian prisoner of war. The Gonellas were permitted to bring the soldier into their home for Sunday dinners. Frankie and Anna Dragna's cousin, Tony Poli, heard similar stories from his parents. Tony explained that the Pomona Fairgrounds housed Italians during the war. "My Uncle, on my father's side, would go and get some of the Italian boys" from the fairgrounds and "bring them to their home for dinner on a Sunday." Tony believes these young men were Italian P.O.W.s rather than enemy aliens. "They took them to some Italian get-togethers and to some dances." After the evening ended, Tony's uncle brought them back to the camp in Pomona.

The number of potentially dangerous enemy aliens that Attorney General Francis Biddle was helping "get away" alarmed officials to the extent that measures were taken to ensure the Department of Justice, and Francis Biddle personally, were doing the job properly: "Members of the Attorney General's office will be asked by West Coast legislators to supply full details of the manner in which the appeals boards system is applied." Going bolder, some involved in this preliminary investigation proved "outspoken in expressions of concern that Biddle," in his "excess of zeal concerning the customary civil rights of the enemy aliens under arrest," might actually "hamper efforts of the military"—efforts that sought "to keep such persons under definite restraint."

Despite the harsh pushback from the public, peers, and superiors, treatment of the families of soldiers and sailors in the fight weighed heavily on Francis Biddle's mind. For this diligence, he found himself countered and questioned at nearly every turn. Aggressive and unbending opposition came from influential military leaders—individuals like Henry Stimson, the Secretary of War, and the more zealous authority General DeWitt. Thankfully, to the relief of many, the president soon came to see just how unrealistic DeWitt's plan was.

After the Japanese were pushed out of key zones and detained, and after Proclamation Number 1 took hold, DeWitt readied for the next portion of his plan: for Germans and Italians to "be ordered out in a continuing evacuation." He estimated the process would probably last several months and affect some 200,000 people. The numbers were far, far greater than he ever anticipated though. Up until then, the president had—to some extent—stepped aside, removing himself of responsibility by repeatedly delegating authority to military leaders. Once he caught word of the magnitude of the general's new objective though—a mass evacuation that would call for efforts across sixteen states, and encompass some 52 million people—President Roosevelt intervened.

Recognizing the impending calamity about to unfold, the Secretary of War received a presidential order to take no further action against German or Italian aliens; at least not without personally consulting the president first. Two weeks later, when DeWitt again pressed for the mass evacuation of Italian and German enemy aliens on the West Coast, Stimpson advised against it, and against any such future action.

Rather than move forward with General DeWitt's plans, President Roosevelt sided with the Department of Justice instead. The president agreed to stay the course of selective internment for Italians and Germans. Jerre Mangione believed the mail flooding the White House may have factored into this decision as well. Letters and postcards came in "from scores of anti-Nazi refugees, among them Thomas Mann, Albert Einstein, and Bruno Frank." Ironically, these messages highlighted that many of the individuals America had categorized as enemies were actually political refugees who were "among the first and the most farsighted adversaries of the governments against which the United States was presently at war."

Unable to trump the power of the president, General DeWitt had no choice but to accept what others had long been pointing out. Removing Italian and German citizens from the workforce would cripple United States war efforts, and to add American citizens of Italian and German descent to the list of those to intern in mass would have been devastating. DeWitt relented that summer.

The San Bernardino Sun, June 28, 1942
"Alien Orders Eased to Meet Labor Shortages"

SAN FRANCISCO, June 27—Lieut. Gen. John L. Dewitt, commander of the western defense command, the Fourth army, tonight announced elimination of "prohibited and restricted areas" in California, thus making available several thousand Italian and German agricultural workers.

Unfortunately, the modification of the governmental plan did not include the Japanese; they had already been evacuated. To cut them loose and send them home now would have been to admit a mistake. But the change in policy that saved the Italians and Germans at the last hour was never one of social concern or fairness. Although the general pushed forward with too much zeal, pragmatics had predominately led the way. For those who had managed to escape interment and relocation, the change in protocol offered a mild safeguard. They were permitted to remain in their homes but a leash tethered them close by. The travel and curfew restrictions persisted and none of their property was returned either. Staying in their neighborhoods, the stigma of being an enemy greeted them every day, and yet, they faithfully and tirelessly continued to contribute to the war effort.

Columbus Day

Near as sudden as it fell upon them, America's Italians got word that an end to their suffering and anxiety drew near. The directives that plagued them would soon be lifted. It came to pass on October 12, 1942, just two and a half months after the Italians escaped mass internment. It had been nearly a year since the attack on Pearl Harbor. Attorney General Francis Biddle gave the official word during a nationwide broadcast at Carnegie Hall. "The regulations applying, up to now, to alien enemies, no longer apply to Italian aliens." On October 19, they would come off the list.

Strategically, the message arrived on the one U.S. holiday Italians held closer to their hearts than any other ethnic group—Columbus Day. Although a great deal of controversy now hovers around this date, it originated as a celebration of heritage for Italian-Americans. The observance became official in 1937, when President Roosevelt declared October 12 Christopher Columbus Day. But the day's roots ran far deeper. The earliest known celebrations took place in New York in 1866 and in San Francisco in 1869.

After making reference to Italian history and denouncing Fascism, Biddle praised the wartime contributions of Italian-Americans: "In each division of the United States Army, nearly five hundred soldiers, on the average, are the sons of Italian immigrants … these men are abundantly represented in the list of heroes who have been decorated for bravery since December 7, 1941." Easing into the issue, Biddle addressed what he believed to be the reason why the mothers, fathers, and grandparents of these brave Italian-American service members were still not citizens; he faulted the literacy test. In a gesture meant to placate both sides of the argument, Biddle explained that he had made a recommendation to Congress that he hoped would alleviate future problems. The suggestion sought to simplify the naturalization process for aliens aged fifty or older who had come to America before July 1, 1942, and had been living stateside continuously ever since. The literacy test would be waved for these individuals. Biddle estimated this simple concession would benefit some 200,000 eligible Italian aliens.

Aiming to calm those troubled by his words, Francis Biddle clarified that this did "not mean that dangerous or disloyal persons" would no longer be "subject to apprehension or internment." Reassuring, he added "we will take no chances." Strengthening his contention that these individuals were of no threat, the attorney general then made a statement that has since been challenged. Going on record, he expressed that fewer than 300 Italian aliens had been interned: "We find that, out of a total 600,000 persons, there has been cause to intern only 228, or fewer than one-twentieth of one percent." This figure was meant to soothe the anxieties and fears some still harbored by showing how unlikely an act of Italian espionage really was. The Italians, he explained, could be trusted.

Although the governmental mindset and directives had changed, the process used to arrive at this conclusion—no matter how painful, laborious, and costly—could not be undermined. It could not have all been in vain; could not be viewed by the American public as a mistake or failure. All the dollars spent and the suffering endured still required justification. Knowing this, Francis Biddle exclaimed "the test of time, of actual performance, was essential. We wanted proof. We were right in requiring it."

Many Italian-Americans came to view Francis Biddle as a savior for their people. Working for his administration, and witnessing his efforts firsthand, Jerre Mangione was certainly of this opinion. It is true that Biddle's hands were restrained, if not completely tied, during much of the enemy alien situation. Even his speech on Columbus Day 1942 demonstrates a level of censorship. The announcement brought good news: soon the civil rights normally afforded to non-citizens would be restored. Yet Biddle's words also delivered a quiet backhand. Nowhere in the ten-page speech is there any mention of suffering or hardship. Because these actions were not made known to the public, much of what happened remained a secret for more than half a century. Sadly, more than seventy-five years later, many are still unaware of what truly happened.

Attorney General Francis Biddle addresses an audience to announce Italian aliens will no longer be classed as enemy aliens and will be "free to participate in the war effort" beginning October 19, 1942, Carnegie Hall, New York, Columbus Day, October 12, 1942. (*Author's personal collection*)

At Carnegie Hall, Francis Biddle failed to admit wrongdoing on the part of governmental agencies. Not a trace of remorse resonated. Much more tragic was the lack of something that would not come for nearly sixty years—an apology. Rather than extending sincerity or empathy, Biddle instead highlighted the pragmatic effect of the new decision—these Italians were now "free to participate in the war effort without the handicaps that have hampered them up to now." The statement reverberated in the headlines that followed: "Italian Aliens Win Freedom to Aid in War." Perhaps subdued by the governmental censorship curtailing the press, even journalists lacked sympathy. In close at the podium in New York, Biddle faced the cameras and uttered a near warning to those soon to be pardoned: "See to it that <u>all</u> Italians remain loyal."

The government was careful to ensure that a victim was not identified—the trampling of civil rights strategically omitted—as without a victim, there can be no aggressor or bully. The approach allowed the government to wave all blame and retain its hero status. Conversely, Biddle used the word "exonerated," suggesting Italian aliens were guilty of something other than simply being Italian.

A week more and they would be removed from the list. At least they could rejoice at that. But first General DeWitt exercised one final flex.

The San Bernardino Sun, October 13, 1942
"No Change on Coast"

San Francisco, Oct. 12—Italians on the Pacific coast will remain under military restrictions despite Attorney-General Biddle's announcement they would no longer be classed as enemy aliens after next Monday, unless Lieut. Gen. J. L. DeWitt countermands his proclamations governing them in the western defense zone. General DeWitt's restrictive orders governing movements of enemy aliens, including Italians, were superimposed on similar orders issued by Biddle. The military orders can be withdrawn only by another order from the western defense command. General DeWitt and his aides made no comment tonight on the attorney-general's action.

Stubborn as the general was, not even he could dismiss the futility of going up against the president. Out-gunned, he ultimately relented.

Response and Reasons

There is no question that economics figured into the decision against a mass internment for the remaining Axis nationals. Facilities required maintenance and the detainees needed to be guarded, fed, clothed, and provided with medical attention, and some even argued those security guards could be better used in the fight overseas. But dollars were only one of several hot issues. Race was another.

Prejudice and discrimination are often listed among, if not cited as, the primary reasons why the Japanese received separate treatment. Whether or not this is true, it was no secret that the Japanese stood out when compared to the other Axis nationals. Even the newspapers noted the fact. In February 1942, the *Bakersfield Californian* "pointed out that Japanese are easily recognized where Germans and Italians are not." Historically, Italians were not treated like white Americans, but their physical features did allow them to blend in far more than the Japanese, and the same could be said of the Germans. Regardless of where U.S. residents of Japanese descent were born—America or abroad—their physical appearance posed an issue. The shape of their eyes and the shade of their skin stirred negative feelings in those still shaken by the attack on the home front. For many, these traits reminded them of the death of young American servicemen—of sons, and nephews, and cousins, and neighbors; those recently taken without provocation. These physical traits served as a trigger. Sadly, this made the Japanese much more susceptible to reprisal—acts of vandalism and violence.

For Americans stuck in this fearful or hateful mindset, to look upon anyone remotely Japanese—perhaps even someone of Korean, Vietnamese, or Chinese descent—was to look upon the face of an enemy. The events that took place influenced the thoughts and behaviors of American citizens on a large scale. Fear, hatred, and mistrust boiled in abundance. That being said, just how much this actually influenced governmental actions and policy is a completely separate matter. The distinction, however, is commonly overlooked. History books still sell a cause-and-effect story about the Japanese attack and America entering the fight. The problem with portraying the event like a hand quickly flipping a switch is that it negates a hefty list of precautionary efforts that took place long before the bombing of Pearl Harbor.

Despite the popularly held belief of a racial military or governmental agenda, several points combat the level race actually played. The Institute for Research of Expelled Germans explained that despite the obvious fact German and Italian citizens were classed as Anglo-Saxon—or white—while the descendants of Japan were not, the vast majority of those who were arrested after the attack were actually of European descent. Also highlighted by this research is the lesser-known fact that the Japanese were allowed to return to their homes after the war, while other internees remained in detention camps for nearly another three years. Also, unlike Japanese detainees, a number of German and Italian aliens found themselves deported. Perhaps putting it best, Fox blamed "economics, politics, and morale" for what came to pass then elaborated that race served "as a reinforcing factor."

Hate, fear, and economics aside, what ultimately led to the abandonment of the mass internment for those of Italian and German descent was the inability to execute the plan and the repercussions for trying. Simply put, it was not feasible, and if it had been, going through with it would have been severely detrimental to the war effort. In an article about the enemy alien situation in Kern County, the *Bakersfield Californian* inadvertently touched upon the primary reason the effort was abandoned. "Several thousand axis aliens and their families reside" in the area, but of these individuals, only "about 500 are Japanese." A comparable statement could be made about nearly every city all across America. Numbers presented a major obstacle for the military's objective. Comparatively, far fewer Japanese resided on American soil. This stemmed primarily from immigration laws, which capped the number of immigrants permitted to enter the U.S. from Asian countries years before it began restricting Europeans.

It is far easier to control a small population than it is a large one, especially when that population is densely consolidated in a specific area. This proved to be another key factor that allowed for the Japanese interment. Geographically, Italians and Germans had dispersed themselves throughout the country. Additionally, they became integral to a wide range of industries. The same could not be said of Japanese nationals, who primarily clustered together along the coast as fishermen. Although the *Bakersfield California* gently alluded to population size serving as a factor, Tom Treanor of *The Los Angeles Times* preached the point emphatically.

In a December 1941 installment of his column, "The Home Front," Treanor explained that "the practical difficulties of housing so many people, makes wholesale internment a practical impossibility." Alan Rosenfeld was of this opinion as well and offered a perfect example. In a journal article in *Social Process in Hawai'i*, he explained that because of the overwhelming size of the Japanese population on the islands, federal authorities were forced to pursue "a policy of selective internment." Agreeing with Treanor and Rosenfeld, Fox contended: "… had there been several million Japanese in the United States as there were Italians and Germans the Japanese could not have been relocated as a practical matter." Although the numbers aggravatingly plagued the Army's objective and ultimately doomed the Japanese, for others, it became a saving grace: it kept Italian-Americans and German-Americans from internment alongside Americans of Japanese descent.

Tom C. Clark, Alien Control Coordinator for the Western Defense Command, estimated that some 33,600 Japanese resided in California. Clark's figure combines citizens and non-citizens. When compared to the numbers associated with the two other alien groups residing in the state, this figure appears relatively small. Clark estimated there were 100,000 Italian and 71,700 German aliens in California. His estimate was comprised solely of non-citizens. If Clark had included Italians and Germans that naturalized, plus added the American-born citizens of Italian and German descent—as was the case with the Japanese estimate—the result would have appeared astronomical. At the start of the war, 5 million residents in the U.S. were of Italian descent—the largest ethnic group in the country. Making this plan of mass internment all the more laughable, Germans represented the second largest. By Fox's account, "the several hundred thousand Germans and Italians living in the United States and their immediate descendants represented as many as 11,000,000 potential subjects for relocations."

Applying this logic to Hawaii further strengthens the theory. On the islands, an opposite demographic existed, creating a parallel. Dwarfing the other Axis groups, Japanese residents made up roughly one-third of the overall population, and for this reason, as Rosenfeld expressed, these individuals were not relocated. Conversely, Hawaii's Italian enemy aliens found themselves shipped to the mainland. Logistics was but one of the barriers that prevented the relocation of Hawaii's Japanese; impact on the war effort was another. If this group had been removed, production in support of the war would have all but stopped in the area. Making up roughly a third of the population, the Japanese accounted for a significant portion of the working class employed in war-related industries. As Treanor clearly outlined in the *L.A. Times*, on the mainland, the same could be said of Italians and Germans.

Men and women of Italian and German descent proved to be an overwhelmingly essential workforce commodity, so much so that Treanor's warning could not be ignored by governing officials: "The loss of manpower would be serious. Innocent aliens can do valuable work." If the Italians and Germans stateside had joined the Japanese in a mass internment, the war effort would have suffered a supreme deficiency. Italians labored in factories building tanks and planes, they fished the seas providing food and essential oils, and they grew and tended the crops that fed the nation and its service members. Despite the obvious detriment to the war effort, the logistical impossibility of a mass removal of that magnitude, and the astronomical expense involved, Lt General John DeWitt still remained bent on the idea. The exodus of Italians and Germans was set to commence just as soon as the Japanese had been successfully evacuated. Thankfully, this never came to pass.

Although this accounts for several of the reasons why Germans and Italians were not interned in mass alongside the Japanese, it fails to answer one very important question: why were the Italians "exonerated" earlier than the Germans? Several theories have been posed and a number of variables named. Looking over the timeline of events, the upcoming invasion of Europe likely held sway. American troops were not storming in through Germany; they were marching into the continent via Sicily. After invading the island, they pushed forward into the Italian mainland. Leading up to the invasion, a pro-American sentiment was being seen in Italy. Mussolini's praise and favor had dwindled and the Italians had little appetite for a struggle. This could be exploited. The American government showed a sign of good will to Italy when they pardoned their stateside compatriots, freeing them of the enemy alien stigma. The act may have even created greater dissension among the military ranks of "the old country," further softening the U.S. entry into the European Theater of Operations (E.T.O.).

Events happening in Europe, and the news coverage that appeared stateside, slowly began to shift the American view of all things Italian. In May 1942, *The San Bernardino Sun* stated that "not a single anti-American demonstration— even an officially organized one—had been reported in Italy" and that Benito Mussolini was now "leading a hungry, disillusioned and apathetic" country. Still relatively early in the war, Italy's future as an Axis Power sat in question; clearly their war against America appeared unpopular. "Some observers see in Italy a people who dislike their German allies and who care nothing for the Japanese—a people who are looked upon for potential assistance when and if an American-British army lands in Europe to crush Hitlerism." Reports even claimed that Italy welcomed an Allied invasion, as it meant "freeing them from the humiliating grip held by the Germans."

The efforts of Italians in other parts of the world also helped shape a newer image.

The Courier-Journal, August 17, 1942
"Free Italians in Americas Vow Solidarity with Allies"

The Pan-American Free Italy Conference today adopted a proposal by the Argentine delegation that the Free Italians (anti-Fascist Italians) of North and South America state their "absolute solidarity with the people of the United States, Britain, Russia, China, and other United Nations." The conference is composed of representatives of Italians in the Americas. The meeting adopted six resolutions, including one to appeal to governments which have broken relations with the Axis to except from the category of enemy aliens Italians who are known to be anti-Fascist. Another resolution created an office of co-ordination of information for all Free Italian organizations in the Americas. Combatting of the fifth column by anti-Fascist Italians in the Americas was recommended.

The solvency of its troops may have been another factor that contributed to the removal of Italian aliens from the enemy list. No secret to the military brass, men of Italian heritage were by far their largest ethnic force in the fight; hundreds of thousands of Italian-Americans were now serving. But in order for the United States to benefit from this asset, they needed those soldiers, sailors, and airmen to remain focused. Provoking an opposite effect, letters from loved ones back home brought discouraging and heartbreaking news. Such correspondence jeopardized the resiliency and continued allegiance of these young Italian-Americans. Decision-makers must have wondered if they were asking for too tall an order. For nearly a year now, governmental restrictions against Italian aliens had persecuted mothers, fathers, and grandparents. It was becoming a source of anxiety and despair for service members. While the ill treatment of family and friends of Italian-American military members had not yet backfired, some likely questioned how long the situation could persist before it erupted. Mounting anxieties further, despite the level of support the country was receiving from service members of Italian descent and despite how vital Italian aliens were to the war effort stateside, General DeWitt still fully intended to push forward with their mass internment.

Regardless of the reason an exodus was averted, and why Italian aliens were removed from the enemy list, one thing is certain: those that suffered hardships made every effort to move on and to prove their allegiance to America. The *Bakersfield Californian* illustrated well the immediate Italian response. Following the attack on Pearl Harbor, residents of Kern County reacted exceedingly aggressive toward enemy aliens. County officials and citizens there made it painfully known they did not want citizens of Axis countries relocated to their borders, and they even publicly pushed for the internment of all Germans and Italians. While few of Japanese or German descent resided in Kern, many of Italian descent did. After all the heartache and pain, they were still able to show a gesture of kindness.

The Bakersfield Californian, October 26, 1942
"Kern Italians to Hold Bond Drive"

Appreciation for Lifting of Enemy Alien Ban Will Be Shown at Barbecue

Appreciation and gratitude for the lifting of the enemy alien bans on Italians will be expressed by hundreds of Italians of Old River, Panama Pumpkin Center, and Greenfield, on November 1, when they stage a war bond drive and barbecue. The restrictions were recently amended by Lieutenant-General J. L. DeWitt, removing Italians from the enemy alien classification.

Aftermath for an Enemy Alien

Going from harmless neighbor to a feared enemy can happen in an instant. The same cannot be said of making a reversal. Francis Biddle's public announcement may have changed policy but it certainly did not flip an instantaneous switch on the minds of Americans. Easing back to some semblance of the way things were—to trust and friendship and community inclusion—was going to take a bit of adjustment. But in truth, some things lost are never fully restored, and although time is known to heal, not everything can be mended. Despite these difficult truths, life continues.

Hastily thrown together, the contraband program implemented to collect weapons, cameras, and other belongings from enemy aliens had caught most local authorities off guard. Not only were they ill-equipped to receive or store these items, proper protocols for ensuring the safe return of this property were never put in place. Some of the turn-in locations failed to issue hand receipts. In other instances, this paperwork was damaged or simply went missing. As a result, much of what was taken never made it back to its rightful owner. Benito Vanni recalled the F.B.I. agents coming to his home as a child. They removed pieces from his father's shortwave radio then confiscated his binoculars and weapons— two shotguns and two rifles, a handgun, and a saber. Agents interned Benito's father for the duration of the war. After making it back to his family, he headed in to reclaim his property, only to be turned away. Confiscating agents never gave him a receipt, so the items were not returned.

Fishing boats also proved problematic. Much of what came back had either been severely damaged or altered so drastically for military use that the vessels were no longer fit for the fishing industry. The Navy used Giuseppe Spadaro's boat for two years and it came back a mess. Although he spent a lot of money trying to restore it, ultimately, he had to moor it to the wharf and continue fishing with the boat he had rented in its absence. The same could be said for Angelo Maiorano. After four years in the Philippines, his 95-foot boat came back beaten.

Angelo's son, Michael, indicated that "they gave him a $20,000 check, but it cost him $46,000 to get the boat back into condition," a hit that left his father "on his back, flat broke." Although in some instances, Italians received their boats back in decent or even better shape, this was exceedingly rare. For the most part, the compensation did not cover the required repairs.

Two months after the restrictions ended for Italians, laws regulating curfew and travel for Germans were lifted as well. Again, those already interned remained in confinement. Some stayed in imprisonment until sometime in 1948.

The Ogden Standard-Examiner, December 24, 1942
"German Aliens May Celebrate"

San Francisco—Approximately 20,000 German aliens on the Pacific coast, restricted to their homes from eight p.m. to six a.m. since last March, may celebrate Christmas eve in public tonight with American citizens. Lt. Gen. John L. DeWitt, head of the western defense command, lifted the alien curfew proclamation and abolished more than 1,000 zones designated as prohibited to enemy aliens. Alien Italians were released from the curfew regulations on last Oct. 19. DeWitt's latest action in effect abolished the restrictive curfew since it applies now only to Japs, alien and American-born, who have been removed from strategic areas to relocation centers.

When it finally came time to empty the remaining detainment facilities still harboring enemy aliens, the Japanese had already been released. "In a silent effort to avoid national attention, signs were posted at the internment camp Post Offices announcing the release of all internees." Campbell, California, business owner John Perata took a streetcar home from an I.N.S. detention facility in Sharp Park. Recalling the event, his wife indicated "he was too embarrassed to have us take him home." He was not the only one that felt this way. While returning to their homes and families must have been a relief, it also brought a new source of anxiety and embarrassment—reentering their old communities and facing the neighbors that had, and perhaps still, viewed them as enemies, inmates, and traitors.

Although Francis Biddle put the figure of those interned at 16,000 and even publicly went on record stating that this number only included 228 Italians, the research of Tetsuden Kashima offers another set of numbers. Kashima interviewed figures integral to the enemy alien situation—men such as Edward Ennis, Director of Alien Enemy Control. Further substantiating these findings, which appeared in *Judgment without Trial*, Kashima also offered a series of governmental memorandums—official correspondence with key individuals like Willard F. Kelly, Assistant Commissioner of the Alien Enemy Control Program. Kelly became the D.O.J.'s chief supervisor on the board of parole. According to these official records, the count of those impacted sat far higher than Francis

Exploitation of the enemy alien situation in product advertisement. (*Author's personal collection*)

Biddle let on to Americans. By the time the program finally ended, 16,853 Japanese, 11,507 German citizens, and 2,730 Italian citizens had been arrested and interned—more than 30,000 in all. While this provides a much more accurate estimation than the public was given, the exact figures of those impacted will likely never be known.

4

A Lasting Impact

The struggle for a sense of justice for those who faced hardships began fairly early on. In 1948, when the last of the Italians and Germans were leaving detainment facilities, Japanese-Evacuation Claims were already being filed. To expedite what was turning out to be a very lengthy process, a series of hearings were held in Los Angeles. The year was 1954. During these hearings, a House judiciary subcommittee listened to a number of victims relaying details about the financial losses they suffered. At that time, the government had awarded "approximately $23,700,000 on the claims adjudicated," and was still processing another 3,000 files. Although these reparations in no way repaired the damage, in addition to financial restitution, a formal apology also awaited the Japanese. It came from two U.S. presidents.

Acknowledgment

In regard to the Italians—non-citizens who suffered similar treatment but managed to escape a mass internment—after the war ended, those who lived through the experience chose not to talk about it. Whether shame or fear or some other sentiment guided this decision, collectively, they put the past behind them. Most avoided ever bringing it up. As Patricia Yollin accurately summarized, although "Al Bronzini's father lost his business and his mother lost her mind," and although "Rose Scudero and her mother were exiled," none sought recourse. The Italians did not "want reparations, apologies or pity. They simply want[ed] the history books rewritten to say that" for a time in American history, "it was a crime to be Italian."

After the Commission on Wartime Relocation and Internment of Civilians (C.W.R.I.C.) moved for Congress to acknowledge the injustices suffered by the Japanese, the Sons of Italy's Social Justice Commission looked to the D.O.J. for similar action. The commission requested an acknowledgment and an apology, nothing more. Sadly, they were denied. Grounds for this denial were steeped in the Department of Justice's belief that the internment only affected a small group of Italians—just over 200. This statement, made in the early 1990s, not only demonstrated limited insight, it completely negated the long-term repercussions of the ordeal.

The efforts of two university professors, Dr. Stephen Fox and later Lawrence DiStasi, helped uncover this hidden aspect of American history and ultimately delivered a measure of justice to the Italian people. In Fox's case, when a student in one of his World War II classes asked if he heard that the government forced Italian and German citizens out of areas along the waterfront, he admitted he had no knowledge of the occurrence. After looking into it, though, he was startled to learn his student was right. This fostered a rather shocking realization: he, a professor, historian, and expert on World War II, knew nothing about this tragic event. Thus began a long journey of research, which came to include a number of interviews with those touched by the ordeal. In 1990, these efforts spurred the book *The Unknown Internment*, later retitled *UnCivil Liberties*. These findings unearthed by Fox soon influenced Lawrence DiStasi.

Years before he edited *Una Storia Segreta: When Italian-Americans Were Enemy Aliens*, a collection of vignettes and essays penned by those touched by the event, Lawrence DiStasi organized a traveling exhibit of the same name, which debuted in 1994. Although only slated to run for one month, the exhibit toured the country for years, educating the public about this secret injustice. Eventually, it caught the attention of politicians and congressmen. Progress was in the air. In 1997, it even looked as if all the hard work was about to pay off; at last the truth would come out. That year came the introduction of several bills that called for the declassification of F.B.I. records pertaining to wartime internment. Policy had kept these documents confidential for decades. Also serving to hide the bigger truth from the American public and the world at large, were the government's efforts to censor the media; they actively ensured many of the details about internment were not included in the reports that appeared in the papers and were being broadcast over the radio.

Moving forward, in 1999, the House of Representatives passed the "Wartime Violation of Italian American Civil Liberties Act." The act itself did not declare any injustices, it merely called for a year-long investigation—a Review of the Restrictions on Persons of Italian Ancestry during World War II. This entailed rifling through "well over a thousand boxes" of confidential files; documents that, for half a century, had been locked away at the National Archives in Washington, D.C. More files were dug up in a variety of regional archives as well, and, of course, internally with the F.B.I.

In addition to historical data, the review also called for interviews. Elderly Italians touched by these events came to Washington and testified during House and Senate hearings. Seventy-one-year-old Rose Scudero spoke to the board twice about her experiences being evacuated from Pittsburg, California. Rose was twelve when the directives forced her family from their home in late February 1942. Trying to put others in her shoes, she explained: "… picture going home today and your mom tells you she got a letter from the government and because she isn't a citizen, she has to leave the house and your father and your siblings. And you don't know where you're going or for how long."

Compiled, the review came to nearly 250 pages. The document showed "deliberate policy" kept the measures impacting Italians hidden from the public, and admitted these events had "never been acknowledged in any official capacity by the United States Government." Finally, the wartime measures restricting the freedoms of over 600,000 Italian-born immigrants and their families were included in an official public record. In summary: roughly 50,000 were hit by curfew laws; more than 10,000 West Coast Italians were forced out of their homes and kept from coastal areas; thousands were arrested; and hundreds sent off to military camps for internment. Equally as important, came the acknowledgment of an unspoken rippling effect. "The impact of the wartime experience was devastating to Italian American communities in the United States, and its effects are still being felt" by survivors and their children.

Going further, although not all encompassing, the review even listed individual names of some of the Italians impacted. This included nearly 2,000 who were taken into custody; 100 and some ordered to relocate; 442 jailed over curfew, contraband, or travel violations; plus, 418 of the interned, 315 fishermen prohibited from fishing, thirty-three ports labeled off limits to Italian fishermen, and six wartime restrictions that affected Italians as a result of Executive Order 9066. Finally, the world would know the truth. But it was not to be. Another event far overshadowed the findings and even rivaled the attack on Pearl Harbor.

The Review of the Restrictions on Persons of Italian Ancestry during World War II was released to the public on November 27, 2001, a short time after the September 11 terrorist attack, which toppled New York's Twin Towers. Amid the chaos and heartache felt throughout the world, few heard or gave little thought to injustices suffered nearly sixty years prior. Close to a decade passed before the impact of this tedious review finally took hold. In 2009, California designated October as Italian-American Heritage Month, in remembrance of the Columbus Day release of Italians from the enemy alien list. In 2010, the state also offered a formal acknowledgment to America's Italians, expressing the "deepest regrets of these acts." At last the record reflected that "the treatment of Italian Americans during World War II represented a fundamental injustice."

In order to acknowledge that these events happened, to remember those whose lives were unjustly disrupted and whose freedoms were violated, to help repair the damage to the Italian American community, and to discourage the occurrence of similar injustices and violations of civil liberties in the future.

A Hidden but Lasting Effect

Although the wartime restrictions on Italians lasted but a year, the effects rippled, and to some extent, they continue to do so. In his article, *How World War II Iced Italian American Culture*, Lawrence DiStasi urged readers to "consider what happened to the traditional leadership in Italian American communities." Shockingly, "almost overnight, hundreds of teachers, newspaper editors, writers, and club leaders disappeared." Giovanni Falasca, editor of the Los Angeles-based Italian paper *La Parola*, was among them. After a dark train ride, he spent the duration of the war at Fort Missoula. From what can be seen, the only crime these individuals were guilty of was being Italian and serving as prominent members within their cultural enclaves, and yet they were singled out and treated like traitors and enemies.

A wave of shame, guilt, shock, and fear fell over those who witnessed these incidents. It must have been shocking. Their moral leaders—those admired, considered the best, brightest, and most wholesome among them—were snatched up like common criminals. Following this, to even speak their own language became a crime. Their words were now associated with the enemy. Posters, newspaper articles, and radio broadcasts all urged Italians not to speak their native tongue, to abandon traditions and customs, and to sever all ties to Italy— Americanize or be punished.

Fearful of the consequences and ashamed at being singled out, many Italians chose to heed the suggestions. Sadly, in effect, they gave up much of what it was to be Italian, and despite the difficulties and injustices these individuals suffered, these Italians—too proud to seek out assistance and frightened at the very thought of drawing any further attention—did not seek any sort of recourse. Not one legal case was filed against the U.S. government by Italian aliens or their American-born children. Instead, they chose to forget what happened, exercising a silent attempt to erase the past. Unfortunately, wiping all trace of these tragic events was not the only product of Italian silence. A loss of language was another.

One wartime legacy still felt by Italian-Americans today is the aftermath of curbing the native tongue. F.B.I. efforts, in combination with propaganda posters, advertisements, newspaper articles, and radio broadcasts, linked speaking Italian, German, and Japanese with being disloyal to America. "A powerful message was sent and received," expressed DiStasi, adding that "Italian language and culture, and those who represented either or both, represented a danger to America." In an effort to avoid further persecution or a repeat of what they had already suffered, many of Italian descent did more than merely abstain from using their native language, they over-Americanized. As humorous as it might sound, Yankee Doodle and the Star-Spangled Banner became favorite songs.

Lily Boemker, a high school student in Arcadia at the time of the war, indicated that "in those days, when you're a teenager, you wouldn't even let people know that you spoke Italian." Lily and her family left their home for the city of Eureka after the relocation order passed. American-born, she was lucky enough to make the daily commute to finish out her senior year with friends. When she graduated in June 1942, however, her parents were not permitted to attend the ceremony.

By the time of the first alien registration, Frankie and Anna Dragna's grandmother, Victoria Rizzotto, was a widower. After the death of her husband, Antonio, she came to live with her youngest daughter's family—the Polis. Born in 1939, Biaggio and Angie Poli's daughter, Florence, was too young to remember her parents taking Grandma Rizzotto to the post office to register. In fact, she holds no memories of the restrictions impacting her household at all. Florence contends that not once while growing up did she ever hear her family speak of fear or wartime restrictions. This silence is not uncommon. Like most who lived through the ordeal, her parents simply pretended it never happened. Despite this, Florence still unknowingly felt the effects of the stigma.

"When I was young," Florence explained, "my older relatives would switch to speaking Italian whenever they didn't want me to understand what they were talking about." Laughing, she admitted, "I used to think, how stupid you are, I understand Italian!" Florence learned the language like most children, "by listening." Her family believed she had forgotten, though, and for good reason. When their daughter was about five, Biaggio and Angie Poli stopped speaking Italian at home. Although Florence noticed the change, she never really understood the reason for it. She did, however, overhear them discussing the matter on one occasion.

"My father told my mother 'we're not going to speak Italian anymore around the children.'" Her father added, "Florence is going to school. She has to learn how to speak English." The Italians were no longer on the list, but the war was still being fought, and everything their family and friends had been through remained fresh on Biaggo's mind. Ill thoughts still clung to the Italian identity and to speaking its words. Some still considered them enemies. A little girl did not need to be singled out for reprisal over something as small as uttering words in Italian. Of this, Biaggo was certain. The biggest obstacle standing in the way of his plan of protection was his mother-in-law. As long as she was around, the language would never fully disappear.

Although Victoria Rizzotto had lived in America for decades, she spoke very little English. Florence acknowledged that it was her grandmother's presence that explained how she understood Italian as a child. Regrettably, she no longer can. Using the language with Grandma Rizzotto was something that could not be avoided. Obstinate, she refused to learn. "They would speak Italian to my grandmother but we [kids were] not allowed to speak Italian to her. We had to teach her to speak English." Humorously, Florence recalled these efforts. "Grandma would say *boyd* and *mick*" instead of bird and milk. "Grandma, say bird. You have to say bird. And you have to say milk." Laughing, she unknowingly added a bit of conditioning from her youth—"Because if you don't learn how to speak English, they're going to deport you." It is both odd and troubling to hear a small child caution an elder in such a manner, even in gest.

Teaching Grandma Rizzotto to speak English became a daily occurrence and quickly registered as normal. Florence even viewed the situation as a game. Not until revisiting the past more recently, with the knowing eyes of an adult, did she finally come to this realization about her childhood: as a little girl, a dark secret had been kept from her, and the gift that her grandmother had given was taken away. Like the Polis, the American classroom also shifted gears. During World War II, American schools actively encouraged children of Axis background to shed ties with their native customs and language. In some schoolhouses, Italian- and German-American children were even praised and recognized for speaking only English. The American Legion nudged a step further, presenting awards to Axis children who demonstrated efforts to abandon their culture. In addition to forbidding the young from speaking or learning the language, some families also gave up cultural traditions that seemed off kilter from American norms. Others even changed their names, Americanizing them for acceptance and to blend in.

Florence's brother, Tony, stated that, "in his business," his father, Biaggio, "went by William or Bill. All of his customers knew him as Bill." Tony's father arrived in America at the age of seven. Coming over at such a young age, he lacked the accent his older relatives wore. In a time when American citizens proved skeptical about any dealings with a foreigner—especially those with Axis roots—blending in helped ethnic business owners like Biaggo Poli support their families. Despite this, Tony expressed that his parents went out of their way to buy from Italian merchants—the deli they frequented and the barber who cut their hair were Italian. He also boasted that later in life, their father did ask if he or Florence wanted to learn Italian, but by then the damage had been done. It was around 1953, and Tony was nine. "I don't know if I actually said it or if I thought it to myself," he admitted. "None of my friends at school spoke Italian, so I said no. I had no interest in it."

Not every family was like the Polis. Stevie Niotta's niece was another matter. As a child, Christine Campagna-Ziemantz "wanted to learn Italian" so she could speak with her grandmother. "Grandmother Campagna could not speak English." Unlike Tony Poli's father, Christine's dad refused to teach her. "He was afraid that I would speak with an Italian accent and be discriminated against."

According to Assistant District Attorney John B. Molinari, over-Americanization and the death of the Italian language among California's Italians were not the only lasting changes brought on by the wartime restrictions. During the war, Molinari served as a member of the Citizen's Committee to Aid Italians Loyal to the United States. Because of his prominence and position, the F.B.I. used him as a contact. Occasionally, they came by his North Beach office to ask questions about the loyalties of the local enemy aliens. When interviewed in 1987, Molinari told

Dr. Stephen Fox that after the war, the Italian community in North Beach became "diffused" and "began to disintegrate." Illustrating the change, he highlighted that "the attitude of joining organizations changed" and that there were not "any real strong Italian memberships anymore." To emphasize, he pointed out that before the war "you had two or three Italian radio programs" plus "daily Italian newspapers—morning and afternoon," but "after the war those merged into one, and then it went out of existence" completely. The change is symbolic of so much more.

Part II
The Fight Abroad

The review of the restrictions Italian aliens faced in America during World War II, put together by the House and Senate, rightly credits the courageous efforts of the sons and grandsons of those directly impacted. Honoring the contribution of Italian-American service members, the review expressed that hundreds of thousands performed "exemplary service and thousands sacrificed their lives in the defense of the United States." Like the nearly all-Japanese 442nd infantry regiment, America's Italians also had something to prove—especially those living along the California coast. A stigma plagued their people, and it was up to the bravest and fittest among them to show the country something other than what the rumors had painted—something honest, something worthy, something better. This is the story of a few of those young Italian boys who accepted the challenge.

5

Training

The Boys

Stevie Niotta

Being the youngest son in a medium-sized Sicilian family—three boys and five girls—privacy was certainly out of the question. But being the middle child suited Stevie just fine; his humorous demeanor allowed him to get along with just about anyone. Stevie unimposingly fit in. Most of his older siblings were born back in Louisiana, where their parents, George and Phyllis, met. The second half of the Niotta brood came after the move out west to Los Angeles, where Stevie's father started his first of many business ventures. The family was living in Boyle Heights, not far from Prospect Park, when Stevie entered the world on July 26, 1920. His mother, Phyllis, gave birth right there in the family home on N. Boyle Ave.

The son of an immigrant entrepreneur, Stevie's upbringing swam in a flux of feast or famine. Big George became well-known for fearlessly, and sometimes even haphazardly, jumping into financial endeavors. As a result, Stevie certainly experienced his share of extremes. When his father's deals soared, the family tasted excess, with Big George even springing for new convertibles for the kids. On the flipside, some attempts to make quick cash flew drastically south. The surroundings Stevie grew up in likely prepared him with the adaptability necessary to survive in the uncertain environment he would face and to mentally make it in the fight overseas.

By the time the U.S. entered World War II, Stevie was working with his father in a pair of family-owned endeavors. Prior to that, he delivered newspapers at the original *Los Angeles Daily*. At the family record and jukebox outfit, Wolf Music Company, he started off servicing machines. But before long, he advanced into sales, drumming up new clients from the long list of L.A.'s restaurants, pool halls, bars, and clubs—any old place that might benefit from a little jukebox music.

Stevie Niotta on Catalina Island, selling papers for the *L.A. Daily, circa* 1940. (*Courtesy of Frannie Niotta-LaRussa*)

Stevie got involved in a newer establishment his father picked up as well. Gerries Bar sat at 5710 South Western Ave. There he handled produce purchases for the kitchen, made out the menus, and supervised the staff. Stevie was holding down both jobs when the wartime restrictions struck.

The Niottas were what you might call "a track family." Stevie spent a fair amount of his teens and early twenties watching the horses run. Over the years, his father even owned a few. Traveling as a family, Stevie, his father, his brothers, and his nephews visited tracks all over the state. They frequented the spots close to home—Hollywood Park and Santa Anita Park—but also ventured out, trucking far north to the Bay Area peninsula to race their steeds at Tanforan, and pushing south for Del Mar. Going further still, they even headed into old Mexico to see them race and to compete at Agua Caliente. The war, however, put a temporary hold on the family pastime.

In addition to the travel restrictions that kept Stevie's father close to home, the tracks closed in the spring of 1942. The government repurposed the grounds for something else. Santa Anita and a number of other parks became training camps for the military, but not every track served as a training facility; some became processing centers for the Japanese. Although vehicles belonging to gamblers and spectators normally jammed the lots, tents soon replaced them, covering the large open areas. Barbed wire surrounded it all, and armed guards kept watch around the clock. A number of the individuals moved in for processing remained housed

Stevie in dress uniform. (*Courtesy of Frannie Niotta-LaRussa*)

in whatever temporary structures had been thrown up. Others shipped off to better prepared destinations.

Attorney General Francis Biddle's Columbus Day announcement eased the minds of many, especially citizens fretting over the fate of their alien parents. Stevie Niotta belonged in this category. On October 19, 1942, Biddle kept his promise; America's Italians came off the enemy list. Not so coincidentally, on the very next day, Stevenson George Niotta—the son of a former Italian enemy alien—enlisted in the Army Air Corps.

Tony Amador

The Amadors were longtime Boyle Heights' residents as well. Although Stevie Niotta's family left the area for Lincoln Heights, his oldest sister, Celie, stayed behind. She lived in the old neighborhood with her husband, Johnny Cacioppo, and their daughter, Lolly. The house sat just up the street from the Amador residence. Johnny's sister, Lily, even babysat Tony in his younger years, watching him whenever his parents took the truck out to Bakersfield or ran other errands out of town. "In Boyle Heights they had a wine press that they used to wheel up and down the street," Tony remembered. "Most all the people on the block made their own wine. My father would bring grapes back from Bakersfield for my grandfather, because he lived right next door."

Thinking back on his youthful days, Tony recalled the playground on State Street: "All the guys used to hang out up there. We'd play touch football and we'd shoot dice. We'd play for money. Even when we were teenagers, we used to shoot dice and play for money." When he was old enough to work, he took a job at a local gas station, heading there after his classes got out. But he preferred to spend his time with Lucy. The two became an item around 1940, right when they entered high school: "She was going to Lincoln High and I was going to Roosevelt." Despite the hurdle of separate schools, the pair made it work: "I used to take the streetcar wherever I went." Whenever Tony finished his classes or a shift at the gas station, he rode the tracks into downtown Los Angeles where Lucy worked in a malt shop next to the Paramount Theatre. After class, Tony would head there. Then after her shift, they would ride the streetcar together: "I'd escort her home then walk home from there."

Tony was at the park up on State Street when he got the news about the attack. Born on August 3, 1925, he was only sixteen—too young to enlist. Like many of the teenagers he knew, the itch to head over and get into the fight sparked. Tony had just one reservation, leaving behind his girl: "My family and Lucy's family—the Niottas—were friends." In the late thirties, "her mom and dad had an Italian

Tony Amador, high school footballer. (*Courtesy of Anthony Amador*)

deli in Boyle Heights and it was right up the street from us on Boyle Avenue." Despite this, it was Lucy's visits that spurred their introduction: "She used to come down there to see her sister," Celie, and her cousin, Lolly, and whenever she did, Tony noticed.

Although certain he had found "the one," the war was now brewing and Tony knew he would eventually end up in the fight. "I wasn't drafted," he admitted, "I quit school in my senior year and joined." One of Lucy's friends planted the idea. Kimmey Daher, or "Turk" as his pals liked to call him, "was going in" and suggested they do it together. Tony was only seventeen when he enlisted. Although a bit too young for war and too young for marriage, Tony made a promise to Lucy and even gave her the ring. After he got back, they would marry.

Frankie Dragna

Funny, inspirational, and upbeat are but a few words that accurately depict the brother–sister duo of Frank and Anna Dragna. As their younger cousin, Florence, noted: "Anna found humor in everything." The same could be said of Frankie. A ham, he forever had a joke to tell. More than mere humor, though, Frankie sported a playboy side as well. "Everybody had a crush," remarked his niece, Frannie, admitting that her uncle was a bit of a womanizer most of his life. He played the trumpet, drove convertible sports cars, and dressed exceptionally well. During his days at Dorsey, Frankie was active in Hi-Y and remained a key player on the football team.

In comparison to the reality others faced, Frankie and Anna remained not only fortunate, but privileged. The country had not yet recovered from the stock market crash of 1929, and yet, as Frannie remarked, the Dragnas "didn't know from depression." Frankie and Anna's father, Jack, made his wealth through various channels. He took in a tidy sum bootlegging during prohibition and was also a part-owner in the *Monfalcone* and *Rose Isle*, two of the earliest gambling ships to peddle their wares along the Southern California coastline. Although he now owned a legitimate importing business that specialized in bringing in bananas from South America, he still took in an income from illegal gambling. In addition to owning card houses and night clubs sprinkled throughout the county, he also held an interest in the wire service—an industry integral to off-track horserace gambling. Thanks to this revenue, Frankie and Anna enjoyed the opportunities that the Depression blocked off to most.

The high level of patriotism running throughout the country following the attack prompted many young men to enlist, but Frankie Dragna was not one of them; he simply had other plans. Just weeks after his eighteenth birthday, he fulfilled his childhood dreams: he became a Trojan. From a very young age, he and his sister knew one day they would attend the University of Southern California. In fact, every home Frankie and Anna lived in during their childhood sat no more than a few miles from the campus. Their father was a *Trojaneer for Life* member

Frankie and Anna in front of their Leimert Park home on Hubert, shortly before Frankie left for the war, Los Angeles, 1943. (*Courtesy of Frannie Niotta-LaRussa*)

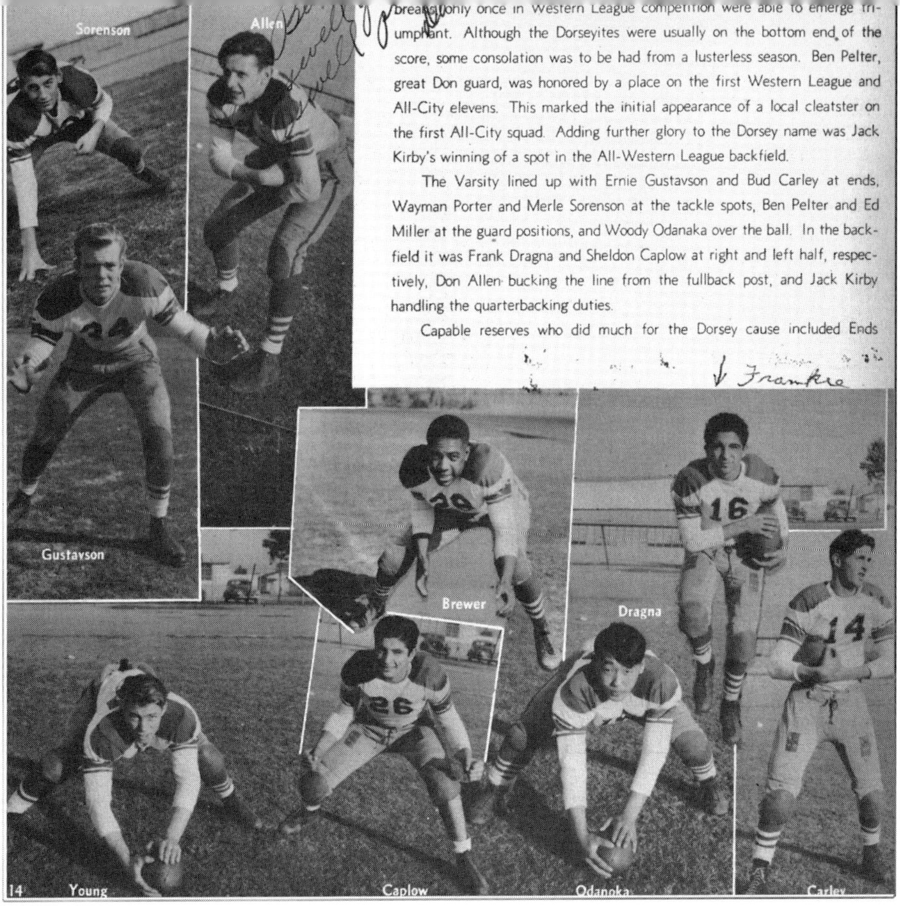
breaking only once in Western League competition were able to emerge triumphant. Although the Dorseyites were usually on the bottom end of the score, some consolation was to be had from a lusterless season. Ben Pelter, great Don guard, was honored by a place on the first Western League and All-City elevens. This marked the initial appearance of a local cleatster on the first All-City squad. Adding further glory to the Dorsey name was Jack Kirby's winning of a spot in the All-Western League backfield.

The Varsity lined up with Ernie Gustavson and Bud Carley at ends, Wayman Porter and Merle Sorenson at the tackle spots, Ben Pelter and Ed Miller at the guard positions, and Woody Odanaka over the ball. In the backfield it was Frank Dragna and Sheldon Caplow at right and left half, respectively, Don Allen bucking the line from the fullback post, and Jack Kirby handling the quarterbacking duties.

Capable reserves who did much for the Dorsey cause included Ends

Above: Frankie Dragna and fellow varsity football teammates featured in the Dorsey High yearbook, 1942. (*Courtesy of Frannie Niotta-LaRussa*)

Below: The Dragna family out to dinner. Anna and Frankie with their parents, Jack and Frances, Los Angeles, *circa* 1944. (*Courtesy of Frannie Niotta-LaRussa*)

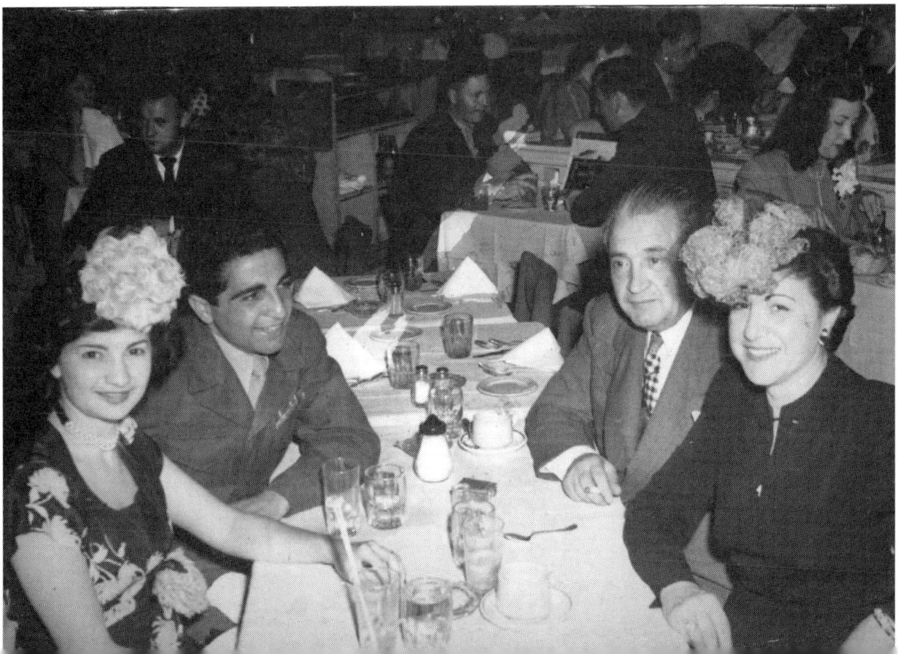

and the family attended U.S.C. sporting events often. Frankie's dream was real. He proudly called himself a college man and even joined a fraternity, but life has a way of altering the plans we make.

A shift in policy removed the blanket of safety protecting students—no more draft exemption. Now eligible for service and required to fill out the paperwork, Frankie obliged. Not long after that, the draft board responded. His induction into the U.S. Army took place on April 2, 1943. Born on August 11, 1924—a full year before Tony Amador—Frankie was eighteen. He was in his second semester at U.S.C. when he got the word. Going off to war never really figured into Frankie's plan, but many others could also say the same. Though no doubt nervous, sad, and likely even scared, he ungrudgingly left school a week later to enter active service. Departing from the campus for what he prayed would not be the last time, he said his goodbye's to friends and to his family before boarding a train for infantry training. As Frankie's former Dorsey classmate, Bill Grinnell, commented: "We were all kind of shocked" after Pearl Harbor. "I don't think any of us figured we would have been drafted within a year. When you're teenagers, you don't really think that far ahead."

Frankie with some neighborhood friends also about to join the fight, *circa* 1943. (*Courtesy of Frannie Niotta-LaRussa*)

Dick Williams

Far off from the mild weather and excitement of the coast, Dick Williams experienced an entirely different kind of upbringing. Unlike the other boys, he could not boast ever having means. Among the have nots and barely scraping by, Dick lived the harsh norm the majority faced amid the prewar depression: "I ended up with seven sisters and a father who left us all, when I was ten years old." Thankfully, they at least had a house in their little town of Cedar Bluffs, Nebraska. The only other thing their father gave them was the family name. "My sisters and I were raised without his presence and without any financial assistance." Putting it lightly, Dick affirmed "it was a pretty rough upbringing. We were what they call a welfare family."

Overcome by a fit of laughter, Dick shook off the harshness of his youth and remarked: "Shoes flapped because you had glue-on rubber soles and the glue would come loose." His family could not afford to replace them: "You'd walk down the street and your soles would slap!" To help out his mother, Dick took whatever odd jobs he could find around town, cutting lawns and shoveling snow. However, landing anything steady proved difficult; just a boy, he still had to attend classes.

The war brought change. Even to Dick's little Nebraskan town. "We were on rationing—sugar and stuff. We didn't have a car in our family, nor did we have a telephone, so it didn't really affect us a lot in that regard. For those that had cars there was the gas and the tires being rationed." In big cities, measures to conserve and limit the use of resources became a major issue. On a much smaller scale, in Los Angeles, Anna Dragna would complain she missed her favorite candy—Milky Way. With sugar one of the first items to be rationed, candy bars left the market quick. Loaded with calories and a caffeine kick, soldiers in the fight received them in their rations. Shipped overseas for service members, these goodies became scarce for civilians, but for Dick and his pals in Cedar Bluffs, candy was never on the menu. "If somebody had money for a candy bar, we'd divide it up. I mean we were that poor, really. Mother would make fudge every once in a while, when we got our ration of sugar." Dick pointed out that "not very many people during that depression had money," but the "farmers were lucky because they had chickens and they had cows, and they ate pretty well."

Shrugging off the struggle, Dick simply explained "that's the way it was," but he recalled good times from growing up in a small town during the thirties as well: "Fortunately, the town where I lived was about a half mile from the Platte River." In the summertime, he swam and fished, and in the winter, when the water froze over, Dick picked up another hobby: "I somehow come to get a pair of clamp-on ice skates." Another fortunate circumstance involved a horse that belonged to his best friend's uncle: "Colonel was the horse's name, and we got to ride Colonel all summer long." Coincidentally, "the airplane that we inherited when we got overseas was called Kentucky Colonel (K.C.)."

Dick's mother often accused him of having his head in the clouds, and perhaps it was—airplanes had always interested him: "I was a model airplane builder when I was a kid." Amid his family's circumstances, Dick's dream of becoming a pilot appeared otherworldly. He came to view such limitations at a very young age, and so, when the war came, all the devastation actually brought opportunity. Many must have felt this way in Cedar Bluffs. "All the guys that were military age at that time—most of them volunteered to go in the service. Everybody wanted to get in and get the war over with. So, they volunteered." Sadly, Dick recalled one young man from his neighborhood who never even made it into battle: "One fellow went in with B-26 training—that Martin bomber they made in Omaha. I was putting up snow fences in Nebraska when I heard he had been killed in a training accident." Danger aside, Dick was determined to join up; that is, once he reached age.

For Dick, many of the measures being taken in his small town seemed humorous, especially considering their location on the map: "As if anybody would be interested in dropping bombs on Cedar Bluffs!" Chuckling, he described the climate: "We had air raid warnings. People'd turn out their lights in a small little town of 400." Demonstrating just how small town it was, more than seventy-five years later, the population still has yet to double. Lacking from those 400 residents in Dick's hometown were the large immigrant communities that could be found in major cities all across America. With less than 500 residents, it is even possible there were no enemy aliens in Cedar Bluffs. Obviously, the wartime restrictions failed to hit Dick or his neighbors the way they did others, especially those residing along the California coast.

Determined to get out of Nebraska and to one day fly, Dick knew what he had to do. Not an ounce of hesitation mounted when he raised his hand and swore in at Offutt Field, Omaha. "Course I finished high school first," he clarified. "I enlisted at the age of seventeen but was not called to active duty until November 23 of 1943, when I turned eighteen." By then, Stevie Niotta had already completed the training that awaited Dick. In fact, when they called Dick to report, Stevie was waiting in England, a week away from his first scheduled mission. The two ended up becoming B-17 crewmembers.

The Air Corps

Although Stevie, Dick, and Frankie all ended up in the Army, their experiences greatly differed. Stevie and Dick took to the sky with the Air Corps while Frankie stayed on the ground. As an infantryman with his boots physically on the battlefield, Frankie encountered another life altogether. The separation between these two sects began immediately. Dick claimed the air crews were an all-volunteer force; if that were the case, then being drafted kept Frankie out. But neglecting recruits from the long list of educated draftees proved to be a hefty error for the Air Corps. The Army desperately needed bright individuals to fill more skilled roles, yet according to a report they gave to the War Department in 1941, they were not getting them. Nearly half the men coming in at this time lacked the aptitude and intelligence required for the technical training. The high demand for qualified men spurred the Air Corps to institute more stringent prerequisites. They requested that at least 75 percent of their new inductees have scores of 100 or better on the Army General Classification Test (A.G.C.T.). Smartly, the War Department listened.

Stevie left Los Angeles for Texas to train during the tail end of 1942. Two years later, Dick followed: "We went down to Fort Leavenworth, Kansas, and from there we went down to Sheppard Field, Texas, for basic training." Sheppard Field opened just two short years before Dick's eighteenth birthday. The facility served as a basic training site for flight crews. Stevie was among the earliest groups of young men to receive training there. Nowadays, the facility is known as Sheppard Air Force Base. Like many other Army air facilities, after the war ended, they fell under a new branch. The U.S. Air Force was sanctioned on September 17, 1947.

Outlining what set the air crews apart from the infantry—or "the regular Army" as he called them—Dick relayed that Air Corps cadets received preferential treatment—even during basic: "They called us combat crews. We didn't even wait in line for chow." As distinguished as it may sound, Dick and Stevie both came in as privates (the lowest rank in the branch), but Stevie, and likely Dick as well, shed the rank after completing basic, becoming a private first class (P.F.C.) during technical school. "The Air Corps was much sought after because we all wanted to fly in those days. But by the time I got in the washout rate was like ninety percent." Like so many others, Dick failed to make the cut as a pilot: "That's how they got their gunners! As many gunners as they wanted." Dick and the others got over it quick, though; the Army had a path laid for them and that path still involved flight.

"Those of us who didn't continue in the cadet program were sent to Kingman, Arizona for gunnery training. That was in the early summer." Training in Arizona during the summertime proved torturous. Like Sheppard, Kingman Army Airfield was also a new addition. Over the years, the spot trained more than 35,000 American service members—gunners—and directly after the war, Kingman became a boneyard for returning planes. By the end of 1945, roughly 4,700 aircraft had been staged in its inventory. Many of these were chopped, melted down, and sold for scrap metal.

"Along with the gunners, all of the flight crew—including the pilots, the bombardiers, and the navigators—we all took the training at those gunnery schools." Although not every bomber station was outfitted with a gun, every member on the aircraft received proficient weapons training. Unlike Dick, Stevie shipped out for additional training before learning aerial gunning. Orders brought him to Scott Field in Illinois, where a radio operators and mechanics

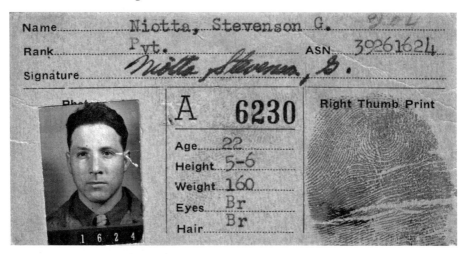

Private Stevenson Niotta. (*Author's personal collection*)

school waited. Scott had been up and running for quite a while. The base opened in 1917, right after America entered World War I. The radio school was a newer addition, which opened in September 1940. Graduates were referred to as "The Eyes and the Ears of the Army Air Forces."

It was at Scott that Stevie first moved up in rank, becoming a P.F.C. On April 28, 1943, he completed the eighteen-week course and received his diploma, becoming an *alumni* member of radio class thirty-two. From Illinois, he moved further south. Instead of seeing the summer in Arizona like Dick, Stevie attended gunnery school in Laredo, Texas. His training kept him there during the stretch of summer heat, a scorcher he wrote home about. In a postcard to his father, Big George, Stevie complained Texas was "hotter and windier than hell." Laredo Army Airfield Aerial Gunnery School opened just before Stevie enlisted. There he took in five weeks of instruction. "This field is right on the Mexico border line and is quite large," he remarked, happy to add that he managed to do a bit of exploring. Scoring a pass, Stevie crossed the bridge into Nuevo Laredo, Mexico for some well-deserved fun.

Texas was not Stevie's only prewar detour. That June, he left Laredo for another destination. As he expressed to his father, "If I make good here, I'll be shipped to Salt Lake Utah, where I'll be assigned to a fighting squadron." Accompanied by his fellow comrades of crew 6-34, Stevie—now an assistant radio operator—moved over to the 2nd Air Force, 2nd Bomber Command. The group was stationed in Geiger Field, Washington. Geiger is where a great deal of heavy bomber training occurred, with Boeing providing the Flying Fortresses. They sat nearby in Seattle. But Washington was not Stevie's last stop either. In late September 1943, he ended up in TAAB, Topeka, Kansas; one final stateside round of bomber exercises before the long flight overseas.

Right: Stevie at radio operators' school, Scott Field, Illinois. (*Courtesy of Frannie Niotta-LaRussa*)

Below: Gunnery school student pass, Stevie Niotta, May 1943, Laredo, Texas. (*Author's personal collection*)

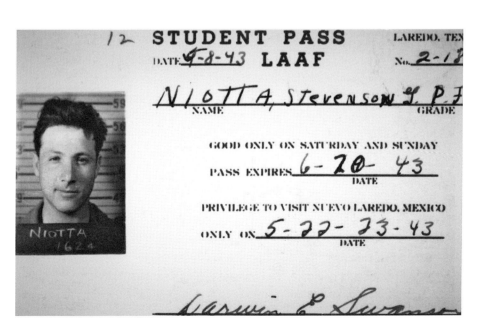

A postcard Stevie sent home to his father, Big George, from Geiger Field, Washington, 1943. (*Courtesy of Frannie Niotta-LaRussa*)

After gunnery school in Kingman, Dick landed in Florida. "No one seems to remember Plant Park," he remarked. "But I do." The tent city they erected there stood right on the baseball diamond of a stadium nestled behind the University of Tampa. "It was where we came together as crewmembers." The young men Dick found himself lumped with would be the lot he served with in the sky. After the new crews formed, a training officer dispersed them for even further training. For Dick that meant the south: "We shipped to Gulfport, Mississippi." Gulfport Army Airfield was another new installation constructed solely for the war effort. There, Dick and his crew ran live exercises, "namely bombing the hell out of Hattiesburg." Commenting on these training runs, he added: "Some will say we never flew a night mission during the war, but for some reason, in the Army Air Corps, we did all our mission training at night." Charging differently, the British Allied forces did the bulk of their heavy bombing after the sun went down. Stifling a short laugh, Dick stated the Brits "thought we were crazy because everybody," namely the enemy, "could see us."

Although daylight made finding the target and accurately hitting it a far easier task, the brightest hours also aided the Germans; the Luftwaffe waited in the air and the anti-aircraft artillery (A.A.) hid below. Each was after an Allied target. This explained the lack of enthusiasm on the part of the British. As for Dick, bombing at night was not a preference. He even kidded: "I like to see where I'm going." Thus far, Dick's crew was far from ready for a fight with the Führer. During one practice mission, they almost lost one of their own.

The day was no different than the rest until Dick's pilot maneuvered in a way that flung the door off the ball turret. This robbed the gunner of the only support he had—essentially, pulling the floor right out from under him. Luckily, the safety strap kept the young man from falling to his death, but when the bomber finally landed, the crew found the disoriented gunner with a mask full of vomit. Returning minus a door, the crew could not cover the incident up. Later that morning, their pilot appeared before the commander. This did not turn out to be the end of the door fiasco, though. About a week later, during a bus ride from Gulfport, Dick caught a humorous earful. He overheard a group of kids talking about a mysterious object they recently saw fall from the sky. Too curious to let it go, Dick asked for a better description. Hearing the shape, color, and size, Dick was quickly convinced; they had seen the final voyage of his crew's missing turret door.

The Flying Fortress

World War II has been called the "largest human effort in history," and for good reason. On the home front, Americans labored tirelessly seven days a week, and many of them were women. The American worker manufactured and assembled parts for tanks and airplanes, ships and radar assemblies, and countless other pieces of equipment. Looking at aircraft alone, from 1941 to 1945, the U.S. built more than 275,000 planes, and they did it exclusively for the war. From this figure, Boeing's B-17 Flying Fortress bomber accounted for nearly 13,000. Unfortunately, less than forty of these marvels still remain. Of these remnants, nearly half are on display or are in the process of being restored, and only twenty-two still fly.

The B-17, the B-24, and, later, the B-29 Super Fortress served as America's heavy bombers during World War II. These oversized planes flew in nearly every overseas theater, and when it came to this department, the Americans had a leg up on their British allies, mainly because the English flyer lacked a ball turret. Dick explained that although the Lancaster "could carry much more than the B-17," it had no way of defending its belly. This proved to be "one very critical weakness" the enemy exploited: "The German fighter pilots during WWII just loved flying against the Lancasters because they just flew underneath it and blasted it from the underside."

Setting itself apart from the other aircraft Boeing manufactured, the B-17 offered a flight deck rather than a cockpit. This made many of the necessary maneuvers onboard much easier for the crew to make. Differences among iterations of the model existed as well. While all Flying Fortresses reached about 74 feet in length and had a wingspan of nearly 104 feet wide—standing more than 19 feet high—other specs varied. Depending on the model, cruising speeds ranged

Flying Fortress postcard, *circa* 1944. (*Courtesy of Frannie Niotta-LaRussa*)

from 150–182 miles per hour, with a max that topped between 287 and 325 miles per hour. Equipped with four engines, the B-17 was no light bird. Empty, she weighed anywhere from 33,000 to more than 36,000 pounds. Loaded, she broke the scales; from 40,000 to 54,000. The extra weight of additional armor engineers added to the later versions slowed the plane down but made it safer.

"I remember reading an article when they rolled out the prototype in Renton." Dick figured he was about ten at the time. Decades later, "how the B-17 got its name" stuck with him. "There was a newspaper reporter up there in Renton, when they rolled it out for public exposure. 'Oh, my God,' exclaimed the reporter, 'it's a veritable flying fortress!'" Apparently the name stuck. The reason Dick never forgot this detail can be blamed on coincidence. It always made him smile that he and that reporter shared the same name. "Now I tell people, I not only flew in it, I named it."

The very first B-17 flight took place on July 28, 1935, just a few months before Dick's tenth birthday. Back then, Boeing simply called her Model 299. Although she broke records early on, the military considered her too big, too complex, and too costly, and they may have been right: one crashed a short time after inception. Because of this accident, the government contract went to a plane manufactured by Douglas instead. In fact, before the attack on Pearl Harbor, only a handful of B-17s existed. The dreadful event was the spark that spurred the plane's rapid production. With such a great demand, Douglas and Vega soon joined Boeing in manufacturing the aircraft. The introduction of the Super Fortress changed this arrangement completely. Boeing almost exclusively handed over production of the B-17 to their competitors.

Fresh out of the factory, a new Flying Fortress set Uncle Sam back more than $204,000. Costly as they were, the bomber crews went through them in great numbers. During the course of the war, several different models emerged, with each attempting to improve upon the last. The B-17G served as the final installment. Dick claimed it was the only one his group flew. The biggest feature that set model "G" apart was the addition of a chin turret, which tucked in beneath the nose. This helped dramatically during head on attacks. Another new feature was the Cheyenne tail, named after the city in Wyoming "where they had a modification setter." The Cheyenne tail offered a wider range of fire for the tail gunner, which made life for the man in the caboose a little easier. But the front and rear stations were not the only upgrades the newer model featured. Portal windows for waist gunners like Dick were now staggered, making it less likely for those firing from the side of the plane to get hit. But getting shot was only one of the dangers.

Because glass shatters and heavy bombers were shot at on a regular basis, this type of plane was never pressurized. In order to breathe, the crew had to wear oxygen masks. No one could survive long without one. But unfortunately, at those temperatures and altitudes, masks ran into problems. Occasionally they froze up, which offset the mixture and spoiled the air. It was hard to tell when it was happening, too. Instead of an abrupt feeling that left the wearer gasping for breath, the imbalance sent a mild fog creeping in. The starved oxygen would make the crewmember groggy, and if they fell asleep, they usually never woke up.

Between all the perils and all the mishaps that could easily snuff a man out, crews went through hell in the sky. This might account for why some felt such a strong attachment to their plane. Many aircraft were named and proudly adorned with nose art. The men even painted the backs of their flight jackets to match, usually adding the name of their plane on a top or bottom rocker. By sheer coincidence, the B-17 Dick was assigned to had the same name as the horse he and his friends rode as children—Colonel the horse and *Kentucky Colonel* the bomber. Yet, despite such a longtime enthusiasm for planes and for flight, Dick never grew attached to the vessel: "Some guys fell in love with their planes. Me, as long as it worked, I didn't care. We had the same plane the whole time, all except for the times when our plane was shot up, and we'd fly a different ship." Quite the contrary, during their stint over Europe, Stevie's crew headed out in over a dozen different B-17s.

As it turns out, the *Kentucky Colonel* that Dick and his crew flew in was not the only one. At the same time Dick's crew was on a run, another B-17 of the same name was shot down over France. Given the high number of B-17s up in the air, multiple planes bearing the same name was not all that uncommon, and the likelihood of there being more than one *Kentucky Colonel* is boosted once the phrase is defined. It is the highest distinction that can be bestowed by a governor in the state of Kentucky. The title is granted to those who exhibit outstanding community, public, or national service.

Dick's crew, *circa* 1944. (*Courtesy of Jenessa Warren and Laurie Williams-Warren*)

Although casualties on the ground with the infantry reached an epic toll, for a time up in the sky—and aboard the B-17, specifically—the casualty rates surpassed those of any other American combat force. The statistics showed a grim reality. Many of the flight crews in the fight were never coming home. According to the World War II Foundation's website: "In 1942, and 1943, it was statistically impossible, for bomber crews to complete a 25-mission tour in Europe." The heavy bomber missions Stevie Niotta's crew flew kicked off in the latter part of '43. They would finish twenty-six before returning home.

The Crew and What They Did

A Flying Fortress crew is made up of ten positions: a pilot and co-pilot, bombardier, and navigator, plus a radio operator and five gunners. On the sides of the plane stood a right and a left waist gunner; covering the sky above and below from their own rotating turret, perched a top and a ball gunner; and watching the plane's six was a man in the tail. Sometimes crews ran lean, however. Although Dick clarified that in *Kentucky Colonel*, "we were always ten," he also admitted some groups flew nine. "They'd only have one in the waist." Dick never experienced this lineup but divulged that a few times *Kentucky Colonel* did go out heavy. They took on photographers.

Pilots

Although two officers typically pilot a B-17, in a pinch, she can make do with just one. Considering the other crewmembers onboard did not know how to fly, the fact that both the pilot and co-pilot were prepared to take the helm must have served as a nice insurance policy. In events where one man was wounded, knocked unconscious, or killed, having a spare flyer could definitely save lives. Dick's pilot was Nick Kantar, and their co-pilot was Don Kofron, though they just called him Pappy. "He was a twenty-seven-year-old. We called him Pappy cuz he was so old." Much later in life, Dick learned that Kofron's military career continued long after the war: "He ended up as a Lt. Colonel and was a Commanding Officer at Udorn Air Base, Thailand."

Navigator

Unlike more traditional aircraft, in a Flying Fortress, not everyone is situated behind the pilot. Two crewmembers sit further forward—the navigator and bombardier. From way up in the nose, the navigator kept track of the plane's whereabouts to ensure the pilots stayed on course, and most navigators did a decent job. Few B-17s got so lost that they ran out of fuel, and, if they were not shot down, most heavy bombers got to and from the target. Like pilots and radio operators, the job of navigator also entailed extensive schooling. He had to be proficient with principles like dead reckoning and celestial navigation in order to determine geographic positioning, and as if these directional duties were not complicated enough, the navigator was also expected to have working knowledge of every single position onboard. That meant they also knew their way around a .50-cal. Those riding in the G-model got plenty of practice in the chin turret. Nearly the entire crew of the B-17 manned a gun—seven to eight of the ten positions. Typically, they packed a M2 Browning.

Bombardier

Even further forward than the navigator crouched the bombardier. He wedged in at the tip of the plane. This was the man who pulled the switch, and when it came time for him to lob a payload of metal on a target below, complete control of the B-17 was his. During a drop, the bombardier even superseded the pilots. Ensuring this, they switched to auto flight. Early in the war, these individuals bombed by sight alone, often taking direction from a lead plane in formation. To be effective in this application required visibility and precision, but due to the constant cloud cover and all-around bad weather of Europe, the art of sight bombing proved too difficult to administer consistently. For that reason, this method could only be done properly during a few months out of the year. With the potential for mass civilian casualties and unneeded devastation below, best estimates were not a pretty concept to consider. Another means of hitting the target was desperately needed and eventually bombers got it.

In time, bombardiers came to rely on radar guidance. Bombing by Pathfinder is the term flight crews used. Pathfinder was a British development—an advanced radar and electronic navigational system that, by the latter half of 1943, when Stevie and his crew reached the U.K., B-17 and B-24 flight formations often employed. The arrangement worked fairly simply: a lead plane, equipped with Pathfinder gear, would head up the formation, and based on radar direction, they gave guidance on where the formation should drop. The line "bombed by Pathfinder" appears several times in Stevie Niotta's flight records. While having this newer technology certainly helped, it still failed to alleviate a bombardier's need for a deeper understanding. With or without radar aid, the bombardier still had to have a working knowledge of groundspeed, direction, altitude, time of fall, drift, identifying the proper target, and many other essential variables. In addition to operating sighting and aiming instruments, he also had to physically release the load—anywhere from 4,500 to 8,000 pounds of metal. In reality, it was not as simple as the mere pull of a switch.

Engineer/Top Turret Gunner

The remaining crewmembers—the enlisted guys—manned stations behind the officers. To the rear and just slightly above the pair flying the plane rested a top turret and its gunner. This was the 'go-to' man the pilots turned to whenever a problem arose, and specifically because he was additionally rated as an engineer. Like the navigator, this called for a vast amount of knowhow. He learned all about the plane, its engine, and its armament equipment. "The top turret was the Engineer. Ours was Don Croft," Dick relayed. "He called out the speed of the airplane on landing and takeoff." Working in conjunction with the co-pilot, he also monitored fuel consumption and engine and equipment operation. The top turret gunner's duties did not stop there, though.

Dick knew a lot about the role of the engineer, and for good reason: "Assistant Engineer was always the job of the left waist gunner." To prepare for the role, before ever leaving the States, Dick clocked in a number of training hours in engineering. Like the other gunners, the man operating the top turret was proficient with stripping, cleaning, and repairing the .50-caliber guns. Going further, he knew the radios, receivers, and transmitters, too. He "also manually lowered the landing gear when it was damaged in battle."

Radio Operator

Just past the top turret is where the bombing doors can be found, and just beyond that point sits the radio operator. Like Stevie, these men all took on extensive training at Scott Field. On mission, they relayed position reports every thirty minutes or so, received transmissions from ground station via Morse code, and recorded mission activities in a log. Not all B-17 radio operators manned a .50-cal., but just to be safe, they all went through the training. When called upon, they left their position and picked up a weapon. Dick pointed out that on the

Right: Top turret gunner, *circa* mid-'40s. (*Author's personal collection*)

Below: Reconnaissance photo of a B-17 in flight, likely taken by a photographer onboard with Rubottom's crew, *circa* 1944. (*Courtesy of Frannie Niotta-LaRussa*)

G-model, "the radio operator had a single .50 caliber that stuck out the top of his hatch." A side duty typically assigned to this individual was reconnaissance photography. They snapped photos to include in their reports. But as Dick also conveyed, sometimes service members with this specific career field (MOS) accompanied a crew.

Waist Gunners

In the midsection of the Flying Fortress, waist gunners protected the left and right sides by firing at enemy aircraft through an open portal. In line with everyone else manning a weapon, they trained to become experts in identifying aircraft; an essential skillset among a gunner. This greatly reduced the likelihood of shooting down one of their own, or an ally. Not tied to a seat or a turret, waist gunners took on a myriad of responsibilities. Dick mentioned serving as an assistant engineer. Another one of these duties included tending to the crewmember beneath their feet.

Ball Turret

Protruding beneath the plane, the ball turret gunner relied on a waist gunner whenever he wanted to climb up and join the crew: "Often times they had difficulty getting out because they had to reach up over their head for two little latches, which they couldn't see." On his back in the fetal position, the man in the ball worked twin .50-caliber guns. "It was a very effective turret. Very accurate," Dick commented, admitting "that the ball turret gunners did better than the rest of us," in regard to hitting their targets. "At least better than the handheld guns," like the waist and the tail.

Like most things round, the ball turret rotated, and with a full circumference range, he could fire in every direction but up. Importantly, this protected everything beneath the ship—a highly vulnerable spot during aerial combat. Whenever the ball sat idle, the enemy suspected it unmanned, and primed for an attack.

Tail Gunner

Way in the back of the plane one final gunner crammed in, but getting there was not easy: "The tail wheel came up between his position and the waist, so to get there you had to squeeze by the tail wheel enclosure." Like the other stations onboard, the position was not ideal; even though the gunner had a place to sit, he "had a bicycle seat and it wasn't very comfortable." He also had "a little door" he could use if he "had to bail out." Protecting the rear, the tail gunner laid fire to anything that snuck up from behind.

Togglier

The position of togglier came about late in the war, when much of the Luftwaffe had already been decimated. During this period, the main threat bombers faced was flak from anti-aircraft guns situated on the ground, but this alone did not necessarily stir creation of the position. Because bombardiers required a high level of training, there were not all that many of them to begin with, and as the war carried on, what began to thin out the number of capable men was the position's location. A bombardier sat right up front in the Plexiglas nose—a spot about as unsafe as the ball turret. This late in the war, a lot of qualified individuals were wounded or worse, while others remained confined in P.O.W. camps. The lucky ones were already stateside, having completed their required number of missions. This lack of bombardiers during the latter part of the war is what eventually spurred the Air Corps togglier. Although more or less an improvisation or skeleton of the full position, it did have an official career field: MOS 509, Overseas Bombardier.

Unlike the heavily trained officers who assumed the role of bombardier, the togglier counterpart was an enlisted man, typically a gunner who had undergone an abridged version of how to handle the machinery. Dick claims these individuals were enticed to learn key aspects of the bombardier's job. If you "volunteered to be a togglier, they would give you an extra stripe. You would be a Tech Sergeant," and from what Dick holds, it was fairly easy: "You didn't have to do anything except toggle a switch." Although the opportunity delivered the promise of a promotion, it came with an added dose of danger. Like a full-fledged bombardier, a togglier took position in the plastic nose, where the flak had a much easier time tearing through the plane. In these tight quarters, these men mimicked the concept of bombing by Pathfinder. They watched "the man in the lead airplane—a regular trained lead bombardier. And when they saw his bombs falling, they just toggled."

What made the cramped quarters of each of these positions all the more tedious to bear was the element of time. "You'd be in there for eight or nine hours"—however long it took before the mission was completed, and during that window of time, the only enlisted member onboard that enjoyed the luxury of a seat was the man in the radio room and the gunner in the tail. The rest were less lucky. Although "it was all standing" and doing it for long periods of time, Dick remained grateful the waist had enough room to do it upright rather than in a squat. At least, they did not stick him in the ball turret; that poor fellow never got to stretch out.

The Life of a Ball Turret Gunner

Like the rest of his fellow crewmates, Stevie wore flight wings. To the "regular Army," the device symbolized a level of separation. It was not uncommon for a soldier to resent someone with wings. In the eyes of the grunt, the tiny metal device pinned to an enlisted man's chest granted him a measure of special treatment. It kept him far and safe from the hell that was the life of the U.S. Army infantry. At least it seemed that way. Enlisted flight crewmembers spent considerable time with the officers that flew the plane, and as a result, they usually established closer relationships with their leadership. This the infantry certainly noticed. The elevated promotion to sergeant that flight crews received solely for being on a plane must have seemed like a gimme' as well. But higher rank was not the only difference the Army instituted. Being in the Air Corps had other bonuses.

As Dick explained, the distinction was instituted all the way back in basic training, where they walked to the front of the line when it came time to eat, and now at their duty stations, they enjoyed separate barracks. These bunks were far less crowded than those designated for the large regiments of soldiers. But unbeknown to the ranks, this consideration had actually been made for the benefit of the infantrymen rather than the enlisted flight crews. It was another decision of leadership. The Army quickly noted the negative impact empty beds had on the morale of ground soldiers. Planes went down frequently, and when they did, often the entire crew went with it. Creating the separation was intended to spare these soldiers the psychological effects of the loss.

After training together and the long flight overseas, Stevie got to know the other members in his crew fairly well. It was evident their survival depended on their ability to not only do the job, but to work together, and to look out for one another. They were a team, and as Stevie soon found out, there was another individual with radio training in his crew. Also sporting the 757 MOS was a kid by the name of Joe Ryan. The guys called him "Old Soak"—a polite way of saying he liked to drink a lot. For whatever reason, Joe ended up as the crew's radio operator. Stevie landed someplace very different. He may have volunteered for the role or it may have been dished out as a punishment. Either way, it was probably the pilot's call. The enlisted men in Stevie's group fell under the direction of First Lieutenant (1Lt.) Robert L. Rubottom, and his co-pilot, Lt. Alander.

Rather than man a radio, as he had been trained to do, Stevie soon discovered he would be squeezing into the ball turret instead. Dick and a lot of others considered it a hardship duty. Some even viewed it as the worst job in the sky. The old story holds that a man with wings enjoying a beer in a pub with his pals got sick of hearing the remarks a man without wings was spouting. Just seeing those little shiny devices always seemed to spark something. The grunts usually barked a snide remark, hoping to look cool in front of their infantry pals. They would mouth this or that about "the clean life" in the sky or about "having it easy" with the officers. At times, a fight would break out. On this particular occasion, however, the ordeal ended very differently. Walking by a table of flight crewmembers, the grunt very audibly griped he sure could go for one of those cake-jobs like the fly boys had. He may have even winked when he made the statement.

To this, the man with wings simply smiled. Standing, he was even polite: "You know, if you want my job that bad, you're more than welcome to it." He had already started unbuttoning his shirt when he added, "Let's trade uniforms." This definitely threw the grunt. He was not expecting that reaction, and for a moment, he stood there unsure how to respond. Finally, somewhat composed, the man without wings curiously poked, "Say, what job you got anyway, bud?" Hearing the casual response, "ball turret gunner," was more than enough. The grunt quickly threw his hands up in surrender then hollered, "No way, pal!" That is the role Stevie Niotta fell in to.

Because of the limited space in the turret bubble, only so much ammo could be packed in with the gunner. Turret operators not only needed to be a good shot, they really had to be frugal and stay cognizant of their trigger finger. Every round counted. For this reason, the regulations only permitted use of short bursts when firing. To stretch their ammo even further, some ball turret gunners took to using just one .50-caliber gun at a time. Stevie's ability as a shooter may have been the catalyst that shoved him in the ball. Records show he was a marksman sharpshooter, both with a pistol and carbine.

Unfortunately, Stevie and all the other unlucky gunners dangling beneath the Flying Fortress only had a diameter of about 3 feet to work with. For this reason, the stories claim that this awful job always went to the smallest guy. While Stevie Niotta may have won the prize at 5 feet 6 inches and 160 pounds, Dick challenged the myth. "There was a lot of people saying the shortest guy got the job. But that wasn't true. There were some tall ball turret gunners." Lester Schrenk was one of them.

Tucked up by his ears is where the gunner's instruments rested. On his back in a modified fetal, he worked the twin .50-caliber Brownings. A pedal by his left foot allowed him to adjust the sight before firing. Dick always "felt sorry for those guys." Going into detail, he added: "They had kidney problems. They would get up in the middle of the night to pee. Something about the position hurt their kidneys and they couldn't control their bladders. They were in this awkward position, practically with their heads between their legs."

The discomfort of the role was not the only trouble associated with being in the ball. As a waist gunner, a 3¼-inch plate of steel protected Dick from bursts of flak. The ball turret gunner, on the other hand, did not share that kind of protection. "The turret was all glass—no armor plate! It was really dangerous." The Plexiglas bubble had only a sheet of aluminum to safeguard the gunner, and because of the limited space, the gunner "couldn't wear a regular flak suit. They had a lighter version." The conditions of the role seemed only to get worse and worse.

Weather as much as weapons plagued the crew. A frozen mask could quickly leave a gunner dead. Alone in the ball, he had no assistance in this predicament. If he drifted, he never woke. But a freezing mask was only one of the risks linked to the drastic temperatures. Although insulation lined their flight suits, at those altitudes and with that kind of wind chill working against them, the cold bit right through. Luckily, the suits issued to turret gunners donned a device that electrically heated. But wired in series like an old set of Christmas lights, they tended to malfunction. Sometimes they even caught fire. Another un-fun factor working against the crew was a lack of restroom facilities. When someone had to go, they did their business down a tube—a completely different way of bombing the enemy. The limitations in the ball turret, coupled with Dick's point that the position left them prone to frequent urination, made the transaction for this gunner far more difficult. World War II ball turret gunner Lester Schrenk approached the subject.

"What I had done, was to find an old oxygen hose, which was about an inch and a half in diameter, and run it up and through one of the slots that discharged the spent shell casings." Schrenk explained that his method worked but also admitted his first attempts proved messy: "I was sprayed by my own urine." While this may sound disgusting, for a gunner up in the air in that weather, the ordeal could prove fatal—or at minimum, serve up a terrific case of frostbite. Anything that got wet froze, and whatever froze usually died.

Plenty of other unsavory details about the ball turret existed, such as the isolation. Other than the voice on the other end of the radio, the gunner remained completely alone. They strapped in while the plane was still on the ground, and for the next eight to ten hours that is where they remained. While it was not impossible for the gunner to climb up into the B-17, it did take considerable maneuvering and effort. The turret had to align properly and the gunner needed assistance getting out. Far more difficult than the climb was the chore of detaching from all the necessary gear. Sometimes, the option to bring the gunner up was out of the crew's hands—when the plane took excessive damage, for example.

Cramped as it was, a parachute was not permitted in the ball. For this reason, in instances where the crew had to bale out, the ball turret gunner was plenty motivated to escape his bubble. Once inside, he could put on his chute, but if flak shot out the mechanical or hydraulic systems and kept the turret from rotating, the gunner faced a desperate situation. Without maneuverability, the ball could not align properly, severing all hope for survival. Another potential fatality for the ball turret gunner dealt with the landing gear. If the assembly took a hit and could no longer function by switch or hand crank, the pilot was forced to crash land. If a ball turret gunner was unable to escape the ball during a crash landing, the only option was to watch the ground until it crushed them on impact.

Out on Leave

Like Stevie, Dick and his pals received a bit of leave before heading over: "Most of us got out on the road and hitchhiked over to New Orleans so we could catch a train to go to our various homes." Hitchhiking with the others, Dick made it to New Orleans. "I remember sleeping on a bench at the train station and then the next day being able to purchase a ticket to my home in Nebraska." After a much-needed week with his mother, his sisters, and friends back home, Dick returned to Gulfport.

Next came Replacement Training Unit (R.T.U.), the crew's last bit of preparations to equip them "to go overseas into combat." After completing the training, Dick and the boys heard some awful news; they would not "get a pass to go into Gulfport." Their last chance for a night out before the fight had been robbed. Adamant about a goodtime sendoff, they decided to go against direct orders: "Somehow or another, someone on the crew obtained passes—ten passes for the whole crew. But of course, they required that the Commanding Officer of the base sign them." Being "a young and stupid eighteen-year-old gunner," Dick did his best with a pen.

In town, the crew had a nice meal, then Dick, "for the first time, imbibed to excess, with just a little bit of whiskey." Drunk, he could not recollect how they made it back to base. A bus more than likely dropped them at the gate. The story they fed the M.P.s escaped him as well. "Unfortunately, I recall being with a pilot in the jeep—with the MP driver—and his wanting to know what my barracks number was." Intoxicated, that escaped Dick, too. "We drove all over the base before they finally found where my barracks was," Dick chuckled.

Although in direct violation of the rules, the M.P.s understood the lot was "to be shipped overseas to combat in the very very near future." Plus, "there was very little they could do to punish" them. "They could keep us in the states or send us into combat." Dick and his crew received their orders shortly after, but before departing on the long flight, they landed in Savannah, Georgia (likely Chatham Army Airfield): "They issued us a new B-17 and all brand-new flying gear." This in tow, the crew boarded the Flying Fortress for Europe.

Dick Williams, *circa* 1943. (*Courtesy of Laurie Williams-Warren and Jenessa Warren*)

Where They Sent the Italians

Not being Italian, Dick found himself in the least likely place the United States military would have sent Stevie, Frankie, or Tony—Italy. Although not always successful in their efforts, the government did attempt to place service members of Axis heritage in theaters far from the homeland of their fathers. The papers even reported on the decision.

> *St. Cloud Times*, December 29, 1943
> "Board Predicts Alien Inductions"
>
> The induction of more enemy aliens into the armed forces is predicted by the selective service system as the result of an army decision permitting the assignment of nationals of enemy countries to combat theaters where they will not fight against fellow countrymen and relatives.

The all-Japanese 442nd Regiment fought the Germans in Europe while the bulk of Italian and Italian-American service members battled in the Pacific. This was the case with Tony and Frankie, who at one point even ended up crossing paths in Luzon. Stevie was another matter. Air Corps members of Italian descent who received assignment to the European Theater of Operations (E.T.O.)—men like Stevie Niotta—typically joined the 8th Air Force in the U.K. Stationed in England, they struck targets in the northern and western regions, which excluded Italy altogether.

After a little more than a year's worth of training—basic, radios, aerial gunnery, and then a barrage of flight exercises—Stevie put on sergeant's chevrons. Dick and the rest of the Air Corps cadets received identical treatment. Every enlisted member on a flight crew saw promotion to a non-commissioned officer (N.C.O.) status before heading over. This ensured better treatment if they were shot down and taken as a prisoner of war.

Dick's assignment linked him with the 15th Air Force in Foggia. The city sat on the back half of the ankle on Italy's boot-shaped mass. Although the Brits heavily bombed the area in their efforts to take it back from German forces, Americans did not settle there until after Italy had submitted. During the initial drive into Europe, when American troops first reached Italian soil, Italy was still in the fight. Allied amphibious forces stormed Sicily on July 10, 1943, and less than two months later, they attacked the Italian mainland. This second invasion occurred a mere five days prior to the Italian surrender. They submitted on September 8, 1943. Although the campaign in Italy continued until May 2, 1945, Allied forces battling there were no longer fighting Italian soldiers.

Johnny Bonome's story is a bit of a rarity. John Guarnieri explained that his family came from Calabria, near the tip of Italy's boot, and that although he was too young to fight in World War II, his older cousin, Johnny, served. Not only did

Johnny Bonome, a first-generation American, partake in the action overseas, he ended up on Italian soil. He was tasked on the Sicilian invasion. Italy had not yet yielded, but as Johnny conveyed to his relatives, the forces he encountered were German rather than Italian. Any internal struggle he wrestled on that assignment surely paled when compared to the next. On September 3, 1943, the Army moved on the Italian mainland. Johnny was there when the strike came in through Salerno, but the battle extended south and eventually made it into Calabria, the place where his mother and father were born. Johnny still had relatives there.

On the Ground

In April 1943, while Stevie sat in class at Scott Field learning about radios, Frankie Dragna began his infantry training. Troops learned their way around the rifle and a variety of small arms weapons—how to load, aim, and fire. The career field also called for lessons in hand-to-hand combat and use of close quarters instruments like the bayonet and trench knife. The men familiarized themselves with hand grenades and camouflage, too, plus a variety of other forms of concealment. They studied the enemy—their uniforms and ranks, even their vehicles and aircraft.

Ordinarily, this process kicked off with thirteen weeks of basic, but a few months before Frankie arrived, the Army altered their routine. Previously, men formed into units and the units that formed would train together then deploy together. Bonds formed during those thirteen weeks. Enduring it all with the men they would soon see action with, they left instilled with a sense of camaraderie. But now with so many units already deployed, and many of them insufficiently manned due to heavy losses, much of the training stateside moved over to another format—Replacement Training Centers (R.T.C.). This is where Frankie received his instruction. Rather than getting a whole unit prepared, the R.T.C. program focused on readying individual troops. These men came in in smaller batches to supplement units that had suffered combat losses. Frankie joined the 43rd Division, which had lost 581 men during the Northern Solomons Campaign alone. In addition to the massive death toll, another 2,059 of their soldiers were wounded.

Trainees that filtered in before Frankie's time learned specific duties under what could only be described as ideal conditions. They would get their seasoning abroad. Allowing soldiers to master their trade before performing it under duress, however, was no longer viewed as an ideal process. Pressed by time constraints and with the growing need for bodies mounting, it quickly became apparent that whoever left for the war, needed to be field-ready before they got there. Beginning in 1943, most of the replacements were forced to learn under the worst conditions the Army could muster—including use of live fire. In an attempt to abandon the customary shooting range and classroom atmosphere for something far more

Frankie Dragna with a fellow service buddy. (*Courtesy of Frannie Niotta-LaRussa*)

realistic, the R.T.C. added several battle courses to the roster. This included infiltration and combat, a three-day field exercise, and village fighting. When it was all done, Frankie joined the ranks of the 745 MOS. He was now a rifleman.

The National Guard

Frankie received orders for the Pacific. There, and perhaps to his surprise, he would join National Guardsmen from Hartford, Connecticut. By now, the Guard had been actively involved in the conflict for some time. They prepared long before America officially entered the fight. On June 1, 1940, President Roosevelt made a request to Congress "for the authority to call the National Guard and other reserves for active military duty." Not even the War Department had intended to go this route: "Army officers said they did not want to disturb the status of the 235,000 guardsmen and 15,000 officers because of the possible effect on private employment." After all, the country was not at war. In anticipation of the possibility, however, the War Department did see the value in building up their ranks. But instead of calling in the Guard, they hoped to reach their goal of 450,000 "regular troops" in another manner: enlistments. Although it took some doing, the president did eventually get what he was after.

Plenty of non-citizens were serving in the U.S. armed forces before the attack on Pearl Harbor. Going back to World War I, the country promised citizenship in exchange for service. It appeared to be an honorable way for a resident alien to prove himself and to become an American. According to law and regulations, "any person who had taken out his first citizenship papers was eligible to enlist in the National Guard." Come March 1938, however, some Guard units "began weeding out aliens from the ranks." An act passed by Congress in November of the year prior spurred the action. The act stipulated that "none of the funds appropriated should be used to pay non-citizens." In response, New York's forty-fifth governor, Herbert H. Lehman, issued the state's Guard units to "oust non-citizens" and to "prevent their enlistment in the future." *The Brooklyn Daily Eagle* claimed the governor's move to purge aliens was aimed at Nazis.

The president's peacetime draft in 1940 put an end to these efforts. It called all eligible men—citizen and not—to register into service. In addition to being drafted, plenty of non-citizens willingly enlisted, joining the Army, Navy, Marines, and National Guard. In peacetime, this was fine, but after the country entered the fight, a red flag quickly lifted. The War Department now faced a difficult situation. According to Lawrence DiStasi: "The military high command seemed to believe that were an Italian American in a combat situation faced with enemy troops which he had reason to believe might include his relatives, he might be inhibited from taking the appropriate action, thus risking lives and/or victory." This prompted a choice, which enlisted and officer enemy aliens were given. They could either stay in the military and fight (earning their citizenship) or they could get out.

For the majority, this may have been an easy decision; they had already willingly joined to secure citizenship. For some, however, came a measure of hesitation. Who, after all, would want to stand on the opposite side of a battlefield from their own cousin or brother? Service members that exhibited any doubt or opposition were relieved of their military obligations; even those who begged to stay in and asked to fight in the Pacific instead. Like all other resident aliens of Axis birth, those ousted from service soon faced wartime restrictions, including internment. Their military training may have even rendered them a threat.

Although DiStasi holds that these alien service members were given a choice, in late February, the decision was made for them.

The New York Times, February 24, 1942
"U.S. Army Aliens Removed From Ban"

WASHINGTON, Feb. 23—All aliens of German, Japanese or Italian nationality serving in the armed forces of the United States as well as all persons of Greek and Turkish extraction who emigrated from the Dodecanese and other Agean Sea islands were removed today by Attorney General Biddle from the category of alien enemies.

This modification applied only "to those who enlisted before" the U.S. declared war. They were granted clearance to remain in the military, but matters were far from rosy for the alien service members who stayed in. Some were spied on, others were limited to stateside service in places like Camp Ripley—a segregated unit in Minnesota, deep in the interior. As DiStasi also pointed out, those who did go overseas typically ended up in a theater where they would not encounter one of their own.

For their efforts in the latter part of war, the 442nd became the most decorated regiment in the entire United States military, and yet some are still shocked to learn that Japanese and Japanese-Americans were ever involved in the fight on the side of the U.S. Perhaps even more surprising, an all-Japanese-American battalion formed in Hawaii back in 1942—not long after Pearl Harbor was struck. A good number of those men were already enlisted prior to the start of the war. When the peacetime draft commenced in 1940, thousands joined the ranks of the Hawaiian National Guard's 298th and 299th Regiments, and roughly half of these individuals were of Japanese descent. The 100th Infantry Battalion was the first group of its kind to see combat. "About ten percent" of its ranks "came into the Army from the Hawaiian National Guard."

St. Cloud Times, December 29, 1943
"Men From Hawaii Fight in Italy"

With Fifth Army in Italy—The little men from the Hawaiian Islands who have fought in the Italian invasion to prove they are as good Americans as any other doughboys have won their place so far as their fellow-fighter are concerned. From the Beaches of Salerno right into the Nazi winter line these troops of Japanese descent have fought and are now fighting some of the hardest battles of the entire campaign.

The National Guard made an immense impact during World War II. Of the twenty-nine initial Army infantry divisions active at the start of the war, eighteen of them were comprised of Guardsmen. Unlike divisions made up of the newly drafted and freshly enlisted, brigades and regiments of the National Guard were already trained. The nation had the president to thank. Roosevelt activated the Guard a full year before the country entered the fight. The preemptive measure doubled the size of the U.S. Army. For most Guardsmen, the activation was anything but sitting around their home unit doing a little light training. Despite the country's peacetime posturing, Guard units shipped out overseas on various assignments. For a unit out of Ohio, that meant flying to China to provide weapons training to soldiers so they could better resist the Japanese.

When the U.S. finally did declare war, the National Guard was far more prepared than the gaggle of young draftees just out of boot, and the active duty component of the military definitely knew it. A pool of officers existed—primarily

Frankie Dragna and some of his infantry brothers. (*Courtesy of Frannie Niotta-LaRussa*)

veterans of World War I—and yet the Army choice to draw the bulk of their officers from the National Guard and from the Officers' Reserve Corps. Come December 1941, members of the Army National Guard were among the first soldiers to see action. The Guard was represented honorably on every battlefield and every conflict during the course of the war.

In the Navy

Right around the time Lucy Niotta's fiancé joined the service, her big brother was just getting back from a tour in Europe. Enjoying some leave before his next assignment, Stevie returned to Los Angeles for a month-long visit. After his leave ran out, he would leave for Texas. News of his baby sister's engagement perked Stevie's ears, but when he discovered Tony had enlisted with the Navy, he began to worry. The Niotta clan really took a liking to Lucy's *beau*. Concerned, Stevie spent some time with the young man before he shipped out, offering his wisdom from the fight.

Unlike Frankie, school did not hold much allure for Tony. It took little convincing to get him to drop out his senior year to enlist. His eighteenth birthday came the month before he finished basic. They sent him just a couple hours south for training. "I went through boot camp at San Diego Naval Training Station." Much of the area has since been repurposed into a popular tourist spot known as Liberty Station. "From there I went to Shoemaker." In the southeastern

Stevie home on leave with his sister, Marion; mother, Phyliss; sister, Josie Niotta-Loveday; nephew, Frankie Loveday; and soon-to-be brother-in-law, Tony Amador, Los Angeles, 1944. (*Courtesy of Linda Amador-Galardo*)

Lucy Niotta with her big brother, Stevie, during his visit in Los Angeles, 1944. (*Courtesy of Frannie Niotta-LaRussa*)

end of Northern California's Bay Area, on a section of farmland near Livermore and Pleasanton, sat a training facility called Camp Shoemaker. She rested in the middle of two other Naval Centers—Camp Parks and the Shoemaker Naval Hospital. Collectively, they called it "Fleet City." Shoemaker handled training and transit for those involved in the fight in the Pacific, but like the name suggested, the installation was fleeting. Not long after the war, the base was decommissioned and dismantled. The farmland that once served as the Naval training center now falls within the Dublin city limits. While at Shoemaker, Tony's orders came through. He received assigned to the U.S.S. *Mississippi*: "I boarded the ship on September 6, 1943, after boot camp." It was the end of the beginning.

Tony Amador, fresh out of
boot camp, 1944. (*Courtesy of
Anthony Amador*)

Tony Amador posing in front of
a war bonds backdrop with pals,
Barnet and Chasin. (*Courtesy of
Anthony Amador*)

6

Life Back Home

Without Stevie around to help, managing the day-to-day affairs of his businesses became rather tedious for Big George, but he managed. At least he could say his son wrote when he could and his two remaining boys had not been taken by the draft board. The pair would receive word in 1944. That April, the Army would call George's oldest son, Michael. But even before that time, the war had kept him busy. The life of the press was habitually hectic and Michael's loyalty to the *L.A. Daily* left little room for assisting in his father's ventures. George, Jr., on the other hand, was still tending bar at Gerries. Business proved less than steady, though; with so many young men off in the fight and the rest of the country chronically working, folks piling in for a beer and a shot had become a rarity, and by the time the Army called up his last son in November '44, he had willingly grown another problem. Despite troubles with patrons and staffing, Big George being Big George, he went out and bought another establishment. The Oakwood Pit BBQ sat at 1744 West Slauson near the corner of South Western.

Stevie, Frankie, Dick, and Tony sent and received letters from their friends and loved ones stateside. They shared their experiences and got caught up on all the bustle happening on the home front. On the receiving side of the mail, the correspondence must have been surprising for everyone. To read of events was one thing, but to see and live it firsthand was a completely different matter. Life in L.A. and in other cities all across America clearly refused to come to a halt after the mass of men and boys filtered out. Aside for some very noticeable changes, the day-to-day happenings continued. Folks still got up and went to work, they read the papers and watered their lawns, and, if they could, they even paid the mortgage. With the war effort now in full effect, though, the term "work" took on a whole new meaning. Unemployment dwindled so fast that even the forty-hour work week became insufficient. Bloody as it was, the fight abroad was pulling the country right out of its long and hard depression.

UNITED STATES ARMY AIR FORCES.

To MY DAD

ON

Fathers' Day

JUNE EIGHTEENTH, NINETEEN HUNDRED AND FORTY-FOUR.

EUROPEAN THEATRE OF OPERATIONS.

Above and below: Father's Day card provided to service members from the U.S. Government. Stevie sent this one to his dad, Big George, 1944. (*Courtesy of Frannie Niotta-LaRussa*)

Nothing would be nicer
    Than to spend this day with you,
But since I am so far away
    The next best thing to do
Is send the best of wishes,
    And then a line to say
That many special thoughts are there
With you this Fathers' Day.

"Steve"

Stevie's father, Big George Niotta, posing for a picture with a service member; likely a customer at his neighborhood restaurant, the Oakwood BBQ Pit, Los Angeles, *circa* 1944. (*Courtesy of Jack Niotta*)

Santa Ana Register, March 14, 1942
"Says War Can't Be Won On Basis of 40-Hour Week"

The war, said W. M. Jeffers, President of the Union Pacific Railroad, today, can't be won on the basis of a 40-hour week in American industry. "I have no quarrel with the 40-hour week as such," he said in a press conference. "But it's a peacetime luxury and it should be suspended until the war is won." Jeffers said he knew of no reason why industry men should not work as much as 60, or even 70 hours weekly. "The working man knows the situation," he said, "and I'm sure the mass of labor would fall in on the program to increase the working week."

After more than a decade of joblessness, hard times, and poverty, wages and the employment rate were finally up. In October 1942, just a hair before the Italians came off the enemy list, the newspapers reported a shocking statistic. According to predictions made by the National Industrial Conference board, the "employment of 62,500,000 Americans in all lines of industry, commerce and agriculture" was expected by the close of the next year. A little more than a month after the board's announcement, President Roosevelt granted overtime pay "at the rate of time and a half for work beyond 40 hours a week." He also instituted wage increases, signing the changes into law on Christmas Eve '42. The boost would assist some 2 million civilians in the government's employ. Going further, the axe fell on the half-holiday on Saturdays that workers had come to know. Calling it a "peace time luxury," he abolished the practice. Six days a week on the job was now the norm.

Rosie the Ethnic Riveter

In addition to its economic benefits, the wartime boom also brought on a great social impact. What Mr. Jeffers from the Union Pacific Railroad failed to mention about the growing workforce was the "working man" was slowly becoming the "working woman." Almost as fast as the men scooted off, women stepped in and picked up the slack; yet American women were doing more than simply going to work, they were showing the nation just how capable they really were. The shift gained momentum once President Roosevelt formed the Office of War Information (O.W.I.) and the War Manpower Commission (W.M.C.)— two agencies geared heavily toward increasing the role of women in defense industries. Tony Amador witnessed the birth of this transition shortly before the Navy called him away. The absence of men in his neighborhood struck him both odd and unsettling.

A big contributor to the cause, the Glenn L. Martin Company, began hiring women in August 1941. Initially, they handled the non-metallic materials used by planes—canvas, felt, cloth, rubber, and asbestos—but later, like a lot of other companies were now doing, they moved their women workers into aircraft production and a variety of other facets. A propaganda push of advertisements flooded magazines and radio broadcasts. This buzz stirred women from the nest in droves and moved them onto the production floor. Charging forward with the ideology, the media forged several icons in order to motivate and perpetuate the war effort. Fictional characters like Rosie the Riveter, Wanda the WAVE, Wendy the Welder, and others inspired women all across America to take on "a man's job" in the service of their country. Welcoming them into the warehouses and factories was a smart move. It sustained production and even helped the drive to sell war bonds.

The Los Angeles Times, December 28, 1942
"Northrop Workers Show 35,000 Visitors How Planes Are Built"

Rosie the Riveter and Joe the Jig-builder yesterday showed the folks how they build dive bombers at Northrop. The day-shifters, turning their day off into "family visiting day," guided mom and dad, sister and Uncle Louie—an estimated 35,000 to 40,000 visitors—down the A-31 assembly line so they could see just where Rosie and Joe get in their licks against the Axis in the sprawling Hawthorne plant of Northrup Aircraft, Inc.

No longer merely tending to the children and the needs of the home, these newly active members of the workforce were earning their own cash and spending it how they pleased. A January 1943 snippet from the *L.A. Times* sums up just how far of a departure from traditional American ideologies this new craze stood. "Two women wearing working slacks and defense plant badges walked into a swanky furrier's last week and each picked out a fur coat." After paying with "a wad of bills," they donned their purchase and walked away: "Rosie the Riveter knows what she is working for and gets it. The furrier, though, is still a little dazed."

The furrier was not the only one in awe by the transformation. Despite this detour from the long-established, some measures still clung to more old-timey gender stereotypes. Security, at least in some areas, beefed up to ensure these new Rosie's were not harassed or harmed. In Philly, "ten detective squads and a number of policewomen" remained on the payroll "to see that women war workers" were not "molested going to and from work." Smartly, they even employed decoys in their campaign against Rosie attackers: "Policewomen will dress in slacks and bandanas, posing as working women."

Miraculously, in less than a year and a half, the long-held American mold of what a woman was, what was expected of her, and what she was capable of doing shattered.

The Long Beach Independent, December 26, 1943
"It Was a Tough Year but 'Mom' Did Her Job"

Washington, Dec. 25—Women hitched up their girdles and went to work in 1943 and Rosie the Riveter was the woman of the year with Frank Sinatra her dream prince consort. Nylon stockings were swapped for rayon, ration coupons for shoes and dates for V-mail. A million-and-a-half women went to work and learned about coveralls, tucked the Veronica Lake-like bobs of 1942 under snoods and turbans; mastered drill presses, lashes and acetylene torches.

While this may have been difficult for some to accept, the country certainly needed it. As one journalist aptly put: "Through four tough years Rosie was a heroine. She riveted the planes that dropped the bombs that won the war. She welded carrier bulkheads and wired torpedoes." These amazing women also "packed the food that kept General Patton rolling through Sicily and across Europe," and evidently, "whatever Generals Eisenhower or MacArthur needed to battle the Axis Powers," American women also "helped build." But exactly who it was that served as the original inspiration for the iconic figure, Rosie the Riveter, still comes into question.

Typically, when folks think of Rosie the Riveter, the yellow Westinghouse poster from 1942 comes to mind. It bears the popular "We Can Do It!" slogan. For

Americans during World War II, however, this image of a woman in denim and a red bandana flexing her bicep did not embody the nation's hardworking women. In fact, most Americans never even saw this rendition of "Rosie" until decades after the war. Feminist use of the nostalgic image during the 1970s and '80s is responsible for its fame, and for what has tied it to the World War II ideology of Rosie the Riveter. Not only was the lady in the red bandana not named Rosie, she did hardly any physical work at all to aid the war effort. Depicted on the poster is seventeen-year-old Geraldine Hoff Doyle. The picture was taken during her first, and only, week as a metal presser at the American Broach & Machine Company.

United Press photographer J. Howard Miller happened to snap Doyle's picture during her brief stint with the company, and apparently the print really sang to him. Westinghouse hired Miller to put together a line of motivational propaganda posters for women; posters that predominately remained on the premises for the benefit of their employees. Ironically, this Ann Arbor, Michigan, plant did not employ riveters. So, if few outside of the confines of the Midwest-based Westinghouse factory actually saw the Doyle-Rosie, what circulated the legend during the war's boom? Another famed image can be given at least partial credit.

One version of Rosie that 1940s Americans were definitely familiar with was Norman Rockwell's. Though not intended to be Rosie either, Rockwell's painting is often associated. It graced the cover of the 1943 Memorial Day issue of *The Saturday Evening Post*. The lady in denim coveralls Rockwell gave to Americans is enjoying a sandwich. Symbolically strewn across her lap is a very phallic and heavy-duty rivet gun. Though brawnier than the Westinghouse version, and dirty from all the hard work, the argument has been made that this Rosie did not live up to the reality of an ethnically-blended workforce.

Contrary to claims over who the "real" Rosie was, the fictional character was more than likely a composite of several young ladies named Rose. In a chance meeting, Rose Will Monroe met actor Walter Pidgeon in an aircraft factory in Michigan. Pidgeon was in the middle of making another of his propaganda pictures and was surprised to learn that a riveter named Rose worked right where they were filming. After catching a glimpse of her on the assembly line, Pidgeon asked her to star in his upcoming war bond film. Even though Jane Frazee played Rosalind "Rosie" Warren in the 1944 release, *Rosie the Riveter*, Rose Monroe is often thought to be the "real" Rosie. Again, the feminist movement lent a hand. Rose Monroe was just the icon they were after. A carpenter's daughter, she grew up learning blue collar skills, and was raised to ignore many of the typical gender barriers. At the age of fifty, that still had not changed. Not only did Ms. Rose Monroe earn her pilot's license, she could boast being the only female member in the local aeronautics club. She even taught her daughter how to fly. Despite the colorful and vetted backing, Rose Monroe was not the only Rosie to help shape the icon.

A "real Rosie" working a drill press in support of the war effort, *circa* mid-'40s. (*Author's personal collection*)

Rosalind P. Walter worked the nightshift as a fighter plane riveter in Long Island. This Rosie inspired the 1942 song "Rosie the Riveter," which predated both the Westinghouse and *Saturday Evening Post* renditions. A third Rosie who also worked as a riveter was an Italian. Rose Bonavita worked for General Motors in an aircraft plant in Tarrytown, New York. During a nightshift in June 1943, this daughter of Italian immigrants broke a plant record with the help of her fellow coworker, Jennie Florio. That night, the pair drilled 900 holes and drove thirty-three rivets in a torpedo bomber. The pair even received letters of commendation from President Roosevelt, and newspaper coverage followed. Before she knew it, Rose Bonavita had become a symbol and role model to nearly 3 million women; women who, just like her, were hustling among the American workforce.

During her wartime efforts, Rose Bonavita lived at home with her parents. Recalling those days, she remembered there only being enough time to eat, sleep, and work. Her typical week included seven twelve-hour shifts. "Before the war, I thought this was strictly a man's job," she indicated, adding "I guess it was Pearl Harbor that changed us. We were all enraged." Ironically, if President Roosevelt had given another nod to General DeWitt, Rose never would have been employed by General Motors. Instead she may have been interned somewhere further inland, leaving American history shy of one of its most iconic heroes. D.O.J. records show that during the first roundups of enemy aliens, federal agents took a Giacomo Bonavita into custody. Although a blood relation has not been confirmed, like Rose, the man resided in the New York area. After being held at Ellis Island, a transfer sent him to an internment camp at Fort George Meade in Maryland.

Like Lucy Niotta, Rose Bonavita also had a sweetheart aboard the U.S.S. *Mississippi*—a Mr. James Hickey. Soon, the ladies heard some wonderful news: after all those miles island-hopping in the Pacific, the *Mississippi* was due for maintenance, and the crew was slated for a spot of downtime. Even better for all involved, the shore leave that waited would take place stateside. In need of an overhaul, the *Mississippi* journeyed all the way to Bremerton, Washington, and while the mechanics tended to her engines, many of the men reconnected with their sweethearts. Rose and James seized the opportunity and got married. The newlyweds even found time to honeymoon. Wanting a big Italian family wedding, Lucy and Tony were still waiting for his enlistment to end, and Lucy's older sister, Anne, had the same idea. She got engaged to fellow with a lot in common with Tony. Mike Campagna's family came to America from the city of Bari, on the heel of Italy's boot. Not only was Mike also an Italian-American, but like Tony, he was serving with the Navy in the Pacific.

For these young couples, the brief but blessed stretch of togetherness they received would have to tie them over. The joyous occasion served as the only time James Hickey saw his beloved during his nearly five years of service. For

Lucy Niotta, the anguish Rose felt was certainly mutual, but with all the Rosie-vibe now rampant across America, she figured she should do her part, too. After graduating from Lincoln High, she left her gig at the malt shop and came to work with her older sisters. Anne and Marion were over at Gilfillan Radio. "When the war was going on," Tony explained, Gilfillan "stopped making radios. They were making radar panels instead. Lucy used to solder the wiring." They needed every Rosie they could get.

GILFILLAN BROS. *Incorporated*

1815-1849 VENICE BOULEVARD •• LOS ANGELES 6, CALIFORNIA

TELEPHONE DRexel 5131

September 8, 1944

Miss Lucille Niotta
Building #3

     On behalf of all of us here at Building #11, I wish to thank you for your unselfish action in giving your blood to aid the wife of Arnold Kirkman.

     It is a privilege to work in an organization where the people come through at a time like this.

             Sincerely yours,

             K. A. Allebach,
             Superintendent, Building #11

KAA:dja

Thank-you letter to Lucy Niotta from her employer, Gilfillan Bros. (*Courtesy of Anthony Amador*)

Each of the "Rosies" that served as models for the iconic figure helped inspire millions of women; women who answered their country's call during a crucial time. During this period, women made up nearly a third of America's workforce, but this figure would not last. According to the *Chicago Tribune*, although nearly 18 million women entered the working world, by the end of 1945, over 2.75 million of them had either been laid off or fired. After the fight, the very same ads that talked women into leaving the household now beckoned their return, urging them to take off the coveralls and resume their domestic duties.

High School Days

Working together on the school paper, Anna Dragna and Bill Grinnell became close friends. Bill even ended up taking her to school, pulling up to Anna's home early in the morning in his Model T Ford. Anna's father, Jack, sincerely liked the boy. Bill was well-mannered and always walked to the door and knocked politely. Thinking back on his high school days at Dorsey, Bill remembered a variety of drives and clubs that supported the war effort. Dorsey's Paper Scrap Club gathered scrap paper from all over the neighborhood then turned it in to be recycled so newer war posters could be printed. Grease-collecting clubs did the same with waste fats, oils, and grease. Like fish oil, these items proved vital to factory production. The school also held scrap-metal drives and fundraiser barbecues. Club members went door to door and involved entire communities. Strangely, war really brought people together.

Recalling personal efforts, Bill talked about the oil fields near Dorsey, which he and some of his pals figured would be a big score. One day, they tested the theory: "We went in and brought down a great big oil barrel." Although not full, he estimated the tank held between 300 and 400 gallons of waste oil. "We dragged it on my car," Bill remarked, referring to the Model T, and after they towed the barrel out, "an oil company came and took it away." But gathering oil was only one of the ways that Bill helped the war effort during his high school days. His real passion was lifting spirits by playing the drums.

Before the war got started, Bill put together a dance band with his pal, Jimmy Dabowlsky. Jimmy played saxophone for their group, the Star Dusters, and while their usual shows consisted of weekend parties and high school dances, they landed something far better after the war got going—a gig entertaining factory workers: "I got us a job playing what they called a swing shift dance, playing from 2 am till 6 am, on Friday nights and Saturday nights." Bill figures they regularly performed to "about five or six-hundred" from "the aircraft industry and so forth." The crowd filtered in shortly after shift and "danced for the rest of the night."

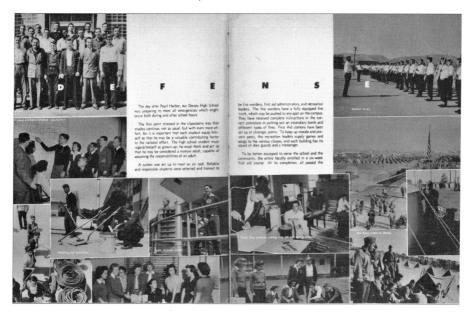

Above: The Army comes to Dorsey and the students prepare to aid in the fight, taken from Anna Dragna's Dorsey High yearbook, 1942. (*Courtesy of Frannie Niotta-LaRussa*)

Right: High school pals, Bill Grinnell and Anna Dragna, Los Angeles, *circa* 1944. (*Courtesy of Frannie Niotta-LaRussa*)

The front page of issue 1, vol. 1 of the Dorsey High student paper *The Sky Writer*, featuring an article co-written by the editor, Anna Dragna, and her fellow staff member, Bill Grinnell. (*Courtesy of Frannie Niotta-LaRussa*)

During her senior year, Anna remained very involved in school affairs. She continued as editor of the student paper *The Sky Writer*, and was even voted class president. The war effort really tied up the printing presses. War posters and other forms of printed media were cranked out regularly and took precedence. Luckily for Anna and Bill, schools were still able to continue the practice of printed journalism and the luxury of an annual yearbook. In addition to showcasing the current student body, many of these annuals also gave praise to former students now away in the fight, those who had fallen, and those listed as missing or as prisoners of war.

While most American high school yearbooks during the war looked relatively similar, some definitely stood out. In contrast was "The Black and Gold," an annual from Honolulu's McKinley High. McKinley's very Japanese population had a lot to do with it. For his brave service, *alumni* Shigeo "Joe" Takata posthumously received the Distinguished Service Cross. Takata, and more than a dozen other Japanese-American students from McKinley, were honored in the pages of the school's 1944 annual. Each of these young men fought in Italy. Despite the "Black and Gold's" bold observance, mention of the school's Speech Club was far more representative of what could be expected from America during this time—and especially in the U.S. territory of Hawaii. "Speak English as you are taught in the classroom—or you will not graduate!" The warning was not exclusive to McKinley. "This is the stern alternative the department of public instruction has presented the students of all public schools in Hawai'i."

One yearbook that stood out stateside was Excelsior Union High's 1942 edition of "El Aviador." The Artesia, California, school not only commented about the internment of their Japanese students, they refused to take out the photo of the campus' Japanese Club.

The Japanese Club was one of the largest and most active clubs at Excelsior under the direction of Miss Marie Wilson. Just before their necessary departure the members held a large party. As many of our firmest friends were among this group, we were truly sorry to see them leave.

Rohwer Center High's 1944 edition of "The Resume" represented another variety of the wartime annual. Rohwer sat inside a War Relocation Center, in McGehee, Arkansas. Like other high schools, Rohwer offered a variety of clubs, and like the other yearbooks, photos captured students attending classes, dances, and various functions. Spanish, needlecraft, Tri-Y, photography, art, glee and other clubs all made an appearance in the pages of "The Resume." The yearbook staff even boasted their efforts. "With camera men without film, the annual fund without money, the staff, under the editorship of Shinya Honda, faced many obstacles with determined efforts to turn out a top yearbook or bust!" While a subtle difference from more typical American annuals can be read in the captions—"From an inauspicious start with even less than barest essentials, our school has been improved greatly in spite of wartime restrictions"—a far more evident divide can be seen in the illustrations. "The Resume" offers a timeline of events depicted via cartoon. This begins with the relocation to the Arkansas facility. Below the date October 4, 1943, rests the drawing of a pair of boots and two suitcases sitting in a puddle of tears. The lone word "segregation" is written.

Although his son was far off in the fight, Jack Dragna was still getting calls from the University of Southern California. Like her older brother, Anna had also received good news from U.S.C. Coursework for a degree in journalism would follow her February 1944 graduation from Dorsey. Anna explained that not long after her acceptance, the admissions office started calling the house. Assuming the tone of the caller, she voiced, "Mr. Dragna, your daughter can use your son, Frank's, service money for school." But this was a subject that Anna's father simply did not want to hear. "My son is going to use it when he gets home from the war," he remarked each time they telephoned. Anna explained that while her brother was away, his room remained exactly as he left it. "My dad wouldn't give away any of his clothes. Superstitious, he kept things exactly as they were." But eventually something did change his mind.

In thanks, every state in America began offering a few hundred dollars to its veterans to allow them to pursue an education. Aiming higher, California divvied out something even better. They agreed to pay for veteran education outright. Smartly, the next administrator from U.S.C. that telephoned mentioned the program. Hearing that his son's continued education was now being paid for, the family patriarch finally agreed to allow the school to use the funds for Anna.

At it had been for Frankie, U.S.C. proved to be a dream for Anna as well. She enjoyed her classes and met a lot of great people. Among them was another Italian. Through her new friendship with Lolly Cacioppo, Anna became close with Lucy Niotta and Lucy's fiancé, Tony. Later, it would spark an introduction with a handsome older fellow—Lucy's big brother, Stevie.

Rationing

During any war, resources and the supply and demand of goods are of major concern. For this reason, rationing is common. The country's program to keep track of food and other items of interest kicked off in 1942, shortly after America entered the fight. Efforts sought to limit dependency on other nations just as much as they looked to ensure U.S. manufacturers had a steady and sufficient supply of raw materials. The program also hoped to calm any potential social unrest on the home front that might arise from shortages. A big concern of the everyday man was the issue of the wealthy buying up everything and stockpiling it. Although a sacrifice for all, rationing effectively curbed this tactic.

As a result of new laws and restrictions, many of the products grown or manufactured in the United States and its territories became reserved for the troops overseas, and in order to ensure wartime production carried on uninterrupted, a variety of other items such as rubber and metal became limited to the general public as well. Rations for sugar, flour, coffee, tires, gasoline, and many other goods were selectively doled out to the American public. The size of the family factored in, meaning some households received a larger share than others. Residents and citizens could only purchase rationed goods if they had a coupon or token for that specific item in their possession. Barbara Guarnieri explained, "My dad worked for a meat company, so we didn't have to use our coupons for meat." Her neighbors were not so lucky, which made for a good swap. "Our neighbor would give us sugar coupons, and we'd give them the meat coupons." Red tokens were used for meats, butter, oils, and fats. The blue ones covered fruits and veggies—canned, bottled, and frozen—and a variety of processed foods. Gas was another hot item.

Although he did not own a car, working at a gas station did end up being a perk for Tony Amador. He devised a clever system. After every tank he filled, Tony drained the excess fuel left in his hose into a small metal can before placing the nozzle back on the pump. By the end of his shift, it added up. Usually he gave what he gathered to his folks. The scarcity of fuel and other resources sometimes presented less of an issue than the location it came from. Much of the supply of coffee and sugar, for instance, was imported, so the two were largely targeted. While fresh fruit could be grown locally, rationing on gasoline and tires severely hampered its transport. Oddly, typewriters also made the list. Although the resources themselves remained in high demand and short supply, the coupons used to redeem them, on the other hand, sat well in abundance.

The Los Angeles Times, March 6, 1942
"Rationing Cards Prove Problem"

County Clerk Doesn't Know Where to Store Sugar Paraphernalia

Sugar rationing cards—3,717,000 of them—were placed under the control of County Clerk J. F. Moroney, rationing agent in charge of the work in the county, by the printers yesterday. Moroney declared that he will have to rent warehouse space to store the piles of cards and accompanying stamps which will be used to control the sale of the precious commodity. "The cards weigh 35,000 pounds," Moroney said, "and their storing and distribution is going to be a problem."

Geneva Convention regulations stipulate that prisoners of war are to receive the same ration as U.S. service members, and they did. But as the papers highlighted, those being interned felt the squeeze of rationing as well. According to *The Long Beach Independent*, the "mess halls at Manzanar set a typical war-time table, with: No eggs, less sugar than the civilian quota, no butter, one cup per day of coffee." In regard to meat, "no steaks, chops, nor roasts" made the menu. "On the average, the meat ration averages well below the voluntary rationing figure requested of all civilians by the Office of Price Administration." The facility's project director, Ralph P. Merrit, added that evacuees at Manzanar had "become self-sustaining to the extent that this year, even after a late planting, they raised more than $40,000 worth of vegetables to be used in the community mess." Not only were they planting enough for themselves, they additionally grew "a corresponding amount of food for civilians."

Tight as it was, Americans faced an even more drastic sacrifice. A complete halt on the production of automobiles meant no new cars for anyone. To meet the high demand for tanks, trucks, planes, arms, and munitions, auto-manufacturing plants quickly switched over, and although a mass of vehicles still waited to be sold on sales lots all across the country, rationing impacted them as well. Automobile rationing commenced on February 2, 1942.

The Los Angeles Times, January 4, 1942
"War Pinch Hits Civilians as New Cars Rationed"

Huge Supplies of Metal, Rubber and Cotton to Be Made Available for War Equipment

Wide World, Jan. 3—When the Supply Priorities and Allocations Board this week took complete control of the sales of new passenger automobiles and trucks our wartime government laid its hands on the greatest single supply of vital raw materials the country possessed. Also, by announcing plans were under way to ration civilian purchasing of motor vehicles, and by earlier rationing of tires, it foreshadowed the most drastic cutting into the normal American pattern of life that the war has yet produced. For the American pattern of living has been built, to an extent that is not even remotely approached elsewhere, around the passenger car.

Initially, restrictions limited sales to fire and police departments, to doctors, key workers, and to traveling salesmen, but before long, only military personnel were authorized. The big change heavily impacted another group of individuals—car salesmen. But at least plenty of other work was now available for the taking. "Salesmen who lose their jobs are encouraged to register with local employment offices for war production jobs." Because Americans still needed to get around, measures were taken to ensure that the cars already on the road stayed running. Contracts designated specific production work. For instance, one Chevy factory out in Saginaw, Michigan, manufactured nothing other than replacement G.M. parts. Greatly helping, carpooling or "Ride Together Clubs" became a big thing. The ads popping up in print dubbed it "a new idea to help you conserve your tires and save on gasoline"—two other items under strict rationing.

The San Bernardino Daily Sun, February 24, 1942
"Drivers Advised to Analyze Cars' Use"

The Rubber Manufacturers association today urged the American motoring public not to drive a mile that is unessential and, on the assumption there will be no new tires till after the war, budget the estimated life of its tires. Donald M. Nelson, chief of the war production board, and Jesse H. Jones, secretary of commerce, said there will be no rubber to spare for civilian use. If the estimated remaining life in the family car's tires is about 10,000 miles, the association said, then their use would have to be limited to about 2,000 miles yearly, which would mean only 166 miles a month, or about 40 miles a week—if the family wanted to keep the car operating a few more years.

As the war progressed, rubber for use by the civilian population drastically shrank. The cap even called for ration coupons for rubber footwear, and before the close of the first full year of U.S. involvement, the government forced Americans to sell their surplus tires to Uncle Sam. Motorists received anywhere from $1.50 to $11.25 a tire. In October '42, the press advised: "The four tires they drove on, plus a spare for emergencies were all that American motorists could legally possess, as the U.S. government began acquiring excess civilian tires." Families that owned a second car were allowed to keep ten. Shockingly, the mandate even came with a threat: "Car owners with more than five tires would be denied gasoline rations when the nationwide registration took place November 9th." Anyone caught falsifying tire statements while applying for gas rations was subject to decade-long prison terms and fines as high as $10,000.

Leaning out America's supply of fuel, tires, and automobiles gave way to a whole new wave of criminal activity. An assortment of stolen, bootleg, and alternative items filtered into the black market, and with a whole new demand to cater to, criminals began stealing the most unlikely wares. Famed L.A. gangster

Mickey Cohen made a bundle on stolen nylons. Discouraging a wave of theft, the papers urged motorists to write down the serial numbers of their possessions. This even included their tires. The number, along with the brand, size, and make, would "assist the police in recovery."

Clark Gable's Car

Anna Dragna's story about a red convertible her father spotted on a car lot during the war is one that her family still shares. He knew the owner of the dealership, Anna explained, and he was playing cards in the shop's break room with a group of guys on the day he saw it. "I want that car for my son," Jack expressed. The dealer was hesitant but finally objected, "That car's being held for Clark Gable!" The famed actor—as the dealer also pointed out—was presently overseas in the fight. Gable's enlistment was prompted by the death of his wife, actress Carole Lombard. Lombard passed away in a plane crash while working a war bonds tour. Given his celebrity status, inserting himself in the war took some doing, but eventually, Gable was successful. Like Dick, he took up position as a left waist gunner on a B-17. Not merely for show, the movie star did actually clock in a handful of rides.

Clark Gable's wealth and popularity, now bolstered by his selfless service abroad, no doubt made it easier to secure himself a car, especially after the war was over. Chevy got back to civilian auto production mere days after the Japanese surrender. That being said, the silver screen heartthrob never did drive that red convertible he was slated. The beautiful machine went to Frankie Dragna instead.

7

Headed for War

Life on a Ship

Life on a ship kept Tony plenty busy. He rarely found time to take care of the little things. Duty called, and when it did, it usually came at the worst possible moment. "When we'd secure from general quarters (G.Q.)," meaning all was clear and they could finally leave their battle stations, "we'd try and wash our clothes—our dungarees and stuff." Even though the ship had a laundry onboard, a lot of the sailors had a hard time getting there. "But whenever we washed our dungarees, they'd sound general quarters." The announcement called for all hands—every single body on board. They literally had to run to their battle stations immediately. "We'd have to take off," and come back and try later.

Tony's shipmate, John Yakushik, experienced the same problem, only on a more embarrassing level. John did his own laundry in the washroom, but because he got so wet in the process, he started the routine of doing the task in the nude, just before he hopped in the shower—two birds, one stone. But being naked long enough to do a load of laundry sometimes became an issue: "I was washing my clothes, then what happens, an air attack, and G.Q. sounded. Boy was I mad! I guess I called the Japs everything I knew."

While Tony enjoyed the view topside, John remained below deck in the power shop. This presented another problem when G.Q. sounded: "Below deck all is watertight, 'Zed'—and there is no way to get to the head [bathroom]." The one consolation these men had was the "buckets with sand" available for usage. But a far worse drawback to being below deck existed. "One of my fears was being rammed," Yakushik admitted, "because I was stationed below deck, and most times," when that happened, "you were entombed." The G.Q. made the night hours difficult, too. "You really didn't get any sound sleep. You'd just start to fall and they'd call general quarters. Then you'd have to go back to your battle station again."

U.S.S. *Mississippi.* (*Author's personal collection*)

Bearded shipmates Paul DeVore and Tony Amador. (*Courtesy of Anthony Amador*)

Back at their defense stations, the crewmembers diligently looked for enemy aircraft or vessels. Trapped in the tense silence, they waited for commands from the loudspeaker. For even the bravest, the blaring call of "air contact!" instilled fear. On deck, divisions of gunners remained heavily armed and ready. Nearly a hundred men made up each division; it took that many to operate a single turret. "I was tier one and I trained the gun out to the target when we'd bombard," Tony relayed about his role in the 1st Division. Sometimes, he pointed at enemy vessels, but usually he aimed at an island to clear it for ground troop entry. Afterward, two of the ship's planes would circle the area to see how accurate the battleship was, and to seek out any additional marks that needed hammering. If so, Tony called for adjustments then the firing resumed. But even with the big guns of destroyers heaving devastation from way out in the ocean, the men who stormed the beaches still ran into enemy fire. The Japanese forces in the Pacific dug in deep.

The U.S.S. *Mississippi* willingly ran toward danger, but battle came to the men aboard as well, and when it did, they were ready. On the defensive, Tony manned a much smaller weapon: "During air attacks, I was on the 20-mm gun." Topside, the *Mississippi* had eighty of them; they replaced some of the older .50-caliber guns. With the threat of the kamikaze a reality, manning these weapons in a fight got plenty hairy. In addition to the 20-mm, Tony also used 5-inch guns. "There was a 5" gun that guys from my division manned, and another 5" gun down from there. The guy I joined the Navy with—Turk—he was on that gun."

Although Tony kept busy during ship life, life at sea was far from constant action. He found time to write Lucy and his mother, mailing letters at the next port. But even with that distraction, sometimes the hours just dragged on. This was certainly the case during midnight watch: "On midnight watch, one of the guys would go and get a big pot of coffee and a couple loaves of bread. And we used to go to the footlocker and get some onions. We sliced onions and made onion sandwiches, and drank coffee." As unappealing as an onion sandwich might sound, apparently they worked wonders at keeping a guy awake, especially with coffee in the mix.

Many seamen had a hard time getting over the vast distances between islands. Naval Officer Paul Barnes commented that the gaps at sea aboard the *Mississippi* could be immense, with "thousands of miles with nothing to see"—that is, nothing other than water. The men managed to stay sane despite it, and at times, the inactivity even spurred hilarious action. Considering most of the crew was between seventeen and nineteen years old, this made sense. The young ones came up with clever ways of entertaining one another. What made the task far more difficult was the order that kept sailors from bringing alcohol onboard. Whether thrown in chaos or caged in boredom, they found a way to hang on to their sense of humor. Many years later, one particular incident remained in Barnes' mind.

Standard battleship practice included stenciling pictures on the navigation bridge. The crew did this to display their war record. Proudly marked on the side of the *Mississippi* were several images: a small island with two palm trees, a

Above: Division 1, operators of U.S.S. *Mississippi*'s turret one; Tony Amador is circled. (*Courtesy of Anthony Amador*)

Right: Tony with his turret, U.S.S. *Mississippi.* (*Courtesy of Anthony Amador*)

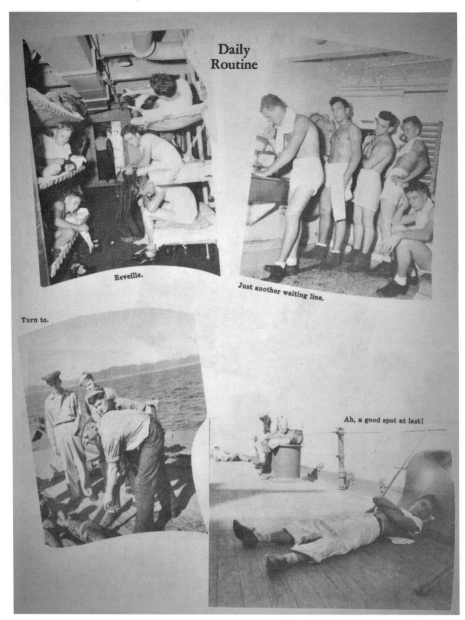

Daily life aboard the *Mississippi*, taken from U.S.S. *Mississippi* war history booklet, exclusive to the officers and crew, 1945. (*Courtesy of Anthony J. Amador*)

OUR SCORE CARD:— 11 ISLANDS BOMBARDED
1 CRUISER SUNK, 1 CASTLE, "SHURI CASTLE AND
9 JAPANESE PLANES SHOT DOWN.

Above left: Portrait of Tony sent home to his "future wife," Lucy, *circa* 1944. (*Courtesy of Linda Amador-Galardo*)

Above right: Battle scorecard of U.S.S. *Mississippi*, *circa* 1945. (*Courtesy of Anthony Amador*)

ship, a plane, and later they even added a castle. They kept count of how many of each they sacked beneath these pictures. Rather than using hashmarks, the men instead painted Japanese flags. At the end of her run during World War II, the *Mississippi*'s "score card" showed eleven islands, one cruiser, one castle, and nine Japanese planes. But sometimes at sea during the long and boring stretches, other items were humorously stenciled on the navigation bridge as well. Interestingly enough, when the three 14-inch guns from the number 3 turret trained a certain way and fired during a bombardment, sometimes the two topside urinals on the deck shattered. "The morning after the bombardment in question, which had broken the urinals as usual, it was noted that two outhouses had been painted on the side of the number 3 turret." There was that humor that kept the spirit going.

Kamikaze

Roughly translated, the word kamikaze means "big wind," or the "divine tempest." But for Allied forces during World War II, it wore another definition: danger and death. "They used to train these guys—these kamikazes. They filled the thing up with bombs and gas, put them in the airplane, and they'd take off." Speaking from experience, Tony added: "And their mission was to divebomb right into the ship." Placing himself back on the deck of the *Missy* to relive these events,

Tony mouthed bleakly, "They knew they weren't coming back." One attack in particular always stuck with him: "We'd just got secured from general quarters and then we got something again. The kamikaze planes. They called air defense." This time, the one-man fighters flew so close that Tony caught a glimpse of one of the pilots. A moment later, the burnt remains of the young kamikaze littered the ship's deck.

Despite popular belief, Collier H. Young clarified that the main role of this specific type of attack was actually conventional bombing. Resorting to divebombing—an outright act of suicide—became an option only if the pilot felt he could not make it out safely. "Mass suicide by men as hard to replace as flyers is, of course, desperate warfare." The high cost of planes and the investment in training a pilot is something that "no air force … can really afford." Speaking of his own experiences with these Japanese planes, though, Young exclaimed that even though this was the case, the Japanese did it anyway—"coldly, deliberately, and ruthlessly."

Although merely a flea when compared to the immensity of a battleship, the kamikaze definitely posed an exceedingly dangerous threat. "We lost some destroyers during some of these engagements where the kamikazes dove into them," Tony sadly admitted. Although these destroyers were not as big as the *Mississippi*, which was a battleship, the vessels were still very well armed, and this actually turned out to be the problem: "They had torpedoes on them and when they got hit," the explosives ignited, taking the entire vessel and hundreds of sailors with it.

The One That Got Away and the One He Got

Near misses, close calls, and dumb luck all played a role at sea during the war, and the same can probably be said about the battle on the ground and up in the air. Chance and statistics certainly had a say in how events panned out. Tony recalled a time when a torpedo was heading straight for him. On that day, the crew of the *Mississippi* was just plain lucky: "It was coming right at us. We had orders to blow it up and I was on the 20-mm at the time. I could see the wake of the torpedo coming right alongside the ship, and we fired down on the water, trying to hit it and blow it up." None of the sailors hit their mark, however. "It kept going," Tony chuckled. "It didn't hit anybody." The crew waited for an explosion but the sound never came: "It just died out and I guess it sunk."

After reflecting on the one that got away, Tony talked about the one he got: "I fired at planes, a lot of planes." On one occasion, he even fired at one of their own. "One of ours chased a Jap plane into where they were not supposed to be flying. He shot the Jap plane down then radioed." The pilot called the ship's crew to let them know he was heading back. Unfortunately, word did not relay to the ship's guns in time. "Before they got the information to the gunners—and I was on the 20—we shot our own plane down!" Thankfully, "the pilot was rescued. He landed in the water and jumped out of the plane. The destroyer come along and picked him up." John Yakushik remembered the incident as well. "I'll bet he was plenty mad!" But according to Barnes, this was not the only occurrence: "In the Philippines, when we were under constant heavy kamikaze attacks, several U.S. planes, which were trailing after attacking Jap planes, were shot down by our task force."

The Putt-Putt

"From Savannah we went up to Newfoundland," Dick Williams relayed about the long flight overseas to join the fight, "and from Newfoundland we went to the Azores." Although this small cluster of islands belongs to Portugal, the Azores actually sit some 950 miles from the country's mainland. On the island of Terceira, rests the Portuguese Air Base, Lajes Field. The U.S. military took up residence shortly after the war started and they still have not moved out. Currently the Portuguese Air Force shares Lajes with the U.S. Air Force. Back when Dick landed to refuel, the U.S. Navy inhabited the area.

In March '41, *The Los Angeles Times* let on to just how strategically important these small bodies of land in the middle of the ocean were: "These islands are for all practical purposes very nearly in the middle of the Atlantic Ocean." The Atlantic being a far sight smaller than the Pacific, the journalist with the *Times* felt it "a conservative statement to say that the control of the Azores is at least as important to our defense and to our interests as a seafaring nation as is the control of Hawaii." The spot proved well-suited for refueling and also as an emergency crash landing site—and it still functions in this capacity.

Although designated as a waist gunner, Dick had his share of additional duties; one of these came into play during their pit stop on the island. As an assistant engineer, Dick operated an auxiliary power unit (A.P.U.), which assisted the plane during take-off: "It was called a *putt-putt*. You would plug into the nose of the airplane when you would land in a field, such as the Azores, where there was no auxiliary power plug in." The putt-putt powered an electrical generator, which fired the plane's four engines. Because the conditions on the airfield where they landed were so ill-equipped, Dick went to work with the putt-putt as soon as they finished refueling.

"My pilot, Nick, had a friend who was flying the same route to North Africa and they kind of had a bet going as to who would get there first." Knowing-well Nick Kantar hoped to win that bet, and was "anxious to take off," Dick ran at the task double-time, but apparently he was not fast enough. "I was out there getting the putt-putt unplugged and I looked up and our airplane was coming right at me!" Eager to get back in the air, Kantar completely forgot one of his men was still outside. "Until I hollered at him!" Dick could have easily been diced by a propeller, or crushed—a close call he would later find humorous.

As it turned out, this was not the only time that Nick Kantar's urge to get in the air in a hurry caused a predicament for Dick. "The engines were starting up. We were on a mission and I had to have a BM"—a bowel movement. Dick was again in a compromising position when the propellers began to whirl: "I was kind of hurrying into the airplane and I dragged the arm of my flight suit through what I left in the ground." In a pinch, Dick did his best to clean up after boarding the plane, but the smell definitely lingered: "Oh boy, thank God there's only one person in the waist that had to be close to me."

"From the Azores we went to North Africa." After a brief stop, they flew further north into Sicily: "There was a terrible, terrible windstorm, and we saw the fighting on the ground. We went through the sand and everything." The conditions less than ideal, their pilot contemplated swinging back toward Africa. Eventually, they did land in Sicily and waited out the bad weather. "Ultimately, the storm calmed down and we went on to Foggia, Italy." After reaching their final destination, the crew got the impression they had been used as a courier service: "In Foggia they took away the new airplane and all the new equipment." In return, they were handed some well-loved and broken-in replacements.

The 15th *versus* the 8th, and the Sentiments of Italians

Stevie's crew made the long ride out to England on October 27, 1943 and landed nearly a week later, setting down on November 2. Assigned to the 8th Air Force's Royal Air Force (R.A.F.) Knettishall, up near Suffolk, Stevie joined the 388th Bombardment Group's 562nd Bomb Squadron. Narrowing it even further, they placed him in the 45th Combat Wing. Dick, on the other hand, received orders with the 15th Air Force's 97th Bomb Group.

"The 97th," as Dick announced proudly, "was the first one to bomb Nazi territory during World War II." The bombardment group was actually part of the 8th Air Force when they made the raid on August 17, 1942, flying over Rouen, France. A month later, they transferred to the 12th Air Force in the Mediterranean, and right around the time Stevie entered the E.T.O., Dick's future squadron moved yet again, settling in with the 15th Air Force out in Foggia. It was in November 1943 that the 15th got situated in Italy. A more strategic placement is what the Allied forces were after with the relocation. From the backside of Italy's boot, the aircrews were better equipped to hit Southern Germany, Austria, Southern France, and the Balkans—targets that proved increasingly difficult for the 8th to reach from way out in England due to unpredictable weather and excessive fuel consumption.

Coming into the fold with the 15th, Dick joined the 342nd Bomb Squadron. "We were the forgotten ones," he conveyed before pointing out the major differences between the 15th and the 8th. Making light of his statement, he remarked "the newspaper reporters would rather go to London than Italy"—and why not? The 15th sat in what, until only recently, was enemy territory. Grudges and hostilities remained. Resentment toward the Allied forces, and the potential for violence, no doubt swayed newsmen from coming. Dick wholeheartedly believed this caused one group to pull more coverage than the other. Referencing the move to Italy, Dick stated: "After our group left England and went over to North Africa," which occurred during Operation Torch, "it seemed like the coverage was all on the 8th. We just didn't get the publicity." Jokingly placing blame on Hollywood's heartthrob, Dick added: "And they got Clark Gable over there!" Dick mentioned Jimmy Stewart as well; Stewart flew Liberators during the war, but he was not the only big name to fight the Axis Powers out of a B-24. Track star Olympian Louis Zamperini served as a bombardier, and just like Frankie Dragna, not only was Zamperini a good-looking Italian, before the war he was also a student at U.S.C. Sadly, he became a prisoner of war after his aircraft was shot down.

Media coverage and the presence of famed service members were not the only factors that set the two air forces apart. Sentiments of the civilian populations greatly differed as well. Even after the Italian surrender, the citizens of Foggia remained far from amicable to the Allied forces, and for good reason. Upon his arrival, Dick heard some pretty gruesome stories. Whether or not these were mere tales, the threat alone was more than enough to keep him on edge. The problem started with the Brits but failed to end when the Italians were done with Mussolini.

"The field that we shared in Foggia, Italy, we shared with the British Royal Canadian Air Force. We were the B-17s and they were the Lancaster. That was the British ace bomber." The 12th Air Force and the British R.A.F. landed in Foggia before Dick's arrival. While British construction of airfields began before the war, Luftwaffe ties to the area went back even further. The Germans used the spot during World War I, and like the Brits, they also built airfields. Conflict waited for the tiniest spark, and once Italy joined the Axis Powers, the dispute ignited. Through force, the Luftwaffe took the British airfields. Fortunately, this control did not last. But taking back Foggia came at a hefty cost; one that the civilian population was forced to pay.

During the struggle for Foggia's airfields, a series of heavy bombing attacks caused upwards of 20,000 casualties. The country will never forget the loss. Sadly, this was not the end of the city's death toll. Despite the signing of an armistice agreement, which declared Italy's surrender, harsh efforts to purge German forces from Italy continued. Following the British grab, the U.S. Army moved in and helped rebuild the wreckage. But the citizens there proved less than thankful. "As you can imagine, folks in Foggia were still very resentful of us—by us I mean American Airmen." For this reason, "they warned us never, never go anyplace alone, especially at night." The stories whispered about those that failed to listen were horrific. "We heeded that admonition and didn't" go out alone "because they were still in the practice of castrating American Airmen if they got a chance—any time they could catch us alone."

Although the Brits welcomed the Yanks from the 8th much more warmly than the Italians greeted the boys from the 15th, Dick did recall a very dangerous drawback to flying out of England. "Those guys had it worse than us. They didn't have fighter escort!" Elaborating, Dick clarified that these bombers were only unattended for part of the mission. This was due mainly to limitations on the fuel supply. "The bombers were very vulnerable for about half the distance to the target, and then returning home." The scenario Dick spoke of was, in fact, protocol, but thankfully, it only lasted a brief stint.

Unfortunately, the idea that B-17 crewmembers could fend for themselves on a bomb run if they all flew together in large packs like wolves was an idea that saw fruition. Testing the theory, the 8th Air Force recklessly sent out bomber crews in mass without fighter escort—and immense losses followed. On the worst of these

Citizens of Licata, Sicily, reading proclamations posted by the U.S. Army following the Sicilian invasion. Notices indicate American troops will remove Fascism and residents of the area will be treated well if they obey, July 20, 1943. (*Author's personal collection*)

horrific days, sixty Flying Fortresses never made it back. The occurrence spurred a temporary grounding of all heavy bombers, and solidified the realization that their leadership had made a fatal mistake. The grim event took place just before Stevie's crew pulled in. Their first mission kicked off once the ban lifted.

Flight book entries suggest that going to and returning from a target without fighter escort was a big deal and certainly not a regular occurrence. Whenever it happened—and at times it simply could not be avoided—crewmembers wrote about the bad feelings associated with the risk. A common theme ran through flight crew journals. Specific targets and areas struck greater fear and anxiety, and the thought of having to go through these stretches without fighter backing made the hazard even more awful to stomach.

Fighting out of Foggia

While the 15th chased targets closer to the Southern end of Germany, the 8th went after the North. The city of Regensburg, however, offered a bit of an overlap. "We bombed the 109 factory there, and the 8th bombed that a lot as well." Perched in the bottom corner of Europe, the 15th also dropped metal on Prague. Dick even called it their "main target." But what ended up being the group's "most effective bombing" was their runs to Vienna. These made up roughly a fifth of the missions that Dick flew on. "They had their oil refineries there, so we bombed there all the time." Sacking this source is what he attributed to the German ineffectiveness "toward the end." Without the fuel to fly, what could the do? "They had all the pilots and they had airplanes but they didn't have any gas or oil."

Foggia's placement—just below the ankle of Italy—put the 15th a short hop from Sicily and Northern Africa. Set so close to the coastline of the Adriatic Sea, they faced the Dalmatian Coast of Croatia. In regard to the advantage of air attacks from this position, military leaders certainly viewed it as an ideal geographic location. Despite the contention of military strategists, Dick always felt otherwise, and likely because of the mountain range B-17s had to scale regularly.

"We flew our missions from Foggia, and always over the Alps." Uttering the word seemed only to trigger all the old difficulties. "We had to make sure that we could maintain an altitude of 16,000 feet." But considering the nature of their missions, achieving this was not always easy. When they went out on runs the enemy attacked, and sometimes bombers hobbled back. "If you lost one engine" from taking flak while bombing a target then "many, many times" you "couldn't maintain altitude." Although B-17s are equipped with four engines, with even just one of them out, the prospect of climbing and holding 16,000 feet could be iffy, and if the plane failed to fly high enough, "you couldn't get back up over the Alps." Either the crew landed somewhere they did not want to land or they crashed into the mountains. The available options were far from ideal.

8

Campaigns:
Welcome to the Jungle

For a well-off college boy from Southern California like Frankie Dragna, marching through the dense jungles of the Philippines while being shot at and eaten alive by mosquitos could not have been any less pleasant. When heavy rain chose not fall, air attacks and troop fire always seemed to, and at times, these horrors even managed to coordinate a joint effort. For even the toughest among them, life in the jungle proved to be anything but easy. Unlike Tony, on a ship, and Stevie and Dick, up in the air, Frankie was forced into close quarters with his adversaries. Infantrymen could see the expressions on the faces of the men trying to kill him. If need be, they took a life with their bare hands.

Although the 43rd Division came together during World War I, at least one of its National Guard regiments predated the Revolutionary War. Among the 43rd's 85th Brigade—known as Custer's Brigade—the 169th infantry regiment could boast such a claim, and this is who Frankie ended up with. But they had already been through a lot by the time he joined them. In late February 1941, while Frankie was still playing high school football, his division mobilized for training. After readying new recruits at Camp Shelby, Mississippi, the group moved west to San Francisco. By the end of September 1942, the force of more than 3,000 sailed for New Zealand. In their new surroundings, they again engaged in extensive training. This theme would never die. Even in between the war campaigns they fought, these men continued to train. According to Lieutenant Colonel Joseph E. Zimmer of the 169th, this "consisted of amphibious landings, infantry-tank team coordination, night patrolling, motorized movements, and battalion assault firing exercises." In addition to New Zealand, they trained at Aitape on New Guinea and again in Luzon.

Northern Solomon's Campaign

Frankie joined the men just over a year after they landed in the Solomon Islands, northeast of Australia. He left the states in late October 1943 and arrived on New

Georgia in the middle of November. It was already late in the fold of the Solomon Campaign. As a replenishing troop, he was called because they had suffered a loss. Not much time had passed since the group took Munda Airfield. The mood was still somber. During this struggle, the 169th assisted in capturing the area, wrestling it from an aggressive force of Japanese. After securing the airfield, they took on a temporary assignment with the 172nd Regiment—clear out nearby Arundel Island. Assisting in this endeavor, they again met with great resistance. Engaged in jungle warfare amid thick dense trees and a continuous downpour, the 169th suffered a big hit: four men killed and another twenty-nine wounded. This is what summoned Frankie to the jungle.

Frankie's regiment had just resumed their guard of the Munda airstrip when he reported to backfill the fallen. These men he joined were plenty seasoned. Frankie could tell right off. He also quickly sensed what he was up against. He may have missed the early jungle skirmishes, but he would face more than his share of action soon, and he did; the Northern Solomon's Campaign was just about to converge with the New Georgia Campaign.

Frankie remained on patrol at Munda for two months, staying until late January 1944, when new orders for the group came down—another airstrip. They hopped islands for the new destination. This time they would protect Vella LaVella. After three and a half months of airstrip duty there, the 169th again sailed for New Zealand. For Frankie, this would be his first glimpse. They landed on March 1, 1944. After all the action the men had seen, they were overdue for a bit of leave. Unfortunately, the furlough was brief; more training waited.

Wartime postcard from Stevie Niotta's collection. (*Courtesy of Frannie Niotta-LaRussa*)

New Guinea Campaign

The New Guinea Campaign began in late January 1943. Frankie was still at U.S.C. then and his future regiment was fighting near Munda. But the campaign would continue until the last day of 1944. Frankie and the rest of the 169th infantry regiment joined the action in Aitape that summer, arriving on July 17, 1944. There they served as reinforcement for the 6th Army's 32nd Division. Unfortunately, they came during the wettest month in an area that averaged 100 inches of rain per year. The group expected torrential tropical downpours. In the wet of Aitape, patrolling continued. Roving, they sought out Japanese troops, and soon encountered what they were after. In fact, confrontations occurred rather frequently as they moved through the neighboring villages along the Driniumor River, and in the surrounding jungles, hills, streams, and swamps.

The month and a half of treacherous work proved fruitful. With the help of the 169th, U.S. armed forces secured the area on August 25, 1944. Their job in Aitape was done and eventually the Australian 6th Division relieved the regiment. Although Frankie's Division suffered fewer losses during this campaign, the 43rd certainly felt each casualty—twenty-eight deaths and fifty-nine wounded. Free of their patrol obligation, the group trained heavy in preparation for their next stop; Luzon, the largest and most populated island in the Philippines. Using aerial photos of their next target, they fashioned their exercises to feel as realistic as possible. Not much needed to be done to the terrain though. Already nearly unbearable—even for the Army infantry—the land proved adamantly trifling on its own. High reeds and muddy primitive roads greeted the boys wherever they went—even mountains stood in the way. But the infantry trudged through on foot, prepping for the invasion.

The Battle of Luzon

Expecting to be struck further south near the capital, the Japanese situated the bulk of their ground forces around Manila Bay. Anticipating this defense, American forces took the fight to Lingayen Gulf instead. They moved in shortly after the new year, landing on January 9, 1945. Confirming aerial photos before launching, "underwater demolition teams went ashore on the landing beaches under cover of darkness." Lt. Col. Zimmer claimed the path appeared just as they hoped; the men reported the beaches "free of obstacles." So, when U.S. troops ran in, they did so in high number and with little ground opposition. An exceedingly large American force fell upon Luzon. The drive pushed more men to land than the first wave of Normandy. Within a few days, 175,000 troops reached shore and secured a 20-mile-wide beachhead. While successful, the march forward was anything but quiet.

Some 2 miles offshore, destroyers, cruisers, and battleships cleared the way, bombarding the land mercilessly. Pointing a turret from the water, Tony Amador, guided the *Mississippi*'s constant onslaught to clear the way for Frankie and his fellow comrades. The 43rd Division landed near San Fabian, inching behind the shells that fell. Overhead, air attacks rained down as they stormed forward.

Frankie's regiment was designated the center landing, known as Beach White Two. Their orders were to take Hill 470. At the highest point of the third ridgeline, roughly 3 miles up, is where the hill waited. On the advance, they took left flank. Driving forward in three separate battalions, they moved through enemy fire and rugged, hilly countryside. They fought the steep slopes of the hill, charging upward, and before nightfall of the second day, they seized their target. The groups moved onto Hills 318 and 355, encountering an elaborate set of caves and tunnels manned by Japanese soldiers—defensive fighting positions (D.F.P.s) all too common on Luzon.

After several days battling a stubborn and dug-in resistance, the regiment finally captured their next target, Hill 560. They took it on January 12. During the battle, the actions of Staff Sergeant Laws—one of Frankie's fellow soldiers—earned him the Medal of Honor. To clear the way, Laws took out a pillbox of three Japanese soldiers in hand-to-hand combat. By the following day, the enemy had taken the high ground, leaving the Army regiments vulnerable on the advance, and still they pressed forward.

It was on January 15—the fifth day of the charge—that an officer gave Frankie a dangerous order: go up that hill, see if you can spot the enemy. Frankie's training warned against such a move, as it compromised his position on the horizon line. To do so would leave him vulnerable to an attack. Hesitant over the risk, he voiced his concern. The order, he soon found out, was to be obeyed regardless. Frankie had been with the group for a little more than a year now, and in that time, he noticed a pattern of the Italian-American soldiers like himself receiving some of the worst duties. He chalked this new order up—being singled out for a dangerous task—as another crappy detail for an Italian. More than sixty years after the incident, Frankie still had not forgotten or forgiven the man who gave the order. After his silhouette appeared, a grenade was lobbed. Frank Paul Dragna took the brunt of the blast in the face. Although lucky to be alive, he came out far from unscathed. The explosion cost him his right eye.

While Frankie laid in a cot with his head in bandages, the infantry continued onward to the Lingayen Plain. Another week of hell and the Battle of Luzon ended. For their part, the 169th Regiment was awarded the Distinguished Unit Citation. But the cuts to earn this distinction ran deep. They lost 248 enlisted men and seventeen officers, plus another 734 were injured. The numbers of those lost throughout the entire 43rd Division proved a far sight larger: 952 killed in action and 3,921 wounded. Reports estimated the number of Japanese killed in combat to be greater than 12,000.

Frankie would hear of the victory and of the names of the men they lost from a hospital bed, but in their care in country, his condition soon worsened; Frankie contracted malaria. More than a month would pass before his health improved enough to travel. He left for Los Angeles on February 21, 1945. He was still only twenty years old. The war would soon end, but like many others, he would have to live with his injuries for the remainder of his life.

9

Campaigns:
In Air with the 15th

As Dick pointed out, unlike the Brits, the Americans flew their heavy bomber missions during daylight hours. This meant that maintenance and repairs happened at night, and because of the limited hangar space, a lot of this occurred outdoors. With security measures keeping bases blacked out during night hours, mechanics turned a wrench by flashlight and the light of the moon. This made the going slow. "Those poor ground crewmembers—the Engineers and so forth—they would work sometimes all night to get the planes ready." After the mechanics rendered a plane safe enough to take up, it moved on to the next batch of workers. Armorers loaded each plane with bombs and ammunition, and when they were through, the refuelers had a go, pumping in thousands of gallons of 100-octane. All this took place before the sun ever rose.

Green Gunners and Taking Flak

According to Dick, in order to season the fresh crews arriving, the Air Corps divided their groups up. They all went out on different planes. Three to five missions with experienced flyers and they returned to the groups they arrived with. After that, the boys were far less green. In August 1944, Dick Williams set out for his first mission out of Foggia. But going up with a different crew had him uneasy. Their abilities were not the issue; they had already gone out and made it back a number of times so they obviously knew what they were doing. Being the new guy in the mix is what bothered him. Dick felt anxious and figured he should somehow stand out or prove himself. The feeling came even heavier knowing the 97th had just received its second Distinguished Unit Citation. Dick wanted to make a good impression but was disheartened to learn they really did not care either way. He figured that out quickly. "They didn't give a damn for you because you were just another guy. You were just a rookie."

Dick made mistakes. That was common for a rookie. His gripe lay in the fact that no one ever corrected him or let him know when he went against protocol. "They just didn't care if they gave you any kind of helpful instructions." He recalled a perfect example. "I field stripped that .50 caliber" and later "I felt like an idiot, because nobody else did." Dick was merely doing what he had been taught in gunnery school. But as he soon learned, a gunner never did that just prior to mission. "I had that gun all taken apart and we're taking off! And they didn't say, 'We don't do that.' No, they just let me do it. It's ridiculous."

Up in the air with this seasoned crew, Dick quickly realized how close he was with the guys he trained with. Over a relatively short span, they had forged a strong bond, and if they lived long enough, he imagined the events to come would bring them even closer. Flight crews depended on each other, and for more than just camaraderie. Every time they went out on a run, it could be their last, and on each go, they trusted the other men onboard with their lives. That became very apparent on Dick's first run.

"The only time I ever heard the flak was flying as a green gunner on my first mission. This flak burst was directly under that B-17 and it just sounded like someone put a shotgun right by my ear and pulled the trigger!" More than noise rattled Dick on his first live run though. "The airplane jumped!" He even saw smoke. Is this the end already, Dick worried? This being his first live experience, he misinterpreted. What he took for smoke, Dick clarified with a chuckle, "was just the dirt in the airplane." All the dust on the floor stirred by the flak flung upward and gave off the appearance of smoke. Dick genuinely believed they had taken a major hit. Recalling the sound once more, Dick added, "Of all the near misses," including "the time we got the one that didn't explode, that was the only flak burst I ever heard." Not only was it loud, it lifted the entire plane. "Probably about another couple feet would have been a direct hit. I don't know. God, it scared the hell out of me." Laughing, Dick repeated his earlier phrase, "My first mission."

Enemy aircraft does not fire flak. Flak is the metal that comes up from the ground—gifted by anti-aircraft guns. Despite all the death from below littering the underbellies of American fighters and bombers, Dick claimed "you didn't call out the flak, no matter where it was." Formation was the primary reason. Heavy bombers like the B-17 and B-24 could not stray from their designated position. "Because you had to fly with all these airplanes, you didn't have the option of any evasive action ... no matter what you saw." Reflecting on the danger, he admitted the flak seemed "like it was always straight ahead." But even when it was, the pilot refused to adjust course. But that never stopped "that crazy ball turret gunner of ours, from always calling out, 'Flak, dead ahead! Flak, dead ahead!'" Considering his vantage point and the dreaded vulnerability of being stuck below, barking loudly about all the metal heading his way made perfect sense.

Talking about the view from the ball, Lester Schrenk commented that you "could clearly see the ground, see flashes of light, and puffs of the smoke from antiaircraft batteries firing at you from the ground." The 360 degrees of sight also allowed these gunners to "see numerous enemy fighter planes taking off from the ground," and to "also see where the bombs exploded, and the resulting fires" that raged. It must have been both terrifying and beautiful. Despite cries from the ball turret, "the pilot had no control because the bombardier up there turned it over to the autopilot. So, for a number of minutes, no matter what happened, you always just flew straight and level." Thinking of the flak and of the enemy fire during these long stretches, Dick relayed "No matter if you knew you were going to get hit, you just flew into it. There was no option. That's just the way it was. That was the only way to hit the target." Frequent as it came, taking flak settled into a norm; so much so, that one of Dick's crewmates even created a game out of it.

"Why don't we go out and count the holes?" It was Thompson who made the suggestion. "He was from Minnesota and we called him Tommy. He was Victor Thompson, our radio operator." The prospect of putting a number to the damage sounded interesting enough, so Dick agreed. "Ok, if you want to." As shot up as they were though, they gave up on the first wing. "We stopped at 100. It was just a sieve! That's all it was." The size of the holes that riddled their plane after completing a mission, ranged drastically. Sometimes a fingertip would barely fit in, other times a crewmember could crawl through it.

Required Number of Missions

Although Dick holds that it was standard practice in the 15th Air Force to mix new crewmembers with seasoned flyers to help them learn the ropes, this procedure did not appear to be exercised in the 8th, at least not during Stevie's tenure. Rubottom's crew never split up, and their early arrival in the E.T.O. might account for why; they got their start when use of U.S. bombers was still relatively fresh. Trial and error in the early days no doubt sparked later change—improvements to protocols that benefitted Nick Kantar's crew and many others. Splitting up the inexperienced men to accelerate the break-in process may have been one of those changes.

Referencing the crews from 1943 and earlier, Dick voiced a pertinent factor limiting such a rotation. "They just didn't have the crews like we had." They lacked the numbers. "In our squadron," he clarified, "we had two separate crews for each plane, which meant that we could fly one day then rotate. But in the early days they didn't have that many men and they didn't have that option." While Stevie's crew did have its down days, for the most part they were up in the air rather consecutively. But even their team faced its share of swapping crewmembers; it appeared that most flight crews were forced to for one reason or another.

"As a rule, we'd fly together as a crew," Dick noted, "but maybe for some peculiar reason the pilot or some other crewmember would finish at different times." One peculiar incident in particular came to mind. "Don Wolf—the right waist gunner when we were training here in the states—he was either a Sergeant or a Tech Sergeant. He'd been in the service a little while; much longer than any of us." After making the long trek to Foggia, splitting up with experienced flyers then returning to their original group, Dick and Wolf were reunited. Although they could say they knew their way around a B-17 a little better, Dick could tell something was definitely off with Don Wolf. "On the first, second, or third mission he just started hollering on the intercom and acting like an idiot, grabbing flak vests and all that." The pilot overheard the commotion and asked Dick what happened. "He was just too passionate. And as a result of those actions, we did get rid of him. He was a qualified Engineer though, so he got a position with another crew." Don Wolf remained in Foggia, but he held a grudge the duration of his stay. "He resented me as long as we were there in Italy because he thought I was responsible for getting rid of him. I wasn't." Wolf's replacement, a New Yorker named Wagner, stayed on in the waist with Dick for the duration.

Dick pointed out another variable that impacted the mission and affected the crew's lineup. A lot "depended on the weather," which "really dictated when you could or couldn't fly." Recalling the perfect example, he stated that "in December of 1944, the weather leading up to the Battle of the Bulge was very bad." Beginning early that month, "my group would try to take off and bomb various targets, but because of the bad weather, we were not able to" complete the mission. But the weather kept Dick grounded for another reason—his health. At least a dozen times his crew briefed for a run that his body refused to let him partake in. "We'd go out to the airplane and do the run up of the engines and wait patiently for the takeoff order." But by the time they got the green light to leave for their target, Dick's lungs would flair up. He just could not shake that nasty upper respiratory infection, and so the crew went on without him, taking another gunner in his place.

Hard as they were amid the icy conditions, the bombings that occurred in early December '44 were certainly worth it; they allowed the tactical Air Force to provide vital air support necessary to aid the ground troops below. It paved the way for the Battle of the Bulge. This epic conflict commenced on December 16. In the mix below was at least one fellow Italian-American Stevie knew—Gasper Cascioppo. Gasper was very close with the Niotta family, and for good reason. His older brother, Johnny, married Stevie's big sister, Celie, and Gasper's sister, Rose, married Stevie's oldest brother, Michael. After fighting bravely with the men of the 776th Artillery Battalion, Gasper returned to his family wounded.

Illness was only one of the factors that differentiated the number of runs crewmembers had under their belts. Injuries also grounded airmen. Health was likely the number one reason accounting for differences among the scorecards of men on the same crew, and these numbers mattered. The count became the standard dictating when a service member could return home. For flight crews, the amount of time they spent abroad mattered very little in regard to when their obligation ended. Instead, the goal hinged upon how many missions they completed. Crewmembers who flew often, who were lucky enough not to get shot down, and whose missions were not aborted due to illness, equipment malfunction, or inclement weather, went home sooner.

The reasoning behind such a system stemmed from a suggestion made by "Bomber" Harris, the head of the R.A.F. Bomber Command. Harris suggested that Americans put a limit on the number of missions their crews completed. After fulfilling this obligation, they could go home. This concept offered a goal and an incentive—something every single airman could look forward to. Harris personally failed to do this with his own troops and later came to realize his error. Luckily for Dick and many others, American leadership took Harris's advice.

"If you were in the RAF, you just kept flying till you got shot down or till the war ended," Dick relayed, stating, "Harris said that was a mistake." Unfortunately for those keeping count, the required cut off kept rising. "When I went overseas, the standard was twenty-five," Dick stated, though "they raised it to thirty" shortly after, and before long, they upped it again, pushing it to thirty-five. Lester Schrenk's time in the skies over Europe occurred prior to Dick's, but overlapped with Stevie's tour. Schrenk indicated that during his days, twenty-five was the magic number. Twenty-five completed combat missions was the initial standard Americans adhered to. These lucky few who completed their objective were guaranteed a ride home. In the 8th Air Force, this also meant you entered the elite ranks of the Lucky Bastard Club. Those that made the much sought-after mark were not entirely off the hook, however. After a bit of well-deserved leave, they continued their service stateside in another capacity. Sometimes they were tasked with instructor duties, prepping the trainees gearing up to head over, and after finishing up the remainder of their term, they received an honorable discharge.

Although the new system gave airmen something to strive toward, as Schrenk grimly remarked, "During the time I was flying, I did not know of a single crew that managed to complete the 25 missions." Schrenk blamed a lack of fighter support: "We had to fly to the target without a fighter escort," during a time when "Germany still had control of the air." His crew was shot down on February 22, 1944, during their tenth mission. All but their pilot survived when *Pot of Gold* crash-landed. Seventy-six heavy bombers never came back that tragic day, and, unfortunately, the Germans were on the ground waiting for Schrenk and his pals. They were escorted off to fifteen months of truly inhumane treatment. It could have just as easily been Stevie and the boys shot down and captured. They were up in the air the day before *Pot of Gold* went down, and he and the rest of the crew returned to the skies just a few days later. Making it through a bomb run alive required skill and team work, but the luck of the draw had a lot to do with it as well.

The leap to thirty-five missions smacked reality into Dick something fierce. He began to feel as if he would never make it back to his mother and sisters. His bad lungs kept pushing him further and further away from freedom. He blamed the jump to thirty-five on preparations "for the buildup in the Pacific"—"they needed crews for the B-29s." To clarify, "they thought they were going to have to do to Japan, what we did to Germany, but the atom bomb took care of that!"

Additional Duties

Although Dick manned a gun in the waist, assisted the ball turret gunner, ran the putt-putt, and took on the responsibilities of an assistant engineer, he still had other duties aboard *Kentucky Colonel*. One included dropping sheets of tinsel-like aluminum foil called chaff out a hatch behind the ball turret. Because it messed with the enemy's radar readings and helped mask their location, flight crews used chaff as a countermeasure. What the Axis Powers could not see, they could not shoot down. But the Americans were not the only ones employing this sort of cover during the war. Several countries devised their own version of chaff during the late '30s and early '40s. The Brits called it "Window" and the Germans, "*Düppel.*"

"We called the airplane dispensing it, the *Mickey ship*." Dick let on that his crew usually handled the chore, meaning he himself assumed the role in bomber formation. Whenever Dick threw chaff, he did it very precisely, dropping handfuls of the aluminum strips every sixteen seconds. This made them less likely to be picked up, and more importantly, less likely to be picked off. But at those altitudes, the freezing temperature presented a problem: "The hatch remained open during the entire bombing run, and every time my oxygen mask froze." Dick knew that if he forgot "to crush the ice" building in his mask, he "would pass out" for good.

Another bad end of chaff was the target Dick wore while dispensing it: "I was lucky. I was on my knees by that little hatch behind the ball turret. We were approaching the target. And there was a group ahead. They were getting peppered" with flak. "We started the I.P.—that's your Initial Point—and we were going straight and level for maybe eleven minutes. I got on my knees and I had this huge box of tinfoil behind me." Dick's thoughts centered on the crew just up ahead getting pegged by the flak: "I knew when the flak was there because it always shut out the sunlight. Then you'd hear gravel going through a fuselage." If they enemy failed to land a direct hit, "it was always the falling flak that you flew through—just falling shrapnel. When I was on my knees and it went dark, I always knew it was a very near miss."

Anoxia and the Italian

Whether Dick threw out chaff, helped bring up the ball turret gunner, or stood at his post in the waist, it was always cold. In addition to the discomfort, this awful fact also brought on a long list of pressing issues. You had to "make sure that your oxygen supply was coming through. Your oxygen mask froze up all the time." By the end of the day, a ring of frostbite set in over the wearer's face. Worse still, the masks failed to function properly when iced over. When the mixture was off, they no longer provided a sufficient amount of oxygen. "They figured three minutes" before pass out, "so you had to remember every three minutes to crush the ice out. They didn't know too much about that then. We called it anoxia, lack of oxygen."

The altitude and temperature impacted the flight crew's communication equipment as well. "We had two microphones. One was in our oxygen mask." Along with the mask itself, it always froze. "Even though you crunched the ice all the time, it still would freeze up." Crewmembers wore the second mic on a throat strap, which proved useful: "That was the one that was always reliable, because the body heat would keep it from freezing."

"It was a real emergency on a mission if you had to leave your post, because you had to disconnect your oxygen. It meant, right away, you were disconnecting your lifeline." Adding to the fear, removing headphones and microphones severed them from the rest of the crew. Calling out for help was no longer simple; the sound of the engines and the wind were far too loud. Regardless of the task the crewmember detached from his gear to complete, there was not much time to see it through: "Unplugged, you only have about three to five minutes before you're dead." Increasing that window, an airman could pick up another five minutes of air through a portable oxygen bottle, but when that ran out, the oxygen-starved airman dropped: "It was so insidious! You didn't know when it was happening," and Dick spoke from experience.

All his down days plagued with lung trouble kept Dick in Foggia longer than the rest of his crew. After his pals headed stateside, he filled in as a spare gunner for whoever needed an extra man. On the mission that Dick got his first taste of anoxia, he was "filling in as a substitute on a crew as a waist gunner. We started over the target and the next thing I knew, we had finished bombing and I was lying on the floor, looking up." Dick passed out and he probably should have died. "When I came to, I was lying on the floor of the radio room. I guess they got me plugged" into some fresh oxygen. "It was after the bomb run, but I have no memory of the bomb run at all."

After the war, Dick read up on the symptoms of anoxia in various flight magazines. Apparently, they had it all wrong. "Really, you don't experience any symptoms. You're just gone and that's it. That was the real seriousness of the matter. You didn't know when it was gonna happen. Anoxia; they call it hypoxia now." Somewhere in one of those wartime articles, Dick read that heavy bombers "lost probably just the same number of men from anoxia as they did enemy action," and he was inclined to believe it. He added "that was a real hazard for anyone who flew at altitude—the B-17 or B-24. That wasn't the case with the medium range bombers, because they didn't fly that high."

Freezing temperatures were not the only threat hampering the oxygen on a heavy bomber; sometimes enemy fire was the issue. On one mission in *Kentucky Colonel*, an Axis fighter shot out their tail gunner's supply: "We were over the target and the tail gunner called me up—'Dick, can you help me?'" Still over the target, protocol forbade him to assist: "If you left your post it was very serious. So, I said, 'not now, Jim.'" Thankfully, the pilot heard Jim Wright's call for assistance. Sensing something was wrong, he yelled to Dick. "Can you get him out of there?" After unplugging from his air supply, he headed to the tail.

Being detached from the oxygen system made getting back to the tail "a real chore." Luckily, these bombers are set up with oxygen stations at each gunner's position. A line on an air tank can be attached to a mask, which put the crewmember on an umbilical cord. "You plugged into them and it gave you five minutes to walk around with." Five minutes went quick though, so they really had to keep track of their supply. Although Dick had an oxygen station in the waist, unfortunately, on that particular day, the ground crew neglected to fill it. "I only had about two or three minutes" of portable air, "so when I left my post, I didn't have much time to get him," and, of course, "the tail wheel comes up in the back, and it leaves a very small area on each side to get around, and get to the tail gunner's position."

Helping Dick out, the others "threw walk-around-bottles" and took turns plugging him into their stations. Getting back to Jim, who now lay unconscious, Dick faced a new problem: "Oh golly, I think our tail gunner weighed about one-hundred and sixty-five pounds, one-seventy, and I at that time weighed about one-forty." The feat called for a team effort: "When we finally got the tail gunner out of there, it required the services of me, the other waist gunner, and the radio operator working in concert." Finally plugged in and breathing, Jim began to come around: "We had him over by the waist and the first thing he did was flail around and hit me. He didn't know he did it of course, but I got it right in the face."

Although Jim Wright survived, the crew lost him as a gunner. The Air Corps felt it necessary to send him home over the ordeal, but the close call did not end up being the last time Dick saw his old pal. More than fifty years after the incident, Jim and his wife came to see Dick in Reno. "He never mentioned anything" about the anoxia incident. Although the pair both survived the war, after his visit with Dick, Jim passed of cancer.

The selection for Jim Wright's position always puzzled Dick Williams. Being in Foggia and knowing how the Italian population felt about the Brits and the Yanks being there, he failed to comprehend the decision to send an Italian-American. They flew him to Italy and wedged him into the tail of *Kentucky Colonel*: "Salvatore Di Pietro. I never did know his history. He was rather silent on that aspect." Like Niotta, Di Pietro was with the 8th out of England, but for whatever reason, they put him in for a transfer to the 15th. Salvatore kept to himself, and flew as the tail gunner for *Kentucky Colonel* for the remainder of their missions. "I don't recall ever going into Foggia with him," Dick admitted, "so I don't know if he ran into any trouble there in town or not."

The Swiss Not So Neutral

En route to Vienna on an Austria run, Dick's crew took too many hits to complete their mission: "We got shot up one day and had to come back alone." That meant leaving the formation and facing the Alps in bad condition: "We were on our way home and one of the pilots called up the navigator. 'Shikora, where are we?'" That was the crew's navigator, Martin "Marty" Shikora: "Of course, Shikora didn't know" where they were, but at least he was "honest about it." Dick, on the other hand, knew their exact location and spoke up over the radio. Surprised his left waist gunner knew where they were when his own navigator had no clue, Nick Kantar mouthed, "How the hell do you know, Willy!?" Smirking, Dick piped: "Look out your window at about 11 o'clock." Nick craned his neck and peered out over the white ridges of the mountains. "Do you see all of those dark marks?" The black flecks in the snow were easy enough to spot. "That's where they always are when we come back from Vienna. So, we're right on course."

The crew took the same route back to Italy and on each occasion Dick noted the black scars on the mountainside where another crew had "salvoed its bombs. In the white snow of the Alps, when you salvoed your bombs, it dug into the earth and you had big black spots where the bombs had dropped." When a pilot flying out of Foggia aborted a mission before dropping his payload and was worried about making it back to base safely, he salvoed. This made the plane lighter, increasing its ability to climb. More importantly, the move decreased the likelihood of crashing. To clear the Alps, the craft had to gain and hold altitude. If they took a beating or if the engines ran less than 100 percent, the best way to do that was to drop weight—hence salvoing. But unloading armaments into the side of a mountain had another purpose as well. It ensured the charges would not explode if the pilot had to crash land, and sometimes that was the only option. The tense decision over whether to bale out or to risk it all and push high into the mountains was one that Dick and his crew eventually faced.

"Munich was where they had SAMs"—surface-to-air missiles. "They actually had guided missiles! We only experienced that once, watching a previous group of B-17s and all these zig-zag lines going up towards it." Confused about what he was seeing, Dick thought, "What the devil is that?" Getting closer, he soon found out. "You could hear them coming and leaving. I didn't realize it" at first, "but they actually had guidance control on them. And it scared the hell out of you because you heard every one of em' coming and going—like sitting beside a railroad with the fast train" charging past. Although not so accurate, "they sure did have a psychological effect." Unfortunately, Dick's crew got a bit closer to death than that.

Everyone onboard understood the crapshoot associated with the Alps. They were also aware that whatever decision the pilot made impacted the lives of everyone onboard. If he chose to bale out, or to land, there were consequences. "They had taken care of that with an agreement with the Swiss Air Corps," Dick highlighted. "The Swiss Air Corps had their own ME 109s," which were highly advanced German fighter planes. The Germans officially called them the Bf 109. "All you had to do was lower your landing gear, and the Swiss sent up their 109s to escort you into their airfields, where you spent the rest of the war." Dick halfway kidded they even had a college set up for the Allied forces. What he really meant was a prison camp waited: "They actually had an Auschwitz guard run their prison. One American tried to escape." Dick had read about this man's horrific account and it came to mind whenever the prospect of lowering their landing gear fell on the table: "They just did everything to him!"

"One day, all of us crew, we would have had justification for landing there, but the pilot didn't want to do it," and after all the awful stories, the rest of the guys were also hesitant. "I'm kind of glad he didn't," Dick admitted, thankful they were lucky enough to maintain altitude. "I don't know how many engines we had out. I think one was smoking, or burning, and I think we had dropped one other. Oh, and then we had an aileron shot out too." An aileron is a hinged mechanism on the plane's wing, which affords the pilot directional control. Managing the plane with one out is exceedingly challenging. Parachuting became a big possibility at that juncture.

"The British had this great parachute. It had a wheel in the front that was like a disc, and they called it a one-release-chute." The American version proved less sophisticated. "The ones we had, had a buckle on each side." Taking off the Brit chute was easy, "You would just hit that one little disc and the harness would just disengage." Although Dick and his crew were initially issued the more user-friendly version, they were not permitted to use it in combat. "I was so aware of" how superior the one-release was "because one day, I got the bailout order."

An 80-mm anti-aircraft shell not only hit *Kentucky Colonel*, it buried itself into the left wing. Although it damaged the aileron, miraculously it failed to detonate. The scene read like something straight out of a Wiley Coyote and Road Runner skit. Luck is the only thing that kept that plane from exploding: "It nicked the main spar and it knocked out one of the ailerons on the left side. And the airplane started into a spin! I pulled the door handle over by the waist to bailout, and unfortunately, I could only get one side of my chute buckled!" Dick was beyond nervous, he was terrified. The other side of the chute refused to buckle: "My hand was shaking and I thought 'Oh my, God, I'm gonna' go down crooked.'" A thankful tone resonated clearly when Dick quickly piped, "And I tell ya,' that it is because of our pilot's flying skill that I'm even alive!" The pilot, with the help of the co-pilot, kept the plane under control. Pilots trained for this type of situation. They practiced take-off, flight, and landing with various combinations of the plane's four engines out. This created a useful and fairly lifelike simulation.

"They practiced landing in the air," Dick commented on how they righted the plane. "They used the one aileron" to get out of the spin and gain control, but the move did not put them in the clear. All the maneuver did was stabilize the aircraft enough to provide an option. If they wanted, they could bale out over Germany: "Of course, we were all chicken. We didn't want to do that!" Despite the damage and bleak prospect of making it back, the boys gave the risky alternative a go. Miraculously, *Kentucky Colonel* limped back to the Alps, but the climb was another matter. Again the pilot posed the question: climb or bale out? "He didn't know how it was going to turn out. Course, he'd never done that before." Still not liking the idea of baling out or crash landing, the crew opted out a second time. Foggia or bust. "It was because of his piloting skill that he landed the sucker. So, I was happy about that."

The Rosary and the Togglier from My Hometown

One day in Foggia, Dick happened to run into a young man from his hometown: "There was a togglier that came over, a kid from my little town of Cedar Bluffs, Nebraska. Said he wanted to hurry up and finish his missions." Dick thought the approach a bad idea. There was nothing smart or safe about the young man's plan, and he voiced his opinion; "Don't do that! You'll be in that plastic nose!" Despite the warning about the dangers of the role, the young man refused to listen. Although not with Dick's crew, he flew in the same squadron; not for long, though: "A week or so later, after my admonition, about four of those flak shells came up. They got the full brunt right in their nose."

Nick Kantor had just finished his last mission, which left Dick all alone in Foggia. "I was flying as a spare gunner" with another crew the day it happened. Although Dick had always flown as a waist gunner, as a sit-in, he manned whatever position needed filling. "I was flying in the tail when those flak shells came up, so I had a direct view." In formation, the line of sight from the tail in the number 4 position offers up a fairly clear picture of the number 7 plane: "The number 7 flies directly behind, and a little bit below." Dick witnessed as the plane carrying the togglier from his hometown "got the full brunt of those four flak shells right in the nose." Doing some heavy math, Dick relayed "You had a full bomb load then—at that time—about 1,200 gallons of gasoline, plus your oxygen." Grimly, he finished the equation: "That's a bad mixture for explosives! There wasn't much left of that B-17."

Locked in formation without the ability to maneuver, any one of the heavy bombers could have taken the blast. That was the risk: "A second or two and it would have been I instead of him that was shot down. Just that distance spared me. I got lucky." Again referencing this "chum" from his hometown who volunteered to be a togglier, Dick solemnly added, "he said he wanted to finish early and he did." Sadly, there were others in the 15th that Dick never got to say goodbye to.

"They showed movies at our briefing room every Wednesday; Wednesday nights. This fellow wasn't in my squadron but he and I were going to see the show. And he had been in town and he bought this rosary to send home to his mother." Although Dick really wanted to catch the beginning of the picture, this other fellow had it in his mind that he needed to get that rosary in the mail. "It was getting late and I told him to send it the next day." He refused, though. He kept on pleading. "I gotta get this in the mail tonight." Frustrated, Dick eventually replied, "My God! There's tomorrow, you know. And a lot of days." To this, he again heard, "No, I gotta mail it tonight," and the young man did, getting up to leave the movie house: "He flew the next day and I guess he must have had a premonition, because he didn't come back. So, you wonder if those guys know."

Did I Ever Tell You About the Plane I Almost Shot Down?

"The first time I flew in the tail gun position, where you have two .50-cal. guns, I had four or five missions to go to complete my tour." Outlining the protocol gunners adhered to while passing over friendly territory, Dick let on that "the first thing you do is clear your guns. This means you take the feeding mechanism out of the breach on each gun that you're firing—or have fired—and pull the trigger to make sure there are no live rounds in there." During this first run in the tail with the new crew, Dick did just that. The problem was that one major aspect separated the tail from the waist—the number of weapons. "I was used to one gun" but the tail had two. After clearing, Dick squeezed. "I pulled the trigger on both guns, which meant I still had one gun with all the shells!"

"As I pulled the trigger I thought, I've made a horrendous mistake, and I saw the tracers for my one gun go right up over the turret of the trailing B-17. That gave me the chills. I thought, Oh my God." Oddly, "not one of those crewmembers ever mentioned the incident." Once again, dumb luck served as savior.

10

Campaigns:
In Air with the 8th

The Many Fortresses of Rubottom's Crew

Stevie Niotta served out all of his bomber missions in the European Theater. Every single time he went up, he left with the same crew, crew 6-34, led by 1Lt. Robert L. Rubottom. Rubottom was from Ranchester, Wyoming, and as young as any of them. Other constants in this group included their Engineer in the top turret, Technical Sergeant (TSgt.) Robert C. Surdam. Bob was a New Yorker, from Spencer. Also on the list was their tail gunner Sgt. Russel C. McNally, who hailed from Maine, plus the man who took Stevie's intended job, another New Yorker, Sgt. Joseph A. Ryan. Ryan manned the radios for all but one of the crew's missions, the last, when TSgt. Warren M. Fleener filled the slot. Flying in the right waist was West Virginian, TSgt. William "Bill" E. Mastin. He only missed two runs with the crew, and like Dick, he also served as an assistant engineer. During the twenty-six missions they completed, two navigators gave direction. Their first was a Texan. After 2Lt. Jack C. Wight left the crew, Lt. Scott joined them. For whatever reason, manning of the other positions under Rubottom's direction rotated.

On the two occasions of Bill Mastin's absence, Sgt. Henry R. Muesse covered the right waist. Muesse was a guy that moved around a bit. He rode in the left waist for two-thirds of his runs but eventually became a togglier. He was Southern Californian like Stevie and lived out in Bellflower. In the crew's first month out, their co-pilot, Lt. Alander, left for another assignment, and he took their bombardier with him, which may have prompted Muesse to go for that extra stripe. Only once did Rubottom's crew ride light, and it did not happen until right at the very end. On March 3, 1944, the boys went out minus a left waist, and like Dick's crew, a few times they also left heavier than the allotted ten.

On two flights during the crew's last stretch in March '44, they carried a photographer. First, they took out Sgt. Marvin J. Queen, then later TSgt. Patrick

Radio Operator Sgt. Joe "Old Soak" Ryan, September 5, 1943. (*Courtesy of Frannie Niotta-LaRussa*)

Navigator 2Lt. Jack C. White. (*Courtesy of Frannie Niotta-LaRussa*)

Right Waist Gunner/Assistant Engineer Bill Mastin, September 5, 1943. (*Courtesy of Frannie Niotta-LaRussa*)

Ball Turret Gunner/Radio Operator Stevie Niotta, September 5, 1943. (*Courtesy of Frannie Niotta-LaRussa*)

Engineer TSgt. Bob Surdam.
(*Courtesy of Frannie Niotta-LaRussa*)

Pilot 1Lt, Robert L. Rubottom.
(*Courtesy of Frannie Niotta-LaRussa*)

Tail Gunner Sgt. Russel C. McNally, September 5, 1943. (*Courtesy of Frannie Niotta-LaRussa*)

Left Waist Gunner-turned-Togglier TSgt. Henry Muesse. (*Courtesy of Frannie Niotta-LaRussa*)

N. O'Keef. Earlier that year, they carried an extra man for another reason. On January 21, they welcomed an engineer. First Lieutenant George H. Sherman joined them over the French Invasion Coast for a "Crossbow Target." The term referred to the German use of long-range missiles on England, and to the countermeasures against those attacks. U.S. Army reconnaissance photos confirmed the presence of such missile sites along the French Coast, near Calais, and in response, they sent out bombers. Dick recalled "crossbow" being the secret name for missions to take out rocket and rocket production sites.

Although Rubottom's men split the bulk of their flights between two heavy bombers, in all the crew flew in more than a dozen Flying Fortresses. At that time in the 8th Air Force, if a bomber was not yet ready, the crew grabbed one that was; quite a departure from Foggia and the rotating crews that Dick Williams talked about. The excessive damage sustained by B-17s in the 8th gave a whole new view to flak holes, too; this type of repair became almost cosmetic. Holes got patched only if they posed a safety issue; the demand for bombers up in the air was just too great. A mechanic devoted his time to more pressing fixes, focusing primarily on safety and functionality. Typically, engines, landing gears, and flying controls saw a wrench first.

Crew 6-34, Rubottom's crew, *circa* 1944. (*Courtesy of Frannie-Niotta LaRussa*)

The long list of planes Rubottom's crew flew in included *Flak Suit, Mister Yank II, Strato Express,* #741 (later called *Thunderbolt, Hi Fever,* and then *Haughty Hazy*), *Tom Paine, Ramp Tramp, Lady Margaret* (also called *Old 66*), *Veni, Vidi, Vici,* and, for their last two missions, a ship that never earned a name, #973 (42-31973). Although many entered the mix, Stevie and his pals spent most of their time between *Boomerang* and her follow on, *Boomerang II.* Formal flight records referred to the first as #986. Not liking the ring, the crew dubbed her *Boomerang,* allegedly because she always came back. Unfortunately, she did not live up to her name. A later bomber the crew spent substantial time on—#153—came to be called *Boomerang II.* Rubottom's men even adorned their flight jackets with a painting of their assigned vessel. And right above it, cursive letters spelled out the proud title of *Boomerang*—sans the "II." Signifying what they accomplished overseas, twenty-six bombs are displayed beneath the aircraft, one for each of their completed missions. The last shell in the lot is a sight larger than the rest, and probably because the voyage was tacked on at the very end for good measure.

Off to a Rough Start

Surprisingly, Rubottom's crew would accomplish what Lester Schrenk never saw done by any B-17 crew during his time in the sky. Despite this success, they sure got off to a rough start. Although operational at the start of its first three missions, due to in-flight malfunctions, *Boomerang* aborted and turned around. Although the crew did not receive credit for these first few runs, luckily the pilot was able to get them back to England safely. While the direct cause for two of these instances remain unknown, a failed supercharger was responsible for nixing their Bordeaux, France, mission on December 5, 1943.

Their fourth stab at a run is when Rubottom's boys finally saw some action. Their first completed run happened on December 13, 1943. But another first also happened that day. No mission prior had ever dispatched so many aircraft, with more than 600 planes deployed. The German cities of Bremen and Kiel served as targets for the day and *Boomerang* went out heavy. With orders for Kiel, up near Denmark, they focused on the city's docks and naval center, where the enemy built their ships. Making their job difficult was the heavy cloud-cover masking their target. Like the rest of the formation, their navigator, Lt. Scott, ended up bombing by Pathfinder.

Boomerang came back, as they hoped she would, but not unscathed. Intense flak welcomed them over Kiel, and as Stevie annotated, "Flak hit the number 4 engine." Thankfully they did not have the Alps to contend with on their way back to the U.K. As they soon discovered, though, touching British soil after a successful mission did not signal the end of the day; in fact, it was far from done. First, a debriefing waited. In an officer's chambers, they would relay the events, provide intel on the target, the number of enemy fighters they encountered and shot down, and also give details about any damage they sustained. After being dismissed, the men ate chow. With their bellies full, they got back to *Boomerang* and grabbed their .50-caliber guns. It was now time to begin cleaning. Only after completing their "chores" were they clear to put a fork in the day.

Three days later, Rubottom's crew left for their next run, which targeted the shipyards in Bremen. This was the home of the German U-boat. This time the bomber formation received a partial escort from the Thunderbolts. But coming home they were again naked. Although not a long run by any measure, crewmembers did report some of the heaviest flak to date, and enemy fighters even tailed them on the return. While *Boomerang* managed to get through without taking any holes, Stevie wrote that "the 96th was attacked by German 109s," and unfortunately, "lost 4 ships in two passes." Later sources tallied this loss at seven.

December 19 is when the group lost their first co-pilot and bombardier; for whatever reason, they left for another crew. The next day, when they revisited Bremen to sack its warehouses, H. J. Teat rode as co-pilot and R. E. Oda as bombardier. The replacements only sat in for one run. Again, the flak over the target in Bremen proved intense: "Every plane suffered battle damage." Stevie confirmed that *Boomerang* was not immune: "Flak was very heavy. We got 17 holes in our plane on the trip." As it had in the fate of Dick Williams several times over, luck played a vital role. "One piece of flak just missed the gas lines." They could have very easily gone up in a blast. Lucky as they were, others were far

Christmas time in the Rocker Club, Knettishall, England, December 1943. (*Courtesy of Frannie Niotta-LaRussa*)

less fortunate. Lt. Ken Eccleston's crew went down and the entire crew perished. Feeling the middle finger of irony, it was their twenty-fifth and final mission.

At the close of their first week as a live fighter crew, *Boomerang* sustained enough damage to be downed. Although she went out six times, she only completed three runs. Conveniently, the repairs aligned with a spot of downtime—the calm came in response to the holiday. Christmas was now upon them and Stevie and the boys enjoyed a full week off. Chances are, they spent some time in the base lounge, an enlisted hangout known as the Rocker Club. Making it as much like home as they could, the establishment even decorated a tree.

Changing Planes (Often)

When the call for the next mission came on the day before New Year's Eve, *Boomerang* still was not operational. Piling into *Veni, Vidi, Vici*, they moved toward the German city of Ludwigshafen, where a "plant three miles long and one and a half miles wide" was about to be sacked. *Interessengemeinschaft Farbenindustrie AG* Chemical Works, commonly referred to as I. G. Farben, produced synthetic fuels and a synthetic rubber known as Buna. It also contributed considerable funds to the Nazi party. By 1937, the company had already purged its Jewish scientists, board members, and employees, but with the war now in full swing, they desperately wanted that labor back. As the Holocaust Education & Archive Research Team (HEART) explained, the decision to build a new plant in Auschwitz hinged solely on the availability of Jewish German labor. About 10,000 of them were being kept in a concentration camp nearby. Farben had all the slave labor it needed to see its construction project through. But come December 30, 1943, the Allies gladly knocked it down.

Because of the denseness of the clouds over the target, *Veni, Vidi, Vici* had to drop by Pathfinder. Difficulties aside, they successfully hit their mark, and that very next day, the boys were out again with a new destination and a new craft to get them there. On New Year's Eve 1943, Rubottom's crew boarded *Flak Suit* (42-31176) and sped toward the Parisian suburb of Ivry where a ball bearing plant waited. Another target sacked.

The new year ushered in even more change for Stevie and his pals. On January 4, 1944, F. W. Miller joined the crew in the bombardier spot. They took a factory in Münster, Germany. Miller stayed on for just that one mission. Although the bombardier seat continued to rotate, 1944 did offer up some permanence. The *Boomerang* crew welcomed Flight Officer (F/O) Zack W. Turner as their primary co-pilot. He was an Arkansas man, out of Van Buren. After two runs on unfamiliar flyers, the boys returned to *Boomerang*.

On January 11, the crew carried bombardier R. C. Tranter. But the boys never got to see him work over Brunswick. The No. 1 engine went out *en route*, sending them limping to England. Many of the other bombers and support were called back as well, due to weather. However, not everyone got the order. The heavy bombers that remained in formation witnessed a hell of a sight. Their outnumbered air support engaged in a three-and-a-half-hour battle with German fighters. In awe, they watched as Col. James Howard took out eight German Me 110s, becoming the first P-51 ace in the E.T.O. For his skill and bravery, Howard earned the Medal of Honor. Throughout the war, only six were awarded to Air Corps' fighter pilots in that theater. Despite the small victory, it came with significant losses. Sixty B-17s went down. For the group's efforts, the division received a Distinguished Unit Citation Award.

January 14 brought the crew their first, and possibly only, "milk run." On this "easy" flight over Pas-de-Calais on the northern coast of France, H. J. Beavers sat in as navigator. Commenting on why "it was considered a milk run," Stevie noted, "No fighters to be seen, flak was inaccurate as heck. No damage to plane." A week later, they returned to Pas-de-Calais, but this time they dropped something different—their Flying Fortress. All the abuse *Boomerang* took under

Rubottom's crew in front of B-17 *Joho's Jokers* running light as a nine-man team. *From left to right*: Togglier Henry Muesse, Tail Gunner Russel McNally, Radio Operator Joe Ryan, Right Waist/Asst. Engineer Bill Mastin, Co-Pilot Zack Turner, Pilot Robert Rubottom, Ball Turret Gunner Stevie Niotta, Navigator Jack Wight, and Engineer/Top Turret Bob Surdam, England, March 3, 1944. (*Courtesy of Jack Niotta*)

the command of Lt. Rubottom and his surly crew called for an early retirement, or, as Stevie commented, "No more *Boomerang* 986." From Pas-de-Calais, she made it over to Ferry Command, where new planes and equipment arrived from manufacturers and from green crews fresh out of training. In addition to receiving new assets and moving them to a variety of areas of operation, Ferry Command also took in damaged goods for retiring.

"We were assigned a new ship, #741 in place of *Boomerang*." Before her days were done, #741 would undergo several name changes. The crews that served onboard called her *Thunderbolt*, *Hi Fever*, and later *Haughty Hazy*. Records show that although the crew grabbed #741, they only used her for a ride home. On their next mission, they took *Mister Yank II* instead. This "Crossbow Target" over the French Invasion Coast on January 21, 1944, does not appear in Stevie's notes. The secrecy surrounding these voyages may have kept it from being included. Packing the Fortress past its ten-man allotment, this was the jaunt they brought an extra engineer. First Lieutenant George H. Sherman accompanied them due to the nature of the run.

A few days later, Rubottom's crew took *Strato Express* out to Frankfurt, Germany, but they never made it. Bad weather spurred a mass abortion. Although the run "was scrubbed after" just "fifty miles in France," the formation had crossed the enemy coast, meaning everyone received "credit for the mission." By now, their numbers were starting to climb. Twenty-five was sounding more and more achievable. They got a second chance to strike Frankfurt again a few days later. They set out on January 29, and during this second stab, the boys finally got to christen #741—the Fortress they swapped *Boomerang* for.

The weather did not hold them back this time; the voyage marked the first time the 8th put up more than 700 aircraft. Another record was also broken that day. While the Brits had raided Frankfurt many times by now, the run marked a first for the Yanks. "Eight/tenths cloud covered Frankfurt, crews said, and bombardiers employed the recently announced new technique to locate the target." As the *Stars and Stripes* also indicated a week or so later, the heavy bombers used Pathfinder to hit their mark. Stevie would clip the article and store it in a box of war keepsakes.

The Stars and Stripes, February 9, 1944
"Frankfurt Blasted by Fortresses"

Out to Obliterate City?

The second attack on Frankfurt in five days, on top of the USAAF's biggest-ever day raid on the city Jan. 29—800 bombers, 700 fighters, 1,800 tons—suggested that the allied air forces were now obliterating the great industrial city with its chemical and aircraft component works.

Although a successful run, Stevie knew some of the men who were unable to make it back: "Lt. Hennessey and his crew went down." After being hit by flak, their plane, *Mary Ellen*, dropped out of formation. Roy Wendell, the plane's navigator, begged for his best friend and co-pilot, Lt. Francis Patrick Hennessy, to bale out, but Hennessy refused. Miraculously, after a crash landing, the pair survived, but half the crew had perished. On the ground, the Germans greeted the remaining five and took them prisoner. Luckily, their captors did not hold them long. After their release, Stevie updated his flight book entry: "Hennessey and Richardson returned 1 ½ month later."

Rubottom's crew boarded #741 for the final time at the end of January. After sacking an aircraft factory in Brunswick, they handed over the plane to its new pilot, Cpt. James E. Zengerle. In exchange, the men received #42-31153, which had at one time been under Lt. Hennessey's command. The crew dubbed their new vessel *Boomerang II* and broke her in on February 4. Bombing by Pathfinder, she laid waste to the railroad yards in Frankfurt. More than just the weather fouled up this mission, though. Complications arose just after they sacked the target. Their navigator got lost.

Leaving Brunswick, Rubottom's crew flew through the Ruhr Valley, which was believed to be the "heaviest flak belt in the world at that time." Stevie holds they were "going in and coming out" up past Cologne. Although reports indicated only moderate flak over Frankfurt, in the Ruhr Valley, it was not only intense, but accurate. The "flak was heavy as hell," Stevie admitted, saying they "lost a few ships" running through the valley. Later reports tallied far greater wreckage: twenty bombers lost, another three damaged beyond repair, plus seven men killed in action, twenty wounded, and an astonishing 203 missing in action. No time to reflect or grieve, the men went out again the very next day.

Although they set out to sack an airfield south of France, they found the target closed in, and moved back north over Paris. Some 133 Flying Fortresses took on a new mark, the main hangars along the airfield at Villacoublay Sud. Many of these hangars were reserved for out-of-commission aircraft; planes waiting to be repaired. Bombing there would save them the grief of facing these fighters later in the air, but the enemy refused to make it easy on them; the airdrome was well guarded. The airdromes in occupied France were among the most developed for German offensive activities. Guarding the operational enemy fighters waiting on the flight line for quick deployment were a series of anti-aircraft weapons and smaller-caliber machine guns. This arsenal also protected the runways, its flight towers, and a mess of scattered structures. Although they gave hell to the bombers above, the shells raining down sufficiently sacked the area.

Over Frankfurt again just a few days later (February 8), the crew took a hell of a beating. The flak was heavy and accurate but the boys managed to make it back. After all the hard charging, the crew desperately needed a rest and a break from the flak, the noise, and the fighting. A two-week absence from flight book

Right: Stevie enjoying leave in Scotland. (*Courtesy of Frannie Niotta-LaRussa*)

Below: Stevie's fellow crewmembers goofing off at Knettishall, England, *circa* 1944. (*Courtesy of Jack Niotta*)

entries suggests they received just that—a well-deserved stint off. Rubottom's crew probably did not soak up much sun under the British skyline, but at least they could relax. Rest was essential for what was about to come. Their first mission back marked the start of the Big Week. Rubottom's crew would fly on four of those seven significant days.

The Big Week

Although the Big Week occurred before his arrival, Dick heard and read plenty: "Their losses were just terrible. A lot of American Airmen were killed. They were just bait. That's what they were." The aim of the mission "was to lay the foundation so the infantry could land on D-Day, on June 6th, and the only way they could do that was to make damn sure that they didn't have a bunch of German planes in the air." The heavy bombers flew "to get the Germans to come up and fight. It wasn't to drop any bombs, just to get as many German fighters as possible," and that is exactly what they did.

The Big Week ran from February 20–26, 1944. According to the Government Publishing Office, up until that point, "Allied bombers deliberately avoided contact with the Luftwaffe." Now they intended to push the other direction. "They deliberately used any method that would force the Luftwaffe into combat." On day one, *Boomerang II* motored to Poland, gunning for the city of Posen. Europe being Europe, the weather fouled their bombardier's visibility. Too poor to hit their mark even with the aid of Pathfinder, the formation sped northwest for another spot to drop. Back over Germany, on the edge of the coast, not far from the Danish Peninsula, the bombers found their new mark—the German city of Rostock.

Making the task hell, on the route in and approaching the drop the bombers encountered German fighters. Twenty to twenty-five aircraft—Me 210s, Me 109s, and Fw 190s—swarmed and shot. Stevie and the crew put in work, and as Dick remarked, they "took a beating on the B-17s." From above the clouds, they spotted several large barrage balloons. Balloons, or blimps, helped defend against enemy aircraft attack. The cables securing them in place damaged low-flying aircraft and dive bombers. Sometimes cables were even charged to explode, but this was not their main purpose. Chiefly, barrage balloons were employed to divert and siphon fighter planes into the line of fire of anti-aircraft guns. While the tactic had little effective against high flyers like the B-17, it did serve as an obstacle. "We dropped our bombs on a barrage balloon," Stevie reported. Although this deflected the blast, lessening its blow, the bombardier still managed to shack his target. "Our bombs hit an aircraft factory and shipyards." Although this completed their mission, danger remained; enemy fighters followed as they headed out. Despite fierce opposition, the bulk of the bomb group made it back.

On day two, the group left for an aircraft factory in Brunswick. With the cloud cover 10/10 and no Pathfinder in the lead, it appeared as though the run might be a complete wash. Determined to make it work, however, the bombers tried another tactic. Rather than using Pathfinder equipment, they went more rudimentary. The lead plane tossed out flares, illuminating the scene below, and it worked.

After a couple days on the ground, Rubottom's crew got word they would give Posen another try—day one's target had become day three's. They set out on February 24, 1944, and for a second time, the cloud cover saved the city from major wreckage. Again, Rostock received the beating instead. In addition to anti-aircraft guns laying into the formation, more than a dozen enemy fighters threatened the bomber groups that morning. Me 210s and various other German fighters attacked in waves, sweeping in every twenty minutes. Hoping to pull the gunners' attention, they employed a diversion. When the line of enemy fighters swooped past, a lone Fw 190 flew slightly out of range. The distraction worked, and in all the mess, the boys took hits.

The "hydraulic system was shot out by flak," Stevie reported, and the "hydraulic pump caught on fire," but the flak did more than just strike their plane, it also tagged their pilot, co-pilot, and navigator. Lt. Rubottom, Lt. Jack Wight, and F/O Turner "all got hit by some bursts." The surrounding bomber crews took their hits as well. *Veni, Vidi, Vici* "lost an engine and didn't have enough gas to come back." Fearing they might have to ditch in the North Sea, the plane's pilot, Lt. Montgomery, requested permission to land in Sweden.

Coasting on fumes with a feathering propeller, *Veni, Vidi, Vici* made it to Rinkaby. Before touching down, they adhered to protocol and destroyed crucial components of their bombsight and radio then tossed the items into the sea. Keeping these assets out of enemy hands was crucial. Stevie indicated, "We got word that all landed safely," and according to the *Wings Palette* website, in exchange for the crew's safe return to Knettishall, the U.S. government agreed to let Sweden purchase nine of the B-17s that had landed there under similar conditions. Allegedly they sold for the low, low price of just $1. Whether or not this is true, Lt. Montgomery's bomber did fly again. It was used in the airline service until the close of 1946.

Wounds and all, the worn crew of the damaged *Boomerang II* was at it again the very next morning. Germany waited to be sacked. The mission targeted an assembly plant and an aircraft engine factory set in the Bavarian city of Regensburg. Unfortunately, the formation proceeded without escort. "They were ahead of schedule going in," Stevie relayed, "and we didn't have any fighter support." The poor decision left them naked; flying bathtubs with a handful of gunners up against stealthy fighters that circled, maneuvered, and stung. After the losses they suffered under similar conditions, the higher-ups should have known better. On the Regensburg shuttle attack just a few months earlier, sixty bombers went down, and several ships that limped their way back from the fight were later junked after they reached England—the heavy damage rendered them unsalvageable.

Drawing German fighters up into the air was the main drive of the Big Week, and as Stevie reported, going up without fighter escort on February 25 was certainly successful. The unattended formation of heavy bombers must have looked like a perfect target. The German flyers ran at the bait. "The Jerrie's attacked us all the way in," but thankfully, backup waited: "Our fighters met us at the target" and helped keep the fleas off. They survived another close one, and this time Stevie even clipped the *Stars and Stripes* article to commemorate the victory.

Stars and Stripes
"No Output Now in Me109 Plant at Regensburg"

Bombed Out, 8th AF Says

The big Me109 fighter factory at Regensburg has been bombed out of production, and at Schweinfurt three of Germany's most important ball-bearing factories have been seriously damaged, Eighth Air Force headquarters announced yesterday. Almost all of the Me109 plant would have to be rebuilt before it could reach its previous output, according to a study of reconnaissance photographs taken after the Fortress raid Feb. 25. The following parts of the Me109 factory were either completely or partly destroyed: the fighter component and assembly plant, all the principal components and assembly shops, five subassembly shops, the main stores building, and three unidentified buildings. Other builders were severely damaged. Heavily crippled in a Fortress raid last August, the plant had been rebuilt by the Germans to the extent that the main assembly portion was in full operation when Fortresses smashed it again in February.

The Germans were not as prepared as they should have been. As Dick relayed, the Air Corps "just decimated the Luftwaffe. They shot down so many airplanes all over Germany; wherever they could get them off the ground." During the course of those six missions, bombers from the 8th Air Force flew over 3,000 sorties. Greatly aiding, the 15th put in over 500. Combined, the strikes totaled some 10,000 tons of metal dropped. Although the Luftwaffe never fully recovered, both sides suffered. The Air Corps lost 226 heavy bombers and twenty-eight fighter planes.

Putting in Claims on Enemy Fighters

A few days of downtime came to Stevie and the boys after their role in the Big Week. They earned it. Their first run back, February 29, brought them to Brunswick. This time; however, their group "led the whole 8th Air Force." Their commanding officer, Colonel David, flew lead ship. The mission that followed Brunswick was to be the first move on Berlin, but before they arrived, the entire formation received an abort order. Adverse weather kept the city safe on March 3, 1944. The flak the formation encountered along the Danish Coast was less than accurate, but the bombers still took hits and several crewmembers suffered cold weather injuries, one even died; waist gunner Sgt. Lutes succumbed to anoxia.

Boomerang II took a beating on its first voyage out to Berlin, so much so that she had to be downed for repairs. Rubottom's crew drew *Flak Suit* for their next mission—this served as their first, and only, light run. Without a left waist gunner to protect their side, the crew of nine climbed in, but they did not get far. In fact, *Flak Suit* never left the ground. "Aborted-takeoff." Having the day "off" on March 6 may have been a blessing, though. The raid on Berlin that followed cost the Allied Forces seventeen fighters, sixty-nine Flying Fortresses, and 701 men.

Stevie's downtime ended on March 8. With *Boomerang II* still unfit, they boarded *Tom Paine* for their one and only run on the bomber. At last Rubottom's crew would get to see Berlin. They set out for the Erkner Ball Bearing Works on the outskirts of the city. Due to a dozen aborts along the way, and the heavy incoming enemy fire, another formation joined their group. Together they huddled for safety, but after reaching the target, they quickly came to a realization. Another Combat Wing had already sacked it. After getting clearance for another mark, they moved toward a factory near Wildau. There a "very determined enemy fighter opposition" offered a surprise greeting. As they did a few days earlier, on March 6, the German fighters waited until after fighter escort abandoned the bombers. That is when they struck.

"30 to 50 enemy aircraft, mostly FW 190s, made these attacks mainly from the nose high in a trail of 10 to 12 aircraft." This tactic of saturation confused the gunners. Even worse, they could not fight off all the aircraft diving in, which meant they began taking hits. "Since it was impossible to fire at all enemy aircraft attacking, some would get through. All of our missing aircraft were shot down on this series of attacks." This included B-17s *Screaming Red Ass* and *Princess Pat*, whose eight survivors were taken prisoner near Celle, Germany. For all the chaos, action, and lives lost that day, Stevie remained modest as ever: "We did a good job."

From his turret, with only one .50-caliber gun functional, Stevie played careful with his shots. His second Browning was down, but this certainly was not the proper time to make repairs. All he could do was time his shots and suppress the enemy. Fw 190s kept trying to blast him from beneath. They stayed on McNally in the rear, too. Returning fire, he got two aircraft from the tail gun. "Fighters McNally got came in from 12 o'clock and out at 6," and Stevie nabbed one as well. Waiting for the right moment when a Fw 190 circled back, Stevie held his breath and squeezed. A surge of heat covered the ball and stung Stevie's eyes as the fighter burst directly beneath him. "Niotta got his fighter coming in at 1:30–2 o'clock, low with one gun out. He shot the plane with about 5 short bursts.

Plane exploded underneath our ship." Stevie noted that his fellow gunner "put in claims for enemy fighters," and that "later the fighters were made good"—the hits confirmed.

While Allied heavy bombers out of England were busy over the skies of Germany, laying waste to Berlin, the Luftwaffe traded blows by striking London. Though only a brief raid, the Axis Powers certainly left a mark.

> The raid, which cost the Nazis nine of approximately 100 bombers, caused heavy damage in scattered areas and a number of casualties. More than 100 flats in one London suburb were wrecked; a nursery was gutted by 100 fire bombs, but nurses carried 22 babies to safety; many houses, apartments, and business establishments were damaged.

The next day, aboard *Ramp Tramp* (42-39861), Rubottom's crew "got another Berlin, Germany raid" to their "credit." But the day was unlike the rest; the boys were part of something larger. Rather than going out with their usual formation, they flew as spares in an enormous operation; one of ten aircraft handpicked out of the 388th Bomb Group to join roughly 600 heavy bombers and a fighter escort of 800. According to the newspaper coverage that followed, "Many pilots who had been to Berlin before reported that the intensity of the flak over the capital was unrivaled, and it was heavy over the entire route as the armada passed from one flak area to another." This time the Germans were definitely ready.

The clouds 10/10, the group got clearance to drop on the center of the city rather than bomb the intended aircraft factory. An estimated 1,400 tons "battered" the German capital. "Huge fires in the capital were reported by the returning airmen, who said they would see great stretches of the city through the breaks in the clouds." Columns of dense smoke rose in pillars, some of them reaching 5,000 feet. Up above, the flight crews watched the flames peeking through. Commenting on the run, navigator 2Lt. William H. Garland called it "the most beautiful fighter-bomber synchronization" he had ever seen. Beautiful as it was, Stevie noted the "flak was heavier than hell."

Back at Knettishall, Rubottom and his men debriefed. In thanks of their heroics, "We got a shot of Black & White Scotch when interrogated." Though appreciative of the gesture, Stevie handed his off to his old radio buddy. "Ryan got mine. I still don't drink." Although they "returned safely," some did not. Nine fighters and thirteen bombers never came back. Lt. Keck's plane made an emergency landing on the U.K. coast, at Beccles, less than 40 miles from home— they almost made it. F/O Dopko's crew, aboard *Little Willie*, had an even rougher go. They baled out after flak hit an oil line and set the No. 2 engine on fire. Although most of Dopko's men were taken prisoner, their navigator and one of the waist gunners managed to escape. The pair trudged along till they came upon a British tank unit.

We Have to Do 26

After five days on the ground, Rubottom's crew readied to head out. *Boomerang II* was all patched up, so on March 15, they took her out to revisit Brunswick. The cloud cover 10/10, it spoiled any chance of hitting the aircraft factory they were after. Instead, they again "dropped on the center of the city." Rough as it was, just the one mission was enough to ground *Boomerang II* again. Stevie and the boys did not share the same luxury. They boarded *Lady Margaret* (42-30778) that next morning; a later crew would call this Fortress *Old 66*. As the men sped toward Augsburg, just outside of Munich, the Germans began launching rockets. Luck on their side, none touched the bombers.

Back in England, Ryan got Niotta's shot again, but something soured their celebration. The brass announced some unhappy news. Before going home, they would have to do an additional mission. "They put another mission on our 25. So, we have to do 26." Exempt from the bonus flight, Augsburg marked the final run for F/O Turner. Meeting his quota, he welcomed the ride back to the states. For Rubottom, Niotta, and the few other originals still among their ranks, they had completed twenty-three, but they still had a few to go.

After a day off, they climbed back into *Boomerang II*. Second Lieutenant John P. Gallien co-piloted in Turner's place. For Gallien, this would be his twenty-fifth and final run, and as if the wreckage they laid two days earlier was not enough, the mission brought them back to Augsburg. The crew readied to drop another dose of metal but never got the chance to deliver. Two bombers aborted over France due to mechanical issues; *Boomerang II* was one of them.

"One of our tokio gas valves wouldn't shut off," Stevie explained. "We lost a lot of gas" and could not make the trip on what was left in the tank. An internal fuel supply known as a Tokyo tank was built into the wings of later model bombers, like the B-17 F and G. The smart modification greatly increased fuel capacity, with more than a thousand additional gallons, but like anything else, they also suffered malfunctions. The crew aborted 80 miles outside of Paris and received credit for the mission. The jaunt not only marked the final run of their sit-in co-pilot, it ended up being their final voyage on *Boomerang II*.

Stevie and Rubottom had just two more flights to go—twenty-five and twenty-six—and they would do them aboard #42-31973. The Fortress was by no means cherry. Their "new" bomber had flown forty-five missions in less than four months. On March 22, they gave her a try and the run proved to be a long one. They moved way out toward Berlin. "The target was the center of the city" and they found it "heavily defended by flak," and once again, "it was plenty accurate." Bombs fell just west of the city's center, striking the suburb of Spandau. Despite the intense flak at the target and on the return, they managed to "get back to the field with the ship in perfect condition." The run fulfilled McNally and Muesse's obligations. They would need two new gunners for their final mission.

The next day, Rubottom and Stevie assembled with their new teammates and left for Brunswick. Aircraft plants were on the agenda. This was to be their last run and a bad feeling likely stuck in their guts. Irony likes to sneak up, so the boys kept looking over their shoulders. What they soon faced was anything but easy. Between thirty-five to forty-five fighters waited at the target. In the firefight that ensued, at least ten aircraft went down. "Fighters attacked our group at 10:30 in a group of thirty or more." Stevie identified the aircraft, "mostly F.W. 190's." Their attacks were vicious but the bombers held steady and took it. Unable to maneuver, the gunners did their best to swat at the mosquitos. The bombardiers and toggliers got ready, but the target below appeared too "closed in" to sack. They dropped their metal in an open field instead.

Two more aircraft were lost in the Ruhr Valley on the way back, when rockets and accurate flak hit. The crewmembers that survived the bale out were captured on the ground. The officers shipped to Stalag; the enlisted, Barth. In his last flight book entry, Stevie coupled two statements—one sad and one relieved: "4 ships failed to return. Mission Completed." For his bravery overseas, Stevenson George Niotta was awarded the Distinguished Flying Cross. Other medals of distinction included two Bronze Stars, three Air Medals, the European Theater of Operations (E.T.O.) Medal with a Star, an Overseas Bar for being in a combat zone overseas, and the Good Conduct Medal. As he himself would have remarked, he did good.

The Lucky Bastard Club

From July 1943 to May 1945, over 500 flight crews cycled through Stevie's Bomb Group. The men of the 388th flew on over 300 missions, each wearing the same aspiration—survive the allotted number, join the Lucky Bastard Club, then go home. But few proved so fortunate. The majority of men serving on flight crews either lost their lives, got shipped back early with injuries, or spent time as a prisoner of war after being shot down. To actually complete the required number was quite a feat. Right waist gunner Bill Shell noted that "26,000 and some many in the cemeteries got purple hearts and things like that. And those of us that finished our missions … we was plain lucky bastards … so they gave us a certificate."

During his tour in the E.T.O., which lasted from late 1943 until March 1944, Stevie completed twenty-six heavy bomber missions, and on March 23, 1944, he joined Bill Shell and other brave men in the sparse ranks of the Lucky Bastard Club. Admittance to this elite faction meant a permanent ride back to the States, which Stevie eagerly welcomed. Although Dick Williams' successfully completed his required allotment as well, being in the 15th, he never even heard about the club. Signed by a commander, these certificates were in fact legitimate. They were never standard Government-issue, though; each Bomb Group that participated in the ritual devised its own.

Stevie proudly showing his Lucky Bastard Club certificate, 1944. (*Courtesy of Frannie Niotta-LaRussa*)

11

Campaigns: At Sea

Island Hopping, Bombardment Style

Tony had just turned eighteen the month before. Fresh out of boot camp, and greener than anything, he was excited to learn about his assignment aboard the U.S.S. *Mississippi*. The destroyer had just arrived in San Francisco after completing her first two campaigns—Guadalcanal then Aleutian—but she needed an overhaul before they could head out on the next voyage. When Tony finally "boarded the ship on September 6, 1943," he was surprised to see his old friend, Turk. The young man that talked him into joining was "on the same ship, only in a different division." With the *Mississippi* down for repairs, the men had a little time to get reacquainted.

Seaworthy come October, they pushed south to San Pedro, near Long Beach, then readied for the long trip out to Pearl Harbor. On the way, they reached Butaritari, a ring-shaped reef—or atoll—in the Pacific Ocean. During the war, Americans called the spot Makin Atoll. It was but one of more than sixteen floating bodies that made up the Gilbert Islands, and it was there that Tony would get his first taste of battle. Four short days before the *Mississippi* pulled in, Frankie Dragna landed in nearby New Georgia. Arriving as a replenishing troop in a seasoned infantry unit, Frankie was just beginning to learn about war as well.

Although heavy bomber strikes from the 7th Air Force hit a week earlier, the Battle of Makin did not begin until the morning of November 20, 1943. Army ground troops from the 27th Division paddled toward the beach. As they moved through the water, several U.S. vessels bombarded the land. They struck the island for an hour and a half, clearing the way for the men to advance. The *Mississippi* was one of those ships, but unfortunately, an explosion erupted in one of its turrets. The blast in turret 2 claimed forty-three lives and wounded another nineteen. Tony worked a turret as well; it was sheer luck that they missed his. He survived his first encounter.

Paul Barnes, the ship's legal officer, recalled the event clearly: "Suddenly there was a loud hiss as gas, smoke, and flames shot out of the rangefinder ports on each side of number two turret, right below the navigation bridge where I stood at my battle station as Officer of the Deck." Knowing the flames could easily catch the ammunition magazines, set them on fire, and potentially blow the entire ship, Barnes worried. Thankfully, the men knew what to do. The fire crews handled the incident quickly, but the report from the boatswain was anything but pretty; nearly all of the men in the top three levels of the turret were either dead or badly wounded. Later it was determined that flareback from the center gun had caused the accident rather than enemy fire.

After the battle's end, a ceremony for the dead was held on the quarter deck. The bodies, sealed in weighted canvas bags, slid into the water for an ocean burial. A bugler sounded taps as the Marines fired their rifles in volley. Although a heavy loss, their fellow vessel the *Liscome Bay* suffered even greater casualties. On the morning of November 24, 644 sailors aboard perished after a torpedo from a Japanese sub struck. The torpedo detonated the munitions below deck, destroying everything in an immense explosion. She sank in twenty-one minutes. Although Army troops had boots on the ground, far more lives were lost in the water that day.

The convoy carried on toward Hawaii but encountered even further action—air attacks from the southwest. The venture proved perilous, but eventually the *Mississippi* reached Pearl Harbor. It was early December and the crew stayed for nearly two months, taking on much-needed repairs after the conflict at Makin Atoll. "We were all somewhat shaken by experiencing the casualties on our ship, and witnessing the spectacular end of the *Liscome Bay*," Barnes recalled. For that reason, all personnel—not just the officers—received three days' leave at the Royal Hawaiian Hotel. During the five or six weeks of repairs that their ship needed, the crew continued to train and enjoy the blessed time on dry land. There they celebrated Christmas and the new year—1944.

At Pearl Harbor, the *Mississippi* received replacements for the sailors they lost during the mishap on turret 2. One of these young men was John Yakushik, who arrived fresh out of boot camp. He got in just before Christmas to fill a role as a ship's repairer. The crew, now supplemented with a batch of green sailors, hit the waters in late January, setting out for the Marshall Islands. Their voyage of island hopping was slated to take them all the way to Japan, but after the chaos at Makin Atoll, they began to question if they would make it.

Mississippi Beach

On January 31, John Yakushik's first day of battle, the crew gave fire support for the invasion of Kwajalein Island. According to Captains William A. Corn and

Lunsford L. Hunter, efforts of the U.S.S. *Pennsylvania* and the U.S.S. *Mississippi*, ensured there would not be a repeat of the Battle of Makin. Too many lives were lost with the sinking of the *Liscome Bay* and the explosion of the *Mississippi*'s turret. To be certain, gunners bombarded the island thoroughly, and without mercy, before dropping the rubber rafts into the water and sending in ground troops.

The November 1, 1945 edition of *Our Navy* highlighted that during its bombardment of Kwajalein Island, the *Mississippi* abandoned protocol, or at very least, they strayed from the tactical rules of bombardment the Navy adhered to. The destroyer went in exceedingly close, within a mile of its target, and in doing so, the men on board made themselves vulnerable to an attack, and they knowingly did it in order to ensure the safety of the ground troops heading in. As *The War History of the U.S.S. Mississippi* pointed out in 1945, the battleship "moved in to a range of less than 1,800 yards from the beach, and at this point-blank range, demolished the Japanese defenses so completely that opposition to our landing forces was negligible."

After the Army landed on the beach, they radioed the ship. From then on out, the point would be known as "Mississippi Beach." Rather than scold the crew of the *Mississippi* for abandoning protocol, the Navy responded very differently. Instead, they adopted the bold approach. Pushing forward, leadership urged the fleet to "move in close" as well. More than seventy years later, Tony still remembers the details: "When we bombarded the Makin Island and the Gilbert Islands, there was a seawall there of concrete, and that was our target—to destroy that seawall so that the Marines and Army could land in there."

After they "destroyed the wall, and blockade, and machine guns," which granted the Army safer access, the ground troops met "very little resistance." In thanks, "one little section where we bombed, they named it, Mississippi Beach, after the ship." Their efforts, as he also illustrated, bolstered a bit of fame. The Marines did a great deal of the fighting on the islands, and now whenever they "called for support fire, they always asked for the *Mississippi*, because we were so accurate with firing on the target."

In an official All Hands memorandum, the *Mississippi*'s commander, Lunsford L. Hunter, indicated that the attack on Kwajalein completely wrecked the enemy command post, and the heavy concrete coming down caved in a series of underground passageways. Tony heard about the collapse: "I was informed that over 250 dead Japs were picked up in the dugouts in the vicinity of this post. Everything in the area was literally blasted out of the ground, and after looking at it, you could not see how anyone could have stayed there and not be killed."

In the Majuro Lagoon a couple weeks later, the crew loaded up on ammunition. Kwajalein left them nearly dry. Replenished, they continued the campaign. During late February, the *Mississippi* hit the Japanese Air Base on Taroa Island then sacked Maloelap Atoll, followed by Wotje on the following day. This marked the beginning of what would become constant U.S. attacks on the area. By now, the sailors of the *Mississippi*, and the warship herself, had put on a lot of miles. The wear began to show. A saving grace came when the crew got word that Hawaii waited in the very near future. For that, they were certainly thankful, but more work had to be done before anyone could enjoy some proper R&R.

After the crew stopped for supplies, the next mission waited. They made a quick stop on the island of Efate's Habana Harbor for replenishing then sailed for action. On March 15, the *Mississippi* entered the Japanese stronghold of New Ireland, and on the 20th, they served as a diversion by bombarding Kavieng. After a few down days at New Hebrides, they pulled out for the Bremerton Naval Yard, in Puget Sound, Washington. *En route*, they would briefly see Hawaii again.

The crew hit Washington on April 24, 1944. The ship received another overhaul and some replacement guns, remaining down for two and a half months. The time on land gave her seamen more time to train. They welcomed the opportunity to let their feet touch solid ground, but the time went by far too quickly. John Yakushik explained that during those three months in Bremerton, the "work went on, around the clock. The ship was remodeled, re-gunned, and the latest equipment was installed." But more than brawn and sweat transpired. The brief stint of shore leave brought immense joy and relief to many. James Hickey found time to marry his Rosie the Riveter fiancé, Miss Rose Bonavita, and Tony Amador spent a handful of days with his family and Lucy out in Los Angeles. Again, the

Above left: Shore leave, 1944. Tony Amador returns home to his family and his beloved, Lucy. (*Courtesy of Anthony Amador*)

Above right: Tony and Lucy during shore leave, *circa* 1944, Boyle Heights. (*Courtesy of Anthony Amador*)

days of leisure fled too swiftly. Once the crew got word their ship was ready, they sailed out for refresher training in San Pedro. From there, they left for Pearl Harbor again and readied to bombard some more.

The Battle of Peleliu

On September 12, 1944, the crew came upon the island of Peleliu—just one of roughly 500 floating bodies of land that made up the island nation of Palau. To strike at the invading Allied forces, the Japanese readied the area, digging deep tunnels and defensive points all along Peleliu's coral ridges. Upon their arrival, the *Mississippi* joined a number of warships in an ongoing offensive action known as Operation Forager. Over the next three days, the *Mississippi, Tennessee, Maryland, Idaho, Pennsylvania,* and a few light cruisers bombarded without end. By day three, the guns of the Bloody Nose Ridge had been knocked out, and the path cleared for ground troops.

The attack began each day at 4:30 a.m., with the surrounding ships alternating bombardment. Time was given to the aircraft carriers as well, allowing them to send out air strikes. The assault continued mercilessly in this non-stop fashion. Swapping back and forth afforded the men a quick breakfast under general quarters and a bit of rest in between bouts. Reveille sounded at 3.15 a.m., waking them long before the sun made an appearance. Not long after that, the bombarding started.

From the observation deck, Officer Barnes had a magnificent view of the action, and from turret 1's right gun, Tony Amador saw plenty as well. Buried in the belly of the ship, John Yakushik was another story. Down below, he prepared for whatever emergency electrical repairs might be needed. Experiencing bombardments from beneath offered a very different perspective: "We, being below decks, don't get a chance to see what is going on, because all hatches are dogged down." But one thing John did note was that the boys "sure can feel the vibrations." For some, the confinement became too much. For this reason, whenever general quarters secured—and at just about every chance they got—the crew below snuck topside for air. Up on deck, they checked out the sights.

During their lunch, the *Mississippi* pulled back from the beach and went on G.Q. John and a few others from the repair crew ate quickly then went up to assess the situation. "We saw our carrier planes, dive bombers and S.B.D.'s, dive bomb the island," striking the land, three or four at a time. During the brief show, he also witnessed one of the ship's planes being shot down by the A.A. fire.

On day three, the green light was given, and the Army and Marines dove into the water. Their mission was to capture an airstrip. Covering the advance, the warships continued to lob metal, sending in rapid fire, and overhead, planes dropped a smokescreen to mask their movements. How anyone or anything

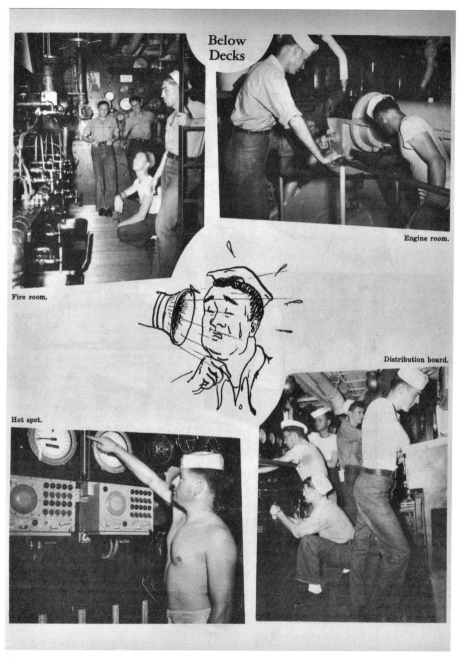

Ship life below deck, taken from U.S.S. *Mississippi* war history booklet, exclusive to the officers and crew, 1945. (*Courtesy of Anthony J. Amador*)

could have survived such a constant and vicious berating is a mystery. But the Japanese on Peleliu were indeed alive and waiting: "Suddenly the Japs began to fire at our landing craft, with all types of guns, mortar, A.A., machine guns, and anything else they had." With a pair of field glasses from up on the ship's bridge, John Yakushik continued to watch the action. Through the lenses, he watched American troops being wounded as they hit the beach. Their tanks were blown to pieces as they landed. The crew's job out at sea was definitely not done. In between newer bouts of bombarding, they ate, caught naps, or played cards. Barnes explained they "continued to provide call fire around the clock—24 hours a day—for the next week." The boys only stopped for a few hours a day, and they only did that to "take on more ammunition."

"Although this was a tiring experience for us," Barnes admitted, he knew that "it was in no way comparable to the hell the First Marines and other ground forces" were going through. In the weeks that dragged on after the *Mississippi* pulled out for her next assignment, these men blasted and flushed out enemy caves "with hand grenades and flame throwers." It was awhile before the "resistance finally ceased." The Battle of Peleliu carried on until late November and earned the codename Operation Stalemate II.

The Flagship and the Pompous Little Popinjay

The *Mississippi* was called away from Peleliu to guard another area in the Palau Islands, the fleet base at Kossol Roads. After fulfilling their duty there, the crew sailed for Manus, a resting port out near New Guinea. Another break was certainly welcomed, but a new tasking had just come down—one of honor. The *Mississippi* would serve as the flagship for Battle Division 3. Unfortunately, the role proved to be far more of a hassle than anything. The flagship hosts the commanding officer, and for that reason, a lot of added protocol must be recognized.

Officer Barnes explained, "the *Mississippi*, unlike its sister ships, *Idaho* and *New Mexico,* was not designed to be a flagship," and for this reason, the crew and its officers were "not used to observing the formalities required by having an admiral aboard." Peacetime etiquette has no place in battle was the thought no doubt running through the mind of every officer onboard. They, after all, were responsible for the actions of the enlisted men. "One day a commander on the admiral's staff chewed" Barnes "out for failure to observe some silly formality." Not too happy about the exchange, Barnes dubbed the high-ranking individual "a pompous little popinjay mightily impressed by his exalted position on the admiral's staff."

On October 12, 1944, bearing the title of flagship, the *Mississippi* left Manus for Leyte Gulf. But something far worse than a pompous little popinjay greeted them on their voyage. *En route* to bomb, the crew encountered a typhoon. Luck alone carried them through it.

Yamashiro and the Invasion at Leyte Gulf

Entering the gulf, minesweepers were sent in ahead. Weaving through the waters, they avoided the perilous mines floating along the path. Clearing the way for the larger vessels, they lit them up with gunfire. The crew of the *Mississippi* quickly came to see that the enemy was anything but stingy. One minesweeper reportedly picked up 137 explosives. The Japanese definitely did not want them on the beach. The going was slow, but once she settled in place, the *Mississippi* readied to bombard. The firing began on October 19, 1944. Once again, they came to provide cover fire for troop advancement. Joining them in the operation were two cruisers from the Royal Australian Navy (R.A.N.) and several U.S. destroyers.

By the second day, Allied troops occupied two of the island's beaches, but the Navy suffered harshly to get them there. A Japanese torpedo bomber—a small plane called a Betty—"sneaked in and dropped its torpedo." It hit the American cruiser *Honolulu* mid-ship and blew "out most of her engineering spacing." Although they were able to shoot down the Betty, the one little plane did a whole lot of damage. Thankfully, the *Honolulu* was able to limp away. After making it back to Norfolk, Virginia, the ship remained under construction for the duration of the war.

On October 21, the fleet took another hard hit. The *Australian* caught fire after a Japanese plane attacked her bridge. "It looked as though the whole cruiser had burst into flames," John Yakushik recalled, and the ship did, but thankfully only briefly. "The flames were from gas spray and they burned quickly." Although the crew managed to extinguish the blaze, the crash took the life of their commanding officer, and many of his men perished as well.

A few days later, amid the Battle of Surigao Strait, the *Mississippi* assisted in sinking the Japanese battleship *Yamashiro*. But the crew's less than aggressive showing raised some questions. While the other warships in the fleet exhibited a fierce offensive, the *Mississippi* fired just once. Speculation circulated. According to John Yakushik, a radar operator explained that they "had something on the screen and it was either a battle wagon or cruiser," but right after firing, their target disappeared. This was only one of the stories John heard. Later rumors held they were nearly rammed by another U.S. vessel, and held off firing to avoid hitting one of their own. Whatever the case, on October 28, 1944, Commander Hunter's replacement addressed the situation in an All Hands memorandum.

Captain H. J. Redfield expressed that the crew of the *Mississippi* deserved "full credit as one of the defending group of ships," and speaking about "the impression" that they could have "fired more shoots at the retreating Japs," he added that the claim was "entirely an erroneous one; the target assigned to the battleships was at a very long range where the chances of hits were small even under ideal daylight conditions."

Survivors of the *Yamashiro* spilled into the ocean, some 600–700 of them, but when American ships went in to pick them up, the floating sailors refused the lines thrown into the water. "Our tin cans," as John called them, "persuaded by spraying the water with their shells. Then the lines were thrown out again, but this time, they were glad to get the rope, and come aboard." For a time, these ships were forced to house prisoners of war.

Over the next few weeks, the crew covered supply and transport ships in the gulf. Like everything else, this too proved difficult. Officer Barnes explained that "following the night battle the Japs started making kamikaze attacks." He also pointed out that historians have credited Leyte Gulf as the first area where these suicide pilots took action: "It was hair-raising to stand on the bridge and watch helplessly as a kamikaze pilot dove his plane as a guided missile." Below deck, John Yakushik felt the vibrations from the guns. Later he caught word that a plane they shot down had managed to steer into another destroyer and crash landed. Another "plane came in" as well but remained out of range. "It got through the firing screen and it strafed" then "dropped a bomb" before crashing into another destroyer. This being the second ship a kamikaze hit during the attack, John believed "the Japs" were specifically after their destroyers. Once their guns were disabled, they could "send in the submarines" to finish them off.

A third destroyer followed and then from the deck, Officer Barnes watched as the nearby vessel, the *Abner Read*, sank after a kamikaze attack. As it went down, the ship salvoed its torpedoes to avoid catching fire and exploding, and when she did, the munitions came dangerously close to lighting up the *Mississippi*. Adjusting position, she avoided the hit. "The torpedoes were coming in at our starboard side, about mid-ship, just where my battle station is," John remembered. The crew below moved over to port side to get further away in case of impact. "The men got orders to try and blow up the torpedoes in the water," but this only caused an accident. A shell exploded in a gun mount and injured eight men.

During their stint in the gulf, the crew ran to their air defense stations a record sixty-two times: "In the twenty-nine days that she operated in Leyte Gulf area, she underwent thirty-eight aerial attacks and one major sea engagement." Aside for the eight wounded in a mishap, they "came out unscathed." At the end of the year, and much to the relief of those aboard the *Mississippi*, the *New Mexico* replaced them as flagship; no more stuffy protocols would heighten anxieties. Instead, the crew spent the holidays gathering ammo from the floating resupply base at Kossol Road. Once loaded, they headed back to the gulf. Not much of a celebration took place, though; it was definitely not the Christmas they enjoyed the year before in Hawaii.

The Invasion of Lingayen Gulf

On the second day of the new year, 1945, the *Mississippi* made its way to San Pedro Bay, just northeast of Leyte. In less than two weeks, on the beaches of

Luzon, the enemy would lob a grenade and take the right eye of Frankie Dragna. The journey to get there was not a quiet one. Sailing for their new target, they witnessed a kamikaze strike the escort carrier *Ommaney Bay*. She did not explode like the *Liscome Bay*, though. Sinking instead, the crew abandoned ship, and 150 survivors came aboard the *Mississippi*.

Though far lesser known, Japanese planes bombed Luzon the very same month they hit Pearl Harbor, and they took control of the gulf shortly after. Three years had passed and they still occupied the area. Tasked with keeping soldiers off the beach, Japan's special attack forces viciously struck, dive-bombing at the destroyers as they prepared to bombard on January 5. On day two of the assault, one of these planes strafed the *Mississippi*, hitting two crewmembers. Only one survived, and others were injured in the chaos as well. But the bombarding continued; nothing could deter them from the mission. They entered Lingayen Gulf then moved near the town of Mangaldan and the gulf's Blue Beach and Harbor. Another bombardment began that day, and as they worked, the crew met the worst batch of kamikazes they had seen yet. Diving Japanese pilots struck more than two dozen U.S. ships; the attacks even claimed the captain of the *New Mexico*.

On January 8, the day before the invasion, Officer Barnes witnessed a kamikaze attack on the nearby Australian heavy cruiser *Australia*. She sat a mere 2,000 yards away. From the ship's observation deck, he watched as the Japanese focused its efforts heavily. Perhaps they mistook her for a troop ship: "By the time two or three kamikazes had crashed on it, the *Australia* looked like a floating junk pile with stacks bent sideways and one turret askew." Despite the beating, the Aussie crew continued to fight. Come the end of the war, she was still being repaired.

After a three-year hold, Allied efforts during this invasion liberated the island from Japanese forces. When the Navy completed its aggressive bombardment on the morning of January 9, some 68,000 U.S. troops invaded. Over the days that followed, another 140,000 soldiers joined the fight, combining with troops from the Philippine Commonwealth. Frankie Dragna was among the brave men that stormed the beach. Providing cover fire for the advance was Tony from turret 1 of the *Mississippi*. Although the two men were not yet acquainted, back home their loved ones were becoming close. Friendship had already sparked between Tony's fiancé, Lucy Niotta, and Frankie's kid sister, Anna. After the war's end, Frankie and Tony would be seeing a lot of each other.

It was D-Day, January 9, 1945, when the *Mississippi* "received her first hit by the enemy." Believing the ground troops had landed safely, the *Mississippi* came off general orders. Given an opportunity to rest, Officer Barnes retired to his quarters. Right after shaving, he heard the explosion. Running up on deck, he discovered that a plane had crashed into the *Mississippi*'s 5-inch gun mount: "The deck around the wrecked gun was covered with flames from the plane's gasoline. Many men were lying around. Survivors were taking ammunition from the ready boxes and heaving it over the side to prevent its exploding in the fire."

Anna and Lucy palling around, Dragna family residence, Leimert Park. (*Courtesy of Frannie Niotta-LaRussa*)

The "kamikaze came in low over the water out of the sun." No one spotted it until it was too late. John Yakushik and his buddy, Ski, had just gotten into the chow line when it struck. The impact threw them to the deck and then "general orders" blared through the ship's speakers. John and Ski scrambled to their feet and charged toward their stations. Below, John later heard what happened from a shipmate who caught the action firsthand. The young man was so close, the fire burned his arm. The pilot came in portside, he explained. The plane grazed the ship's bridge and hit a 20-mm mount. Skipping along the deck, it hit again near two of the 5-inch guns before coming apart. "The motor landed on the galley deck, and parts of it scattered all over, and started burning." Luckily, its bomb bounced over the side and fell into the water before detonating. The casualties would have been far greater if it exploded on the deck. Still, the ship was on fire, and twenty-seven sailors were dead, plus the fire and the shrapnel that came in through the side of the ship wounded another sixty-three. Three men went missing and were never seen again.

Among those injured was Tony's pal, Turk: "He got shrapnel and burns and they transferred him off the ship and sent him home." The event is one that Tony has never forgotten: "We were firing at the plane. I could still see it, see the pilot. I was looking up, and as I went to the right—swinging around—I seen the plane coming in from starboard [right] to port [left]." The safety stops on the turret would not allow Tony to "train the gun any further." This prevented them from "firing into the bridge" and hitting their own.

"The plane was coming in and he was going to miss us, but his wing caught the bridge and threw it into the ship." The "motor wound up in one of the decks above, and the gas from the flames started a fire." Making it worse, the pilot "dropped his bomb at the same time. The bomb hit aft, in the water, and put 300 holes in the side of the ship." Most of the damage came from shrapnel. "That's how some of the guys got hurt. A lot of burns and shrapnel wounds." Thankfully, they were able to put the flames out quickly.

Officer Barnes recalled one of the sailors being transferred to the hospital ship shortly after the chaos; he was waving goodbye with the bandaged stump of an arm. "It was dark when we secured from G.Q.," John Yakushik remembered. Walking toward the toilets he discovered several bodies on the deck being wrapped in canvas and weighted down: "The pharmacist's mates, with help from other shipmates, cast them over the side of the ship." Taps sounded that evening, once more followed by a ceremonial burial at sea. Some of those who perished aboard the *Mississippi* that day had survived the sinking of the *Ommaney Bay*; saved from one tragedy only to succumb to another.

In all, during the nine-day span of the Invasion of Lingayen Gulf, twenty-four U.S. ships sank and sixty-seven more were damaged by kamikazes. On February 10, the crew left Lingayen for Ulithi Lagoon near Palau, where the bulk of the Pacific fleet waited and prepared for the invasion of Iwo Jima. The repairs the *Mississippi* badly needed were the only reason she did not participate. Instead, the crew prepped for the trek to Pearl Harbor for mending. They did not leave empty handed, though. Some 500 troops crowded onboard, more than ready for the long haul back to Hawaii. Stopping briefly in the Marshall Islands, they loaded up on supplies then sailed.

In port, the *Mississippi* received a month's worth of repairs. Anti-aircraft guns were beefed up 300 percent, and the camouflage paint she wore took on a solid gray. The vessel looked completely different. During their time at Pearl Harbor, Officer Barnes received a transfer. After a long flight to San Francisco, he kissed his wife, Betty, and finally got to meet his four-month-old son, Andy. But for Tony Amador, John Yakushik, and all the others aboard the *Mississippi*, the war was far from over.

Shuri Castle

Late in April 1945, the crew motored for Japan to assist the Fifth Fleet. They passed between Tinian and Saipan, and on May 5, they reached Haushi Beach, Okinawa, in the Ryukyus Islands. Fire support for the 77th Infantry began the day after their arrival. The ship's turrets bombarded at Nakagasuku Wan. After laying the initial support fire, duties for the boys aboard the *Mississippi* continued to shift. Next they assisted the 6th Marine Division by providing night illumination, then they bombed Naha Airfield. Fire support went out to the 7th Marine Division as well, and after a short jaunt for replenishing, the crew returned to the area to continue support. The *Mississippi*'s crew helped rescue downed American pilots off Naha then lent further fire support and illumination to the 6th Marine Division.

At the end of May, the crew received a very special mission. They called it "Plan Imperial Special." So far, a destroyer and several air attacks had already failed at the task to breach a 30-foot wall and sack what sat on the other side. The track-record of the *Mississippi* no doubt influenced their selection. She was effective in nearly every major sea landing in the Pacific thus far. According to the military publication *Our Navy*, this was the exact reason why the warship was singled out as the best candidate. The operation lent fire support to the 77th Infantry, but more importantly, it involved cracking a Japanese headquarters that had long been though impenetrable—Shuri Castle.

Reports suggested that flanking the stronghold with ground troops alone would have resulted in the loss of thousands of U.S. lives. The doughboys would have been caught in a crossfire. The cost of that approach was just too great. Leadership decided Shuri Castle had to be crushed before attempting an invasion. Although this seemed to be the best way, thus far it appeared impossible. But the U.S. Navy and Marines had high hopes that the *Mississippi* had enough fight to make it happen. "I know that Shuri Castle, in Okinawa, took twenty years to build. And from what I understand," Tony explained, the "wall on the castle was 20-foot-thick concrete. They said it could never be penetrated. And that was our target."

Although built in the fourteenth century, the castle had received a recent modernization. This included strengthening its defenses. She was "designed to withstand the poundings of modern warfare." An All Hands memorandum from Captain H. J. Redfield, dated June 18, 1945, indicated "One captured Jap Officer had stated, 'you may take Okinawa but you will never take Shuri Castle,'" and after the first battleship tried and failed, they almost believed it. Her 16-inch armor-piercing rounds ricocheted right off—even their direct hits failed to make a dent—and all aerial attempts to shack the fort "penetrated it about as much as an egg dropped on a city street."

"We went up one way," Tony remarked about how they approached the mark. "Turret 1 would fire on it. And turret 2 would fire on it. Then we'd come back." After maneuvering the ship, "turret 3 would fire on it then turret 4. It was like that for three days." The *Mississippi* just kept on pouring out her 5-inch and 14-inch slugs. The reports indicated that turret 2 expended upward of a million rounds, which set the record as the largest amount fired from a turret during any engagement. Though a loud and monotonous ploy, after three straight days of pounding, the unrelenting tactic finally paid off.

The northeast corner of the structure began to crumble first. She cracked on May 27, when all the artillery avalanching in finally breached the ancient stone.

"We destroyed it." But their efforts did far more than just topple a structure that many believed to be unbreakable. With the defeat, the Japanese suffered symbolically, spiritually, and psychologically. The death toll proved enormous as well. According to the ship's official war history, "Dead Japs were scattered all over its underground rooms in pockets of from 50 to as many as 500 in a single sector." Lives were lost, but not American lives: "On May 30th the First Marines entered the castle without loss of a single man. Fewer than 50 Japs opposed their entrance."

The Chaplain

The crew remained in the waters near Okinawa throughout May, circling and moving into position, taking on various targets such as blockhouses. Marks just kept coming in over the radio from scout planes combing the area. "We have air attacks almost every night," John Yakushik commented. "One thing I have to say, they are not as bad as the ones we had, at the Philippines. We have very good air protection here. And very few Jap planes get to our fleet."

Though kamikazes appeared to pose less of a threat in this region, suicide planes had already taken three U.S. destroyers and smaller crafts there in the bay, and things were about to get worse. Air attacks began after dinner on May 25. The men remained at their battle stations until 4 a.m. An attack came from the shoreline as well. John recalled the action: "The damn batteries are after us, again. We seem to be the target. The heavy firing seems to be concentrated on our ship." He considered this the closest call the crew had to date; the shells were coming in and they were very, very close, with missiles landing within 50 yards. Other attempts overshot and landed just past them. Maneuvering to fire upon the beach and take out their artillery, the *Mississippi* just missed being hit by a couple more shells. Luck was surely with them: "Our guns began firing and shelled every bit of the area where the firing came from. Just about every gun went off, from the 14, down to the 40-mm." John holds that all but the 20-mm guns were used. With the beach too far out, they would not have been much use, but what they had to work with was more than sufficient.

On June 5, 1945, the crew felt the attack of another kamikaze. It came in on the starboard side of the quarterdeck. "I seen that one," Tony Amador commented in a somber tone. "It came in low on the water and hit aft just above waterline. Some of the shrapnel and part of the plane went through—below deck—and it killed one officer that was going through the hallway. The stuff came through and hit him in the top of the head." Illustrating further, he relayed "they found parts of the dead Jap on the ship." The ship's doctor examined the remains. Looking at the burnt hand found among the wreckage, the officer gave his assessment: "It was a kid—might have been sixteen or seventeen years old—flying the plane."

Below deck, John Yakushik heard general quarters blaring through the speakers, and by the tone of the voice, he got the sense something awful happened. The voice sounded scared. Those on deck never heard it coming. The pilot probably shut off his engine and came in like a glider: "Part of the plane was on the deck and some of it was on turret 4." Turret 2 caught fire during an earlier attack; now it was turret 4's turn. With only four turrets onboard and Tony sitting at one of them, the odds did not sit in his favor: "The clean-up crew found a hand and leg of the Jap pilot." The young man's parachute turned up as well, dangling from one of the ship's scout planes. In addition to the officer killed below deck, shrapnel also hit a pilot. The ship's doctor could not say for sure if he would be able to keep the leg.

Sadly, the officer killed below deck by the Japanese pilot was a non-combatant, the ship's chaplain. Losing Lieutenant Floyd Withrow "hurt and saddened the crew more than anything else," John expressed. "He was a wonderful Chaplain and everyone liked him." The All Hands letter that followed congratulated the men on their efforts in taking Shuri Castle then noted the loss they suffered: "Our pride must be tempered by an element of sadness in the loss of our Chaplain and the injury of some of our shipmates. The Chaplain was a true padre and we will all miss him keenly."

The Last Stretch

A short time after the loss of their chaplain, the *Mississippi* left Okinawa for Leyte. Although Captain Redfield announced a few weeks of R&R was coming on June 21, when it came time, the men encountered something else. Only four days of liberty were granted once they reached land, but by John Yakushik's assessment, it was more than plenty. "All there is to do is walk around the island," and unless they bartered with the local Filipinos, the two cans of beer a day the men were issued was all they received to drink; it was not enough to get them drunk.

After their fourth day on the island, the group headed to the dry docks, some 40 miles off. There they linked up with the repair ship *Jason*. During the route back to Leyte, the vessel saw to the *Mississippi*'s wounds, mending the ship while travelling alongside it in the water. After making it back, nearly a third of the crew came down with dysentery. One shipmate even died from sickness. A wave of it was hitting a number of naval ships. It was only a matter of time before the *Mississippi* was affected.

A month and a half after they reached Leyte, an astounding announcement came over the radio. It was August 10, 1945, and the crew got word that Japan was willing to surrender. If they were allowed to keep their emperor, they would submit. All the boats in Leyte Harbor blew their whistles and sirens over and over as the men cheered and hollered. "We had our searchlights on," John Yakushik remembered. "The crew were waving them through the sky. We also sent up rockets. Our foghorn was going full blast. That was really something to see."

A week after the announcement, the *Mississippi* returned to Okinawa. The ship landed on August 21, 1945, but only stayed a couple days before receiving orders for Tokyo Bay. The directive came as a standby effort, just in case the Japanese had other plans. Tony and the boys reached Sagami-Wan Bay and held in place until all the formalities of the peace treaty were in order. When it came time, the ship proceeded to Tokyo Bay. It was September 1, 1945, the day before the signing. An overwhelming sight awaited them when they arrived; an immense fleet had gathered. Captain Redfield's All Hands called it "one of the largest concentrations of Naval power in the history of the world." In addition to destroyers like the *Mississippi*, Task Force 38 also made a showing, and the men witnessed yet another marvel during their brief stay in Okinawa. "Off in the distance," John, Tony, and all the others "could see the volcano, Mt. Fujiyama."

On September 2, 1945, the Japanese Empire officially surrendered. The crew of the *Mississippi* hung around a few days after witnessing the ceremony, pulling out on September 5. From there, they moved toward Okinawa to gather troops to transport back to Hawaii. The ship made it to Pearl Harbor on September 20, but did not stay long. By early October, they touched Colon, Cristobal, in the Panama Canal. Eight days later and the Port of New Orleans welcomed them. From late November 1945 until May 1946, the ship remained at Norfolk, Virginia. Her crew departed at different times, saying their farewells. Although thankful to be on the final stretch home, after all they had seen and been through, no one was the same.

Waiting for his turn to disembark, Tony got word from home: "I had a telegram from Lucy." She mentioned her sister, Anne, and her fiancé, Mike Campagna. "Why don't we make it a double wedding?" is what the message asked. "I answered her back" with the casual line, "It's okay with me." By the time Tony got back to Los Angeles, "everything was set up already!"

While Tony Amador was off with the crew of the *Mississippi*, Michael "Mike" Joseph Campagna served aboard the U.S.S. *Columbia*. The vessel bombarded in Munda just before Frankie Dragna's arrival, and it also patrolled Vella LaVella with him. The ship coordinated with Tony and the *Mississippi* as well, in Palaus, Peleliu and Leyte, and Mike joined Tony and Frankie at Lingayen Gulf when Frankie stormed the beach at Luzon, days before being wounded. Like Tony, Mike also faced close calls; one of them too close. On January 6, 1945, while still *en route* to Lingayen Gulf, kamikazes dove into the deck of the *Columbia*. Thirteen were killed in the explosion and another forty-four wounded. The planes attacked again on January 9; this time claiming twenty-four lives and wounding ninety-seven. In each instance, the men of the *Columbia* put out the fires and bombarded their targets, receiving a Navy Unit Commendation for their valiant efforts. Unfortunately, Mike was one of the young men caught in the wreckage.

U.S.S. *Mississippi* at the Panama Canal, 1945. (*Author's personal collection*)

Christine Campagna-Zeimantz explained that although she saw the scar on her father's chin every day growing up, he said very little about how he got it. On one occasion, however, he did admit remembering "the grins on the faces of the bomber pilots as they shot at the ship." Although he rarely mentioned the war, other signs suggested what he went through. Mike frequently woke in the middle of the night startled by nightmares.

By the time Tony Amador parted ways with the *Mississippi*, Mike Campagna and Frankie Dragna were already at home recovering from their injuries. Tony bid farewell to the Navy on February 24, 1946. The record of the *Mississippi* and its crew speaks for itself: "She had delivered 12 million pounds of steel to the enemy in a dozen operations, ranging from the misty Aleutians, to the sunbaked Solomons, and the typhoon filled China Sea." When asked to sum up the achievements of the men onboard the U.S.S. *Mississippi* during the fight, Tony relayed, "we shot down nine planes and we bombarded eleven of the Aleutian Islands going all the way through the Pacific." He then qualified, so as not to overstate his part, "I was only involved in nine of those landing invasions for the Marines and the Army."

Mike Campagna home and healed after a kamikaze attack, spending time with his fiancé, Anne Niotta, Los Angeles. (*Courtesy of Caitlin Meininger*)

12

The Return

Not only did Italian-Americans serve in every branch of the U.S. military during World War II, representing the largest ethnic force in the fight, they also earned more Congressional Medals of Honor than any other group, with at least thirteen awarded. From the ranks of the Army Air Corps, this included Major Ralph Cheli. The regular Army boasted quite a few: 1Lt. Willibald C. Bianchi, 2Lt. Robert M. Viale, Master Sergeant Vito R. Bertoldo, TSgt. Peter J. Dalessondro, SSgt. Arthur F. DeFranzo, and P.F.C.s Frank J. Petrarca, Joseph J. Cicchetti, Gino J. Merli, and Mike Colalillo. On the Marine side, this included Sgt. John Basilone and Cpl. Anthony Casamento and Cpl. Anthony P. Damato. Damato, who received the award posthumously, even had a destroyer named after him—the U.S.S. *Damato* (DD-871).

John Basilone is perhaps the most well-known among this group. He, too, had a destroyer named in his honor, the U.S.S. *Basilone* (DD-824), and according to the National Italian American Foundation, after making it back from the war as a Medal of Honor recipient, he joined a group of actors on a war bonds tour. Although he was "credited with raising nearly $1.5 million in ten days," the limelight was not his calling and he requested to return to the fight. In February 1945, "after single-handedly" destroying "an enemy strong point" at Iwo Jima, he was killed in action. Posthumously, he was awarded the Navy Cross.

The National Italian American Foundation holds that Peter J. Dalessondro "was believed to be the second most decorated World War II veteran." In addition to the Congressional Medal of Honor, he was also awarded "three purple hearts, two Silver Stars, a Bronze Star, and the French *Croix de Guerre*." Another high honor in the war for Italian-Americans was achieved by Army Air Corp flyer Dominic Salvatore Gentile, who "was awarded the Distinguished Service Cross by General Dwight Eisenhower for breaking Eddie Rickenbacker's record of enemy planes destroyed," who had twenty-six confirmed. Like Basilone, Gentile also returned stateside and saw success selling war bonds.

The long list of Italian-American contributions to the fight abroad—land, air, and sea—also includes the deeds of Army Ranger Henry Mucci. In 1945, this Pearl Harbor attack survivor led 121 Rangers in what is widely believed to be the most successful military rescue in all of U.S. history; the Rangers freed more than 500 survivors of the Bataan Death March.

Despite the hardships they faced stateside, America's Italian citizens also made a big impact on the war. Some Italian families sent as many as six of their sons to the fight, and a large number of those that stayed behind contributed to war effort production. They made up nearly 5 percent of the workforce—roughly 800,000. In addition to this, through the efforts of the Sons of Italy and the Italian newspaper *Il Progresso Italo-Americano*, more than $16 million in war bonds were sold.

Wedding Bells and Boyle Heights

Tony Amador wasted no time getting back to the life he left behind. One week after his ship docked, he married his childhood sweetheart, Lucy Niotta. The ceremony at Los Angeles' Sacred Heart "was a double wedding," Tony bragged, and all healed up after surviving a kamikaze attack, Lucy and Tony's friend, Turk, even served as bestman. Surprisingly, between the two newlywed couples, not one

Tony and Lucy with Turk and a date after returning from the war, Los Angeles, *circa* 1945. (*Courtesy of Anthony Amador*)

of them owned a car: "We did all of our transportation by bus or streetcar." That was one thing the war had not altered.

"We spent our honeymoon at the Biltmore Hotel in Los Angeles." In another year, the spot would host the reception for another Niotta wedding—the union between Stevie Niotta and Anna Dragna. Reconnecting on an in-town honeymoon, Tony and Lucy walked through Pershing Square for breakfasts at Clifton's Cafeteria: "We'd get on a bus and go to Santa Anita to see the races" as well. To the delight of those who loved betting on the horses, the tracks had reopened.

Family and his sweetheart were not the only familiar comforts Tony returned to. Boyle Heights also waited. But somehow, just as he had, the area changed, and as the days carried on, this change continued. With the influx of returning service members taking up residence, plus the construction of the 10 and 101 freeways, Boyle Heights slowly became something else. The new freeways sectioned off and divided the neighborhood, causing an awful housing crunch. Italian communities left for the suburbs, moving further east to spots like Alhambra, San Gabriel, and Rosemead.

Change hit the Jewish communities of Boyle Heights as well. Brooklyn Avenue, the Jewish neighborhood near Tony's stomping ground—where he bought clothing from Zellman's and corned beef sandwiches and hotdogs from Canter's Deli—the old hangouts there slowly disappeared. Not long after the war, the deli Tony loved so much moved from Boyle Heights to Fairfax, as did the majority of the Jewish community. It all seemed to shift in a wave. To fit the new dynamics, Brooklyn Avenue eventually even changed names. Zellman's, which opened in Boyle Heights in 1921, may have been on one of the last holdouts. Just before the year 2000, the shop closed its doors for the final time after a seventy-eight-year run.

In the early years before World War II, when much of Los Angeles was segregated—and predominately white—Boyle Heights offered a diverse collection of ethnicities and cultures. This is no longer so. According to more recent statistics published in *The Los Angeles Times*, the area houses a 94-percent Latino demographic. Brooklyn Avenue became Cesar Chavez Avenue, and the trail of kosher butcher shops and delis and Italian markets gave way to taco shops and panaderias.

For his service and bravery as a young man, the United States Navy awarded Anthony J. Amador the World War II Victory Medal, the Navy Occupation Service Medal, the Philippines Liberation Medal with two Bronze Stars, the Asiatic Pacific Campaign Medal with one Silver Star and two Bronze Stars, the National Defense Service Medal, a Presidential Unit Citation, and the Philippine Presidential Unit Citation. Like so many other young men who fought, were lucky enough to survive, and came back a decorated hero, the rest of his life waited.

Right after their honeymoon, Tony reentered the workforce: "After we got married, I went to work in a steel plant." Although he only stayed with United

Pipe and Steel, in Vernon, for about a year, his next position proved long lasting. The all-veteran organization G. I. Trucking Company took Anthony on: "The two guys that owned it—one was a Marine Sergeant, the other a Marine Captain, in the Marine Air Force." Among good company, he stayed "thirty-nine and a half years, and retired from there."

By the close of the 1940s, Tony and Lucy had their first child, a daughter named, Toni. Early in the 1950s, came their second, Linda, and then, in 1960, their final, Mark. At last, Tony had a son to carry on the family name. Tony and Lucy enjoyed a long and fruitful life together. Sadly, after fifty-seven years of marriage, Lucy passed. Tony, now in his early nineties, currently resides in Las Vegas, Nevada.

The Points System and the Ruptured Duck

In all, Stevie served eight and a half months overseas. It was the summer of 1944 when he left the European Theater of Operations. Two weeks later, on July 12, he hit American soil. Promotion to the rank of technical sergeant followed, as did a bit of well-deserved leave. His father, Big George, had been back at the racetracks ever since they reopen. He even purchased another runner, Liedevin. Revisiting the family tradition, Stevie accompanied his father down south to Old Mexico's Agua Caliente racetrack and watched the horses run, but Stevie's stay with family and friends in Los Angeles was only temporary. The time flew quickly and the new assignment waited.

Although Stevie completed his required number of missions abroad, the U.S. Army Air Corps was not quite through with him yet. Dick had a name for the clause that kept Stevie from returning to civilian life. He referred to it as "the points system." Officially, it went by another title—the Advanced Service Rating (A.S.R.) score. Like the required number for bomber crews, the A.S.R. served as another factor that determined when a military obligation had been met. Sensibly, the system revolved around the premise that those who fought the hardest and longest should finish out the soonest. It just made good sense.

For an enlisted man to fulfill his quota, he had to accrue at least eighty-five points, but there were only four ways he could do this. Service members earned a point for each month of service, plus another for each month served abroad. If they had a family back home, that helped, too. Enlisted men with a dependent child under the age of eighteen earned a dozen points right out the door. Certain campaign medals and combat awards—such as a Bronze Star—qualified as well, in some cases to the extent of five points each. Similar to the change in the number of allotted missions required of bomber crews, the number of points necessary to meet the A.S.R. standard eventually rose as well. The minimum reached eighty-eight by the war's end.

English Ace Visits Sisters Here

Tech. Sgt. Steve Niotta, veteran of 26 missions over the English channel as turret gunner and radio operator and wearing the Distinguished Service Cross with oak leaf cluster, is spending a 30-day furlough with his sisters, Marion, Anne and Lucille Niotta of Plant3. With the Daily News before enlisting, Steve has made real flying history in the Western European theatre.

✩

English ace news clipping from the *L.A. Daily*, salvaged from a family album, 1944. (*Author's personal collection*)

Hometown hero TSgt. Stevie Niotta happy to be back in Los Angeles for a visit, 1944. (*Courtesy of Frannie Niotta-LaRussa*)

Still not having enough points to rate an honorable discharge, Stevie left Los Angeles for Texas, where a point a month waited. He spent time in San Antonio with its 78th Flying Training Wing, and at Hondo, and Lubbock Army Air Field. By the end of the year, he earned enough points to switch his status to Class 1-C. All said and done, he racked up eighty-eight total. Air Technical Service Command in San Bernardino, California—the Army Air Corps' Separation Base—cut Stevie's official special orders. His papers arrived on September 19, 1945.

For his participation in the Normandy and European Air Offensive Campaigns, Stevie was awarded the European-African-Middle Eastern Campaign Medal (EAME), and for his heroic service with the 8th Air Force in the E.T.O. came the Distinguished Flying Cross, an Air Medal with five Oak Leaf Clusters, two Bronze Stars, and the Good Conduct Medal. Commenting on the Distinguished Flying Cross, Dick explained that "all of the officers—the pilots, the navigator, and the bombardier—were eligible" for the award after they fulfilled their "required number of missions." If they were capable of doing that, the award was automatically granted. Enlisted members did not have it so easy, though. They had to do something extra to merit acceptance. The same went for a Bronze Star. Commenting on Stevie's medals, Dick expressed, if he got "two bronze stars and the DFC, he must have done something very exceptional." Proudly, Dick even added "Heroic! He was a real hero." Stevie's wife confirmed Dick's contention. Anna Dragna-Niotta clarified that he "received the Distinguished Flying Cross" because he "shot down a German fighter plane that was threatening their Fortress."

Stevie's discharge paperwork came a week after Frankie Dragna's. Like Stevie, although Frankie's fighting days were over, returning stateside had not fulfilled his military obligation. By the time he sustained his injuries, Frankie had accumulated less than sixty points. Sitting in a hospital bed for a month, minus an eye and suffering with malaria, he gained a couple extra, and although the awards he rated helped as well, he still sat shy. Participation in three campaigns afforded him the Asiatic-Pacific Theater Medal and three Bronze Battle Stars. Although he had an Expert Infantry Badge and a Combat Infantryman Badge, these did not garner A.S.R. points. For his sacrifice, he later received the Purple Heart, which pushed him over the sixty-point mark. Ultimately, though, Frankie never met the government quota, earning only sixty-six points in all. For this reason, Frankie did not receive an honorable discharge until six months after he made it home.

With the war ending, the War Department instituted a redesignation of their point system. Amazingly, giving an eye in the service of his country still did not automatically qualify, but with a score between sixty and seventy-nine points, Frankie now fell under the "Liquidation Forces" clause. Finally, they granted him eligibility. From a hospital bed in the Birmingham General, in the city of Van Nuys, he got the good word. It was September 13, 1945. On the other side of the world, Tony and the rest of the crew of the *Mississippi* were watching as Okinawa slowly shrank behind them. Next, they would reach Pearl Harbor, back to where their fight first got started.

Mere weeks before his discharge, Frankie turned twenty-one. Since climbing that hill to look for the enemy and taking shrapnel in the face, he had spent roughly eight months in various hospitals and medical facilities. Malaria made for a difficult and lengthy recovery. Even after checking out of the hospital in Los Angeles, Frankie continued to suffer from malaria-induced episodes. More lasting, though, he lost an eye—an injury that would stick with him for the remainder of his life.

In addition to his release papers, Frankie also received a tiny golden button of gilded brass. The device, which bore an eagle wrapped in a circle, had been designed to slide through the eye of a buttonhole. To the wearer, it signified that he had endured, that he made it through alive, and that he did it honorably. "The boys all said it looked more like a duck," though, Frankie remarked. "That's why it earned the name, the ruptured duck."

When metal was still in short supply because of the war effort, the men who rated the device were given plastic versions. These could later be traded in for the real thing. The lapel version was exclusive to ground troops. Crewmembers with the Air Corps earned another version, one that Stevie Niotta was given. Although

Frankie back in Los Angeles wearing shades after healing. With friends and a date at the famed Ciro's, Hollywood, April 27, 1945. (*Courtesy of Frannie Niotta-LaRussa*)

it still bore the gilded brass "duck," its backside held a stick pin with a frog, so it did not have to be worn through a buttonhole.

She Finally Got that Milky Way

Although the bootlegging trade linked the Dragna and Niotta families during the roaring twenties and the early part of the thirties, which sparked business and friendship ties, these bonds died out around the time prohibition ended. Despite the fact that Lucy Niotta and Anna Dragna were jointly baptized as babies—when Lucy's big brother, Stevie, was about seven—Stevie only really came to know his future wife, Anna, after the war was over. The pair got acquainted through his niece, Lolly Cacioppo. Lucy's visits to see Lolly and Lolly's mother, Celie, in the old neighborhood brought her past Tony Amador's home often enough for the teenage boy to take notice, and once Lolly met Anna Dragna at U.S.C., she fell into the fold with Tony and the Niottas.

A smile brightens Frannie Niotta-LaRussa's face whenever she recalls the story of how her parents, Anna and Stevie, came together. Slyly, Anna Dragna tricked her father, Jack, into letting her out on dates. The large gap in age between Stevie and his oldest sibling, Celie, worked in everyone's favor. Not much older than Celie's daughter, Lolly, Stevie grew up thinking of her as more of a cousin than a niece. This is typical in larger families. This closeness between Stevie and Lolly turned out to be quite beneficial whenever Anna wanted to see Stevie. Knowing well that her father would demand a chaperone, and would want to know who that individual was, Anna played an ace whenever she asked to go out to the movies with her girlfriend, Lolly.

Although already twenty years old, by American standards and U.S. law, Anna Dragna was still a minor. Going further, her father maintained a very proper household. That being said, hearing that Lolly's Uncle Steve would be accompanying them on their outing always seemed to satisfy Mr. Dragna's concerns. Clearly, he pictured a much older gentleman. Matters would have been very different had he known a mere seven years separated Lolly from her uncle, or that the young war hero was romantically interested in his daughter.

It did not take much courting before Stevie knew Anna was the one, but before he could act on those feelings, he had to get her father's blessing. Luckily, hearing the honest sentiments of a decorated veteran like his son, Frankie, was enough for Jack Dragna. He sensed right off that Stevie was a good fit. Knowing how much Anna loved her Milky Ways, and how she had "suffered" without them during the course of war, Stevie humorously decided to incorporate the candy into his proposal. He hid the ring in a box of them.

Like the Amador and Campagna couples, Stevie and Anna married at Sacred Heart, with Frankie Dragna serving as Stevie's bestman. For the reception at the

Left: Anna and Tony, Los Angeles. (*Courtesy of Anthony Amador*)

Below: Newlyweds Anna and Stevie Niotta toast with their maid of honor, Frances Lucchese, and bestman, Frankie Dragna, Biltmore Bowl, Biltmore Hotel, Los Angeles, 1948. (*Courtesy of Frannie Niotta-LaRussa*)

Anna and Stevie Niotta on a European vacation shortly after the war. (*Courtesy of Frannie Niotta-LaRussa*)

Biltmore Hotel, Anna's father reserved their largest hall, the Biltmore Bowl. Guests enjoyed a live performance by family friend, Jimmy Durante, who entertained the crowd with his old pal Eddie Jackson. After a honeymoon at Niagara Falls and a visit with family friends out in New York, the newlyweds returned to Los Angeles. Stevie resumed work with his older brother, Michael, at the *L.A. Daily*, this time as a circulation manager. But with the new decade came more promising ventures.

In November 1950, Stevie joined his brother-in-law, Frankie, in opening a carwash out in North Hollywood near Toluca Lake. She sat at 10760 Riverside Drive. Stevie and Anna had become parents as well. Phyllis arrived in March '49 and Jack in January '51. Stevie, Jr., and Frannie would join them a few years later. Jack Niotta vaguely recalls the family carwash but still tells his father's stories. Every Saturday, his dad fed the carwash employees: "He would cook up a big pot of pasta and bring in Italian loaves of bread." But apparently the guys down at the wash were not Italian. Laughing, Jack remarked, "They'd put the pasta on the bread and eat pasta sandwiches!"

Unfortunately, "two new carwashes were built on either side within a few blocks" of the Niotta-Dragna business, so "they went under." Soon after, the family relocated to San Diego, where Anna's father helped them get situated in another business. For Stevie, it was a return to the pre-war days working with his father, Big George, when they still had their own jukebox business, the Wolf

Above and below: Stevie Niotta at the Niotta-Dragna carwash, *circa* 1951. (*Courtesy of Frannie Niotta-LaRussa*)

Music Company. With this new endeavor in San Diego, which included vending and gaming machines in addition to jukeboxes, Stevie became a part-owner. He again took a very hands-on role, serving as Maestro Music's secretary and treasurer. He remained in the industry for more than thirty years.

Stevie stayed a San Diegan for the remainder of his days and was a longtime member of the city's Italian American Civic Association. Heart failure took him on November, 16, 1997. He was seventy-seven years old. In mere months, his marriage to his beloved wife, Anna Dragna-Niotta, would have reached its fiftieth anniversary.

Swinging for the Fences

Carl Paul Maggio's sports memoir *Swinging for the Fences* offers a fun postwar tale that briefly mentions Frankie Dragna. Maggio played right field for the American Legion Baseball Team back in 1951—the year they celebrated the title of League Champions. More than six decades later, as an octogenarian, Maggio fulfilled his lifelong dream of throwing the opening pitch during a Dodgers/Angels game. Back when Maggio met Frankie, he was still just a little boy. Frankie had recently left the hospital following malaria treatment. Their chance meeting illustrates well the sort of man Frankie was. It also throws a lens on the public image surrounding the Dragna family name.

Like many neighborhood kids in Los Angeles during the 1940s and '50s, not only did Carl Maggio love to play baseball, it meant just about everything. On one particular day, though, his skills on the diamond tested his nerve. Carl hit a homerun, something any ball player should be proud of, but unfortunately, the ball landed somewhere it should not have landed: "As the ball left my bat, I exclaimed, 'Oh, no! The ball is headed for that house!'" Carl pleaded for "a do-over but knew it was too late. Of all the houses in the neighborhood you didn't want to hit, that house was the most dreaded one."

As much as Carl begged for the missile he launched to change course, "not only did the ball hit that house, it managed to locate the huge, stained glass bay window displayed proudly." Understanding the severity of the situation, Carl's pals promptly split, leaving him to contemplate his options: "Run like hell" or take it like a man? He imagined that window cost about $500. That was $500 at a time when "the average income was less than $500 per month." Weighing far heavier than "the financial ramifications though, was who lived inside the house." That large ornate window belonged to the Dragna family, or more precisely as Carl put it, "the house was owned by Jack Dragna, the purported head boss of the West Coast Mafia!" With the rumors abounding, Carl feared the worst. "Would his mafia henchmen set my feet in cement and throw me into the Pacific? Would they point a machinegun out of a car and mow me down as I rode my bike to school?" He began to imagine "the Boss' angry tirades" as his henchmen dragged him in "to face the Italian tribunal."

A child's mind can run wild, especially when the papers fill it with fearful tales. Despite the terror and anxiety eating at Carl, he chose to do the right thing, and to his surprise, he encountered something and someone very different than he imagined: "Standing in front of me was a handsome young man, wearing a broad smile on his face, and holding a baseball in his right hand." Too nervous to speak, Carl merely mumbled, but the man seemed to understand: "Before I could get a comprehensive word out of my mouth, he interrupted, 'Boy, you really hit that ball a long way. You must be one of the stars in the neighborhood.'" Hearing this, Carl apologized emphatically then offered to pay for the damage. The young man was not interested in the money, though: "Oh, you're forgiven. No problem. And don't worry about the window. We'll take care of it. I never liked the way it looked anyway." After returning the ball, the stranger then kidded, "I have no use for this window crasher, and it looks to have quite a few more hits left in it. But do me one favor, keep swinging for the fences and have fun doing it."

Carl Maggio found out later that the handsome man he ran into was not Jack Dragna, "but his son, Frank, who was a student at USC, attending on the GI Bill." One day, young Carl would call U.S.C. his *alma mater* as well: "Frank had returned from the war as a decorated hero, having received the Purple Heart, among other impressive metals for bravery." Carl contended that "Frank didn't need to show" him "any medals to prove himself," though: "His actions that day demonstrated the class and kindness of a man who would forever be my hero."

The Sins of the Father

With so many Tonys in the family, Tony Rizzotto went by the nickname Sonny. Like his cousin, Frankie Dragna, he also served abroad, fighting on some of the very same battlefields. Acting as a squad leader in the Army's 128th Infantry Regiment put him in Luzon, Papua, and New Guinea. Sonny and Frankie had the Purple Heart in common as well. Mike Rizzotto explained that his father was wounded in the Philippines, taking rounds in the right leg and in the left arm. Further mirroring Frankie's story, Sonny even contracted malaria. It is no wonder this pair of cousins got along so well after they reunited in Los Angeles. Thankful to be alive, the two decided to celebrate their luck together.

Tony Poli, who was born mere months after the Italians were removed from the enemy list, still remembers the war stories his uncle shared. Sonny Rizzotto and Frankie Dragna "were hellions on wheels when they got back from the service; going out and partying and having a good old time," and they had an ongoing gag with the ladies, too, saying "they were going to get them in the movies, because some family member had connections in Hollywood." In addition to hamming

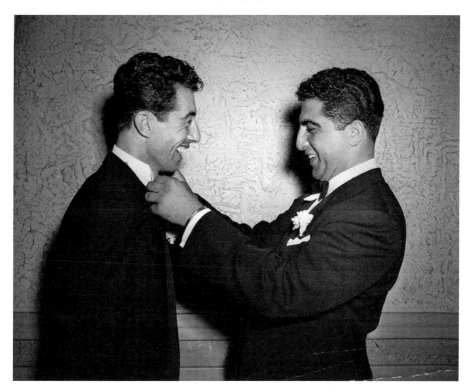

War hero cousins, Tony "Sonny" Rizzotto and Frankie Dragna. (*Courtesy of Frannie Niotta-LaRussa*)

it up with the girls, Frankie and Sonny also did a bit of brawling. Relaying these events to his nephew, Tony, Sonny laughed: "I knew we were going to get into a fight whenever Frankie took his eye out at the bar and set it in somebody's drink." Nearly losing his life in the line of duty and going half blind for his country in the process certainly had not robbed Frankie Dragna of his sense of humor or spirit. But something other than the casualties of war would bring him down. Forever overshadowing his heroism and sacrifice were the sins of his father.

Frankie healed and eventually resumed his coursework at U.S.C., but his problems were just beginning to hatch. The second half of the '40s proved frustrating but only served as a precursor. "He went to the war and he came back," Frankie's niece, Frannie, remarked, indicating that is "when they started making trouble for him." The authorities had been watching Frankie's father closely for some time, and moving into the postwar years of the '40s and into the new decade, the L.A. Gangster Squad kicked off a campaign of petty harassment. After this controversial task force was disbanded in 1950, over use of questionable and unlawful tactics, Captain Lynn White's Intelligence Unit picked up where the squad left off.

Members of the L.A.P.D. did far more than just target Jack Dragna, they also went after his family. Frankie was too young to have been a bootlegger and was never involved in any of his father's gambling affairs. As Frannie and other family members contend, he was never groomed to take part in illicit business. Frankie Dragna was a war hero and a law student. Unfortunately, this purposeful separation did not grant any sort of immunity from the rousting efforts of the L.A.P.D.

Like the other members of his family, detectives tailed Frankie wherever he went. They followed his red convertible to and from the house on Hubert and on the campus at U.S.C. Sometimes they even pulled the vehicle over and rousted everyone inside. Shaking Frankie and his frat brothers down, officers ordered them to empty their pockets then lean on the car as it was searched thoroughly. Authorities also threatened the small business Frankie started a few years later—a neighborhood deli. Parking their squad cars out front of the establishment regularly, they loudly heckled and drove off the clientele. Situations such as this were put on record in October 1950, when Jack Dragna and his lawyer, Sam Kurland, appeared in Chicago before the Special Committee to Investigate Organized Crime in Interstate Commerce.

Addressing a senator and the other members of the committee, Mr. Kurland indicated that the L.A.P.D. followed Jack Dragna "with three cars" and that they also followed "his son, with three police cars." Officers kept at it "night and day." Frankie's mother, Frances, was not exempt either. Three squad cars tailed her wherever she went, too: "They have 27 police cars following him in shifts." Kurland adamantly pointed out that these efforts were "not for the purpose of following him, but merely for the purpose of annoying him." Police presence was very obvious: "One goes in front and one goes in back, and one goes on the side."

Regarding police interference in Frankie Dragna's deli, Mr. Kurland offered: "He has a son working 12 hours a day in a delicatessen. They follow him. They stand out in front of the delicatessen all day with three police cars." Ultimately, the shop closed due to a lack of customers, the police drove them away, and although Frankie's nephew, Jack Niotta, holds that the family carwash folded due to competition, bad press likely played a role as well. The hearings Jack Dragna appeared at in late 1950 were more than just a big story in the papers. Proceedings were held in cities all across the country, and many of them were televised. The name "Dragna" made a negative splash in the headlines one month before the carwash opened.

In February 1950, agents went further than mere rousting, making an arrest. After a bomb went off in the home of Jewish gambler Mickey Cohen, police hauled in the Dragna family. During the two-day hold in police custody that followed, Frankie, his Uncle Tom, and Tom's two sons, Louie and Frank, were never formally charged with a crime. In addition to being denied legal counsel, they were refused all requests to make a phone call. Officers bullied them further by refusing to let them sleep. More detrimental, the L.A.P.D. granted full access to press photographers. When the degrading photos hit the papers, articles claimed "conspiracy to commit murder" and labeled Frankie Dragna a gangster.

Frankie's rights had been violated and he pursued justice through the legal system. Suing for false imprisonment, he filed a case against the chief of police, the captain of the Intelligence Squad, and ten other Los Angeles officers.

The Los Angeles Times, April 8, 1950
"Frank Dragna Sues Police for $350,000 in Damages"

Frank Dragna, 26-year-old WWII veteran yesterday began suit in Superior Court for $350,000 false improvement damages against Chief of Police W. A. Worton and Capt. Lynn White of the Police Department.

Frankie contended that officers "issued statements to the press branding him as a member of a gang and asserting that an arsenal had been found in his home." Commenting on these accusations, Frankie "stated in his petition that there was no such arsenal or any weapon whatsoever found in his house." Both before and after his service in the war, as he further declared, "he was a student at the University of Southern California and had never been involved in any dispute with law enforcement officers."

Frankie's court case lingered on for years, sapping his already depleted faith in the legal system. Despite all the tedious legwork, courtroom fees, and headaches, Frankie never saw justice. The decision came down in March 1954. The papers reported the final verdict: "Judge Caryl M. Sheldon upheld arguments that police officers are immune from suits based upon their actions in the performance of their duties."

Although a bachelor for the bulk of his life, Frankie did marry shortly after the war ended. He and his beautiful new bride, Nadine, were deeply in love, but the police and media involvement in his personal life caused a huge rift in their marriage. In great part, the tactics of the L.A.P.D. and newsmen lent to the couple's divorce. "Nadine was crazy about Frank," stated Frankie's cousin, Florence, and that although "she loved him very much, there was too much going on." The newspapers drew a lot of attention, people talked and Nadine became embarrassed, and so the pair began to fight often, with Frankie in a rage because of Nadine's refusal to be seen anywhere near his parents. They divorced in December 1953, not long after the passing of Frankie's mother, who died of cancer that summer.

After the carwash flopped and his sister's family relocated further south, Frankie opted for a change of scenery. He followed Stevie and Anna to San Diego, where he held part ownership in a local tavern, but that soon fell through as well. Due to a licensing dispute over the Gold Rail, Frankie lost the establishment.

Being a disabled and decorated war veteran who could also boast being a U.S.C. *alum*, Frankie should have been able to find work easily, but that was never the case. Lamenting over what her cousin went through, Florence expressed that Frankie was singled out for much of his life. "It was very, very difficult for him when he was in school," but his troubles did not end after he left the university, or even after his father passed away in February 1956: "Later it was very difficult for him to hold down a job with any well-known company because of the name." Florence even urged him to change it.

Despite more than a decade of hard luck, come the early '60s, Frankie heard some encouraging news about a promising position. His brother-in-law, Stevie, had a nephew down at Sterling Liquor, and the young man put in a good word for him. Recalling the event nearly fifty-five years later, George Niotta exclaimed that Frankie had the job solid: "My boss called me up and said, 'Frankie's got the job, a hell of a personality. We really like him.'" Despite the assurance, the offer never panned out. George later discovered that mention of the Dragna family name a short while after the interview killed Frankie's chances: "We had a couple trucks hijacked and the Police Department uncovered the perpetrator. It was an inside setup with our own people—the driver and some outside group that was going to fence the booze." Although unrelated to Frankie, his name came up in conversation when officers on the scene questioned George's boss: "This Sergeant that cracked the case said, 'If I were you, I'd lay off of him,' and so they did."

Right around that time, Frankie filed another lawsuit, this time over defamation of character. The papers were once again calling him a gangster. "Although he is now dead," the article stated in reference to Frankie's father, "the Dragna name is still feared in the California underworld." The tabloid journalist then alleged that Frankie had "taken his [father's] place in the rackets."

Once Star-Banner, February 9, 1962
"Gunmen Rule West Coast Underworld"

The two Frank Paul Dragna's are known in the underworld as "One Eye" and "Two Eyes." The son, who has a glass eye, is active in San Diego. The nephew keeps his two good eyes on the Dragna enterprises in the L.A. area. Both "One Eye" and "Two Eyes" have been schooled in violence, have been arrested but not convicted of "conspiracy to commit murder."

Bolstering the unsubstantiated claim, the reporter conveniently neglected to highlight just how Frankie came to lose that eye. It was a point Frankie's lawyer stressed heavily in the courtroom. This time, thankfully, Frankie did see a bit of justice.

Being a syndicated column, readers all across the country read the article, but now, thanks to the courtroom win, newspapers that ran the story would be required to print a retraction; it came as an apology and admitted the claims made by the journalist were both unsubstantiated and unfair. Rightly, the circumstances of how Frankie came to be injured were finally included. While certainly a victory, the small win paled when compared to the decades of ill treatment that followed. Rather than owning a bar, Frankie instead found himself pouring drinks. For lack of a better way to make an honest living, moving into the 1970s, Frankie continued to tend bar. He served drinks in numerous establishments, including San Diego's Lafayette Hotel. During the day, he sold appliances.

Life with Anna

While the shame of being labeled a gangster and the inability to find steady work continued to push Frankie into the shadows, all the negative press had another effect on Anna. Over the decades that followed, the media coverage surrounding their father and family name continued to resurface. It proved nerve-racking, frustrating, and problematic. Even worse, it was not going away. There was always the worry of the neighbors finding out. Continuing to carve the image of herself that far contrasted what the media portrayed, Anna took an active and positive role in her community and politics. Marrying out of the Dragna name likely made it easier for her to accomplish this.

During the 1960s, Anna became heavily involved in Frank Curran's campaign for San Diego mayor. Then, in the '70s, she worked on Senator John Tunney's campaign. She also utilized her schooling in journalism to edit the monthly newsletter for the Italian American Civic Association. Although a member, she began to feel that the women within the organization needed their own voice. Eventually, Anna rallied with several other spouses and co-founded a separate group, the Italian-American Women's Association. She even served as their first president. Come the late '70s, Anna found yet another avenue to give back. She began work as an instructional aid and remained with San Diego's Unified School District for a full decade. She retired in her early '60s and assumed the fulltime role of grandma.

After suffering the loss of her husband, Stevie, in 1997, Anna once again came to live with her older brother, Frankie. Neither remarried and Frankie never had children. The two lived together in San Diego for fifteen years. For a long time, Frankie prevailed against respiratory issues but finally passed on November 3, 2012. Sadly, he still harbored the resentment and pain that had lived with him since the end of the war. He was not at peace when he left and requested that no services be held in his honor and that his body be donated for medical research. It was a wish his family sorrowfully granted. A couple years later, his sister followed. After nearly two decades apart, Anna Dragna-Niotta was laid to rest beside her husband, Stevie. She passed on July 16, 2015.

The Other Dick Williams

With a name as common as his, Dick figured it was only a matter of time before he ran into another Richard Williams. Apparently, one was sitting right there in Naples, Italy, with him. Although each was waiting to head home, they never got the chance to meet. "I was there with what they called the Repple Depple," Dick recalled. It had been awhile since the last of the guys on his crew departed for the states. His damn lungs refused to let him leave Italy, but now it was finally his turn to see home. But before long, all the men who came to the Repple Depple were gone as well. Newer and newer arrivals kept replacing them. Groups filtered in, then checked out, but not Dick; he stayed planted.

"After about three and a half weeks I thought 'what the devil is going on here?' I knew nobody, and yet people were coming and going all the time." At last, Dick finally inquired: "I've been here a long time," he complained, which caused them to check their files. It was then that Dick discovered the problem. The paperwork they had belonged to another Richard Williams altogether—a man who had already shipped out. Someone else got his golden ticket home. Coincidently, not only did this other Dick Williams have the same name, his first four serial numbers matched as well.

The error painfully apparent, the staff pushed Dick to the front of the line. Leaving Italy, he detoured in Africa: "I got on the airplane to take off from North Africa, from Dakar to Brazil, and fortunately that DC4 has four wheels!" Dick clarified, "We had a blow out on takeoff." When the plane started jittering, he really began to worry. "I thought, after all my missions I'm going to die on the way home? Really!"

It Goes Full Circle

For his service abroad, Dick Williams was honored with several awards: "We gunners got an Air Medal after the first five missions and we got an additional Air Medal for the next ten—incremental." In all, Dick ended up with four, plus five Presidential Unit Citations. After surviving the flight back, he reentered small-town life. Looking around, he quickly noted how little had changed. They built an American Legion, which played movies in the auditorium on Saturday nights; that was about it. The same could not be said about Dick; he had been through far too much. Although the town of Cedar Bluffs did eventually see a small measure of growth, Dick was not around to witness it happen. He left Nebraska entirely.

After taking an interest in court reporting, Dick ended up in a school in Minneapolis, some six hours away. Thinking over his stay there learning the trade, Dick let out a quick laugh then dove into a humorous story about his former dorm roommate: "He had been in the Navy and we always razzed him."

Chuckling, he explained why: "You know what terrible duty he had during the war? He played in the Navy band in Hawaii!" Releasing a mess of pent up laughter, Dick chimed: "Oh God, Dean—that must have been terrible duty." Humorous as it was, when compared to what Dick and the others went through, to be selected to stay on as a musician was actually quite an honor.

Before Pearl Harbor was hit, nearly every ship had a band. Even the Marines competed in the battle of the bands. Once Americans entered the fight, though, most of the big bands were disbanded and nearly all of the musicians were put in other positions. "They realized that having a band on a ship was unnecessary," contends MSgt. Sandoval. "They retrained most of the guys because they were going into a war posture." But the music was not entirely gone: "They kept a handful of people as a fulltime band at Pearl Harbor for MWR (Morale, Welfare, and Recreation) reasons." MSgt. Sandoval's grandfather, Orville Edmiston, was chosen among this select few, as was Dick's college roommate. In all, perhaps fewer than two dozen musicians remained in Hawaii for the duration of the war. These talented young men backed a variety of famed acts such as Bob Hope, Bennie Goodman, and Artie Shaw. Few as there were, Dean and Orville probably knew each other. Hearing MSgt. Sandoval's story, Dick eloquently conveyed: "All the little coincidences in life do influence us directly."

Eventually, Dick's new profession took him further west to Nevada. It was there that he ran into one of his old crewmates from *Kentucky Colonel*: "I walked into a hotel in Reno and there was Wagner, our right waist gunner." Wagner was still in uniform, only now he wore a badge. Time had changed his old friend some, but Dick recognized him right off; his voice gave him away. Excited, Dick approached: "He was sitting with another cop in Reno, and I walked up and said, 'Hi.'" But apparently Dick had changed as well: "The last time he saw me, I was nineteen. There in Reno I was thirty-two." Wagner failed to recognize him, and in a rather "stand-offish" tone, he responded: "I don't think I know you, fella." To this, Dick simply voiced, "You don't remember, Willy?" That did the trick. It was good to see an old friend and to catch up; and it still is.

Dick enjoyed his new line of work so much that he put off retiring until the age of eighty-five. He could probably boast being the last of the breed that got the job done without email or a computer. He is now over the age of ninety, and still refuses to learn: "I always assumed I'd be dead or retired by the time it mattered. Why start now?" Despite retirement, from time to time, Dick still proofreads articles for reporters in the trade.

Commenting on what became of his childhood desire to fly, Dick relayed: "I always wanted to be around airplanes, so I just enlisted. I said, boy this is a way I can learn to fly an airplane." Although he came into the military out of a love for flight and out of a desire to pilot an aircraft, his washout during the cadet program cut short his best shot. Never a quitter, though, Dick kept the dream alive. He had a whole lifetime to keep at it, and eventually his dream came true.

After settling in Reno, he and some friends started a glider club. Dick finally learned to fly—or soar as they call it—and as a throwback to his former war days, he earned his wings on a surplus glider from World War II.

Dick married in 1958, and shortly after a Hawaiian honeymoon, he and his new bride, Beverly, started their family. In all, they had three daughters and one son. Inheriting a love for airplanes from his dad, Craig Williams flies Boeing 737s for Delta Airlines. Dick became a grandfather, too. Before becoming a cartoonist for Disney, his granddaughter, Jenessa, attended Cal Arts University. There in Santa Clarita, California, the young lady befriended a fellow student, a musician by the name of Domi LaRussa. Coincidentally, she too had a grandpa who served as a gunner on a B-17. His name was Stevenson George Niotta.

Suggested Reading

Una Storia Segreta: The Secret History of Italian American Evacuation and Internment during World War II, edited by Lawrence DiStasi
UnCivil Liberties, Stephen Fox
An Ethnic at Large, Jerre Mangione
The Lucky Bastard Club, Eugene Fletcher
The Lucky Bastard Club: Letters to my Bride, Roy R. Fisher, Jr.

Bibliography

"$25,000 Bond Set in Alien Registration," *The San Bernardino Sun*, April 23, 1941.

"4 Men Held on Lottery Charges," *Santa Ana Register*, November 21, 1936.

14th Amendment. U.S. Constitution. Retrieved from www.law.cornell.edu/constitution/amendmentxiv

"200 Aliens Housed At Former CCC Camp," *The Long Beach Independent*, December 16, 1941.

"2,944 Aliens Arrested," *The Petaluma Argus-Courier*, December 24, 1941, p. 1.

"A.C.L.U. Protests," *The San Bernardino County Sun*, February 23, 1942.

"Additional Areas for Removal to Be Named," *The Bakersfield Californian*, February 3, 1942.

"Alien Enemy Control Unified Efforts Sought," *The Los Angeles Times*, February 11, 1942.

"Alien Is Suicide," *The Petaluma Argus-Courier*, February 10, 1942, p. 11.

"Alien Orders Eased to Meet Labor Shortages," *The San Bernardino Sun,* June 28, 1942.

"Alien Plotting Bared; Spurs Coast Cleanup," *Oakland Tribune*, February 5, 1942, p. 1.

"Aliens En Route to Montana Camp," *The Los Angeles Times*, December 27, 1941.

"Aliens Flocking to Register Unit," *The Los Angeles Times*, February 4, 1941.

"Aliens Given Until Tonight To Leave," *Lubbock Morning Avalanche*, February 24, 1942, p. 6.

"Aliens to Lose Radio, Cameras," *The San Bernardino County Sun*, December 28, 1941.

"Aliens Warned," *The Richmond Item,* May 13, 1938.

Amador, T., personal interviews, ongoing beginning June 24, 2016.

"American Citizenship: Sweeping Reforms Planned," *The Los Angeles Times*, December 21, 1906, p. 5.

"American Life after Pearl Harbor," *The Saturday Evening Post,* September 8, 2016. Retrieved from www.saturdayeveningpost.com/2016/09/08/personal-essay/american-life-pearl-harbor.html.

Anderson, J., "1942 Shelling of California Coastline Stirred Conspiracy Fears: History: Submarine's attack did little damage. But it whipped up support for Japanese-American internment," *The Los Angeles Times*, March 1, 1992. Retrieved from www.latimes.com/archives/la-xpm-1992-03-01-me-5256-story.html

"An Enemy Alien, But Happy," *The Des Moines Register*, February 20, 1942, p. 4.

"Army Expels Five Italians," *The San Bernardino Sun*, October 11, 1942.

"Army May Guard All Areas Banned To Aliens," *The Los Angeles Times*, February 2, 1942.

"Army to Evacuate Aliens," *The Oregon Statesman Journal*, March 4, 1942, pp. 1-2.

"Arrest Five for Bombing of Cohen Home Near L.A.," *The Elwood* [Indiana] *Call-Leader*, February 14, 1950.

"Axis Aliens Must Surrender Radios and Cameras to Police," *The Los Angeles Times*, December 28, 1941.

"Ban On Alien Fishing Will Be Requested," *The San Bernardino Daily Sun*, January 1, 1938.

Barnes, P., *World War II from a Battleship's Bridge* [Unpublished manuscript, 1993].

Battalion History, [n.d.], 100th Infantry Battalion Veterans Education Center. Retrieved from www.100thbattalion.org/history/battalion-history/.

Bell, A., "Santa Anita Racetrack Played A Role In WWII Internment," *The Los Angeles Times*, November 8, 2009. Retrieved from articles.latimes.com/2009/nov/08/local/me-then8

Biddle, F., "Americans of Italian Origin: An Address by the Honorable Francis Biddle. The Columbus Day Celebration," October 12, 1942, Carnegie Hall, NY. Retrieved from www.justice.gov/sites/default/files/ag/legacy/2011/09/16/10-12-1942.pdf

"Biddle Lifts Ban against Italian Aliens," *The Los Angeles Times*, October 13, 1942.

"Biddle Warns Against Persecution," *The Los Angeles Times*, February 2, 1942.

Big Week, [n.d.], The United States Army Air Forces in World War II. Retrieved from permanent.access.gpo.gov/lps51153/airforcehistory/usaaf/ww2/atlanticwall/awpg4.htm.

"Board Predicts Alien Inductions," *St. Cloud Times* [Minnesota], December 29, 1943, p.7.

Boeing B-17 Flying Fortress, [n.d.], The Aviation History Online Museum. Retrieved from www.aviation-history.com/boeing/b17.html.

Branca-Santos, P., "*Injustice Ignored: The Internment of Italian-Americans during World War II*," *Pace International Law Review*, vol. 13, no. 1, pp. 151-182, 2001. Retrieved from digitalcommons.pace.edu/cgi/viewcontent.cgi?article=1207&context=pilr.

Brightwell, E., "California Fool's Gold—Exploring Lincoln Heights," *The Pueblo's Bedroom*, March 8, 2012. Retrieved from www.amoeba.com/blog/2012/03/eric-s-blog/california-fool-s-gold-exploring-lincoln-heights-the-pueblo-s-bedroom.html.

Brooke, J., "An Official Apology is Sought from U.S.," *The New York* Times, August 11, 1997. Retrieved from www.nytimes.com/1997/08/11/us/an-official-apology-is-sought-from-us.html.

Buel, A., "Who Was the 'Real' Rosie the Riveter?," September 1, 2013. Retrieved from www.centralmaine.com/2013/09/01/who-was-the-real-rosie-the-riveter__2013-08-31/.

Buntin, J., *L.A. Noir: The Struggle for the Soul of America's Most Seductive City* (Three Rivers Press, 2009).

Bushor, N., personal interview, September 13, 2016.

Campagna-Ziemantz, C., personal interviews, January 4, 2017, January 10, 2017.

Campaign Report, January 31, 1944. Retrieved from www.backtonormandy.org/the-history/air-force-operations/airplanes-allies-and-axis-lost/lancaster/RAF55833.html?tmpl=component&mapinfo=1.

Carnevale, N., "No Italian Spoken for the Duration of the War: Language, Italian-American Identity, and Cultural Pluralism in the World War II Years," *Journal of American Ethnic History*, vol. 22, no. 3, 2003.

Chawkins, S. "State Apologizes for Mistreatment of Italian Residents during WWII," *The Los Angeles Times,* August 23, 2010, pp. 102. Retrieved from articles.latimes.com/2010/aug/23/local/la-me-italians-20100823.

Chen, C., [n.d.], World War II Database. Philippines Campaign, Phase 2. Luzon: 9 Jan–15 August, 1945. Retrieved from ww2db.com/battle_spec.php?battle_id=27.

Christgau, J., *Enemies: World War II Alien Internment*, (Authors Choice Press, 2001).

"Citizenship Denied Former Ship Gambler," *The Los Angeles Times*, June 29, 1944.

"Coast's Japs Marshal Friends for Hearing," *The San Bernardino Daily Sun*, February 24, 1942.

"Comparing the American Internment of Japanese-, German-, and Italian-Americans during World War II," Institute for Research of Expelled Germans, 2009. Retrieved from expelledgermans.org/germaninternment.htm.

"Congress Aids Women to Regain Citizenship," *The Fresno Bee*, June 23, 1940, p. 3-A.

Crews, [n.d.], 388th Bomb Group. Retrieved from www.388bg.info/Crews.html.

Crowl, P., and Love, E., *United States Army in World War II. The War in the Pacific. Seizure of the Gilberts and Marshalls* (Center of Military History, 1993). Retrieved from www.history.army.mil/html/books/005/5-6-1/CMH_Pub_5-6-1.pdf.

"Curfew Restriction Provided as Meanderings of Aliens Curtailed," *The San Bernardino Daily Sun*, February 5, 1942.

Daniels, R., and Olin, S., *Racism in California: A Reader in the History of Oppression* (New York: Macmillan Company, 1972).

Dedicated to the Officers & Men: War History of the U.S.S. Mississippi, 1945.

"Deny Citizenship to Jack Dragna," *Nevada State Journal*, June 30, 1940.

DeZeng, H. L. IV, *Luftwaffe Airfields 1935–45:* France, July 2017. Retrieved from www.ww2.dk/Airfields%20-%20France.pdf.

DiStasi, L., (ed.), *Una Storia Segreta: The Secret History of Italian American Evacuation and Internment during World War II* (Heyday Books, 2001).

Dorr, R., "Actor Clark Gable Served in Uniform, Flew Combat Missions in World War II," *Defense Media Network*, August 11, 2010. Retrieved from www.defensemedianetwork.com/stories/clark-gable-served-in-uniform-flew-combat-missions-in-world-war-ii/.

Dragna, A., personal interviews, 2015.

"Drivers Advised to Analyze Cars' Use," *The San Bernardino Daily Sun*, February 24, 1942.

Dunn, G., "Mala Notte," *Una Storia Segreta: The Secret History of Italian American Evacuation and Internment during World War* II, edited by Lawrence DiStasi, pp. 103-114 (Heyday Books, 2001).

Elkins, A., 'The Origins of Stop-and-Frisk,' *Jacobin Magazine*, May 9, 2015. Retrieved from www.jacobinmag.com/2015/05/stop-and-frisk-dragnet-ferguson-baltimore/.

"Employment: To Reach 62,500,000," *Woodstock Daily Sentinel*, October 17, 1942.

"Enemy Aliens Get U.S. Cards," *The San Bernardino County Sun*, January 16, 1942.

"English Ace Visits Sisters Here," *The Los Angeles Daily News*, unknown date, 1945.

Evans, M., "Roy E. Wendell Dies; World War II Veteran, PR Executive was 91," *Newsday*, February 23, 2016. Retrieved from www.newsday.com/long-island/obituaries/roy-e-wendell-dies-world-war-ii-veteran-pr-executive-was-91-1.11503041.

Executive Order 9066. Authorizing the Secretary of War to Prescribe Military Zones. February 19, 1942. Retrieved from www.foitimes.com/internment/EO9066.html.

"FBI Tightens Curb on 256,000 Aliens," *The New York Times*, April 1, 1942, p. 23. Retrieved from www.foitimes.com/internment/NYTimes.jpg.

"Fifty-Ninth Congress. Closing Session," *The Los Angeles Times*, February 28, 1907, p. 4.

"First Evacuation of Axis Aliens Completed," *The Bakersfield Californian*, February 16, 1942.

"Flying Baroness Once A Guest At White House, Held as Alien," *St. Louis Post-Dispatch*, December 10, 1941, p. 3-A.

"Forts Blast Bremen, RAF Hits Struttgart," *The Stars and Stripes*, December 16, 1943. Retrieved from www.stelzriede.com/ms/html/mshwm17.htm.

"Forts Blast Frankfurt; Kassel Hit," *The Stars and Stripes*, October 5, 1944. Retrieved from www.stelzriede.com/ms/html/mshwm24.htm.

Fox, S., *UnCivil Liberties: Italian Americans Under Siege During World War II* (Universal, 2010).

"Frank Dragna Sues Police for $350,000 in Damages," *The Los Angeles Times*, April 8, 1950.

Frank Dragna vs. White. November 4, 1955. Retrieved from scocal.stanford.edu/opinion/dragna-v-white-26712.

"Frankfurt Blasted by Fortresses," *The Stars and Stripes*, February 9, 1944. Retrieved from www.wartimepress.com/archive-publication.asp?TID=The Stars and Stripes - London 1944 02 09&MID=The Stars and Stripes - London 1944 January - April&q=9327&FID=1120.

"Free Italians in Americas Vow Solidarity with Allies," *The Courier-Journal* (Louisville, KY), August 17, 1942.

"German Aliens Curfew is Lifted," *The Petaluma Argus-Courier*, December 24, 1942, p. 1.

"German Aliens May Celebrate," *The Ogden Standard-Examiner*, December 24, 1942, p.1.

Gold, M., "Era Ends as 78-Year-Old Men's Store Calls It Quits," *The Los Angeles Times*, October 4, 1999. Retrieved from articles.latimes.com/1999/oct/04/local/me-18604.

Goldin, C., and Katz, L., "The Power of the Pill: Oral Contraceptives and Women's Career and Marriage Decisions," *Journal of Political Economy*, vol. 110, no. 4, pp. 730-770, 2002. Retrieved from dash.harvard.edu/bitstream/handle/1/2624453/Goldin_PowerPill.pdf?sequence=4.

Gonella, F., "Sundays in Colma," *Una Storia Segreta: The Secret History of Italian American Evacuation and Internment during World War II*, edited by Lawrence DiStasi, pp. 37-38 (Heyday Books, 2001).

Grinnell, B., personal interview, December 7, 2016.

Guarnieri, B., personal interview, November 24, 2016.

Guarnieri, J., personal interview, November 24, 2016.

"Gunmen Rule West Coast Underworld," *Once Star-Banner*, February 9, 1962.

Hacker, M., "When Saying 'I Do' Meant Giving Up Your U.S. Citizenship," *Prologue*, Summer 1998. Retrieved from www.archives.gov/files/publications/prologue/2014/spring/citizenship.pdf.

"High School Yearbooks from World War II," The National WWII Museum. Retrieved from www.ww2yearbooks.org/home/#books.

Hillson, F., "Barrage Balloons for Low-Level Air Defense," *Airpower Journal,* Summer 1989. Retrieved from www.airpower.maxwell.af.mil/airchronicles/apj/apj89/sum89/hillson.html.

Hoover, J. E., "Alien Enemy Control," *Iowa Law Review,* vol. 29, March 1944, pp. 396-408.

Hull, W. R., and Druxman, M., *Family Secret* (Hats Off Books, 2004).

Huntzinger, E., *The 388th at War* (Newsfoto Yearbooks, 1979).

"Hysteria Against Aliens To Be Kept Down," *The Bakersfield Californian*, December 9, 1941.

"I. G. Farben: I.G. Farbenindustrie AG German Industry and the Holocaust," Holocaust Education & Archive Research Team, 2010. Retrieved from www.holocaustresearchproject.org/economics/igfarben.html.

"In Defense of Our Country," *Altre Voci*, vol. 24, no. 3, 2005. Retrieved from www.italiancenter.net/pdfs/newsletter_archives/2005-05.pdf.

"Inspiration for Iconic Rosie the Riveter Image Dies," *History*, December 30, 2010. Retrieved from www.history.com/news/inspiration-for-iconic-rosie-the-riveter-image-dies.

Irvine *v*. California, United States Supreme Court, No. 12, February 8, 1954. Retrieved from caselaw.findlaw.com/us-supreme-court/347/128.html.

"Isadora Duncan to Land Today at Ellis Island," *The Washington Times*, October 2, 1922.

"Italian Aliens Win Freedom to Aid in War," *The San Bernardino County Sun,* October 13, 1942.

"Italian American Racism During the WWII Era, & Italian Slur and Slang Definitions," [n.d.], Winshaw Historical Society. Retrieved from www.wishaw.50megs.com/_/Italian_American_Racism.html.

Kamisar, Y., "On the Tactics of Police-Prosecution Oriented Critics of the Courts," *Cornell Law Review*, vol. 43, no. 3, 1964. Retrieved from scholarship.law.cornell.edu/cgi/viewcontent.cgi?article=2428&context=clr.

Kashima, T., *Judgment without Trial: Japanese American Internment during World War II* (University of Washington Press, 2003)

Kearney, M., "It Was a Tough Year But 'Mom' Did Her Job," *The Long Beach Independent*, December 26, 1943, p. 6.

Kent, M., *U.S.S. Arizona's Last Band: The History of U.S. Navy Band Number 22* (Silent Song, 1996).

"Kern Italians to Hold Bond Drive," *The Bakersfield Californian*, October 26, 1943, p. 9.

Kerr, G., *Okinawa: The History of an Island People* (Tuttle Publishing, 2011).

Lacovetta, F., Perin, R., and Principe, A., *Enemies Within: Italian and Other Internees in Canada and Abroad* (University of Toronto Press, 2000).

"L.A. Gangster is Indicted for Tax Evasion," *Santa Cruz Sentinel-News*, March 11, 1954.

Law, A., "Women Do Lot to Keep 'Em Flying. Tour of Plane Plant Reveals Proportion High," *The Los Angeles Times*, November 28, 1943, p. 13.

"Lehman Orders Purge of Aliens in National Guard; Aims at Nazis," *The Brooklyn Daily Eagle*, March 13, 1938.

Leighton, A., *Governing of Men: General Principles and Recommendations Based on Experience at a Japanese Relocation Camp* (Princeton University Press, 1945).

Lingayen Gulf, [n.d.], Pacific Wrecks, Inc. Retrieved from www.pacificwrecks.com/provinces/philippines_lingayen_gulf.html.

Lothrop, G., "Unwelcome in Freedom's Land: The Impact of World War II on Italian Aliens in Southern California," *Una Storia Segreta: The Secret History of Italian American Evacuation and Internment during World War* II, edited by Lawrence DiStasi, pp. 161-194 (Heyday Books, 2001)

MacMillen, F., "War Pinch Hits Civilians as New Cars Rationed," *The Los Angeles Times*, January 4, 1942.

Maggio, C., *Swinging for the Fences: How American Legion Baseball Transformed a Group of Boys into a Team of Men* (Wheatmark, 2013).

Mangione, J., *An Ethnic At Large: A Memoir of America in the Thirties and Forties* (Putnam, 1978).

Mangione, J., "Concentration Camps—American Style," *Una Storia Segreta: The Secret History of Italian American Evacuation and Internment during World War* II, edited by Lawrence DiStasi, pp. 117-131 (Heyday Books, 2001).

"Many Declared to Be Escaping Internment; Biddle Leniency Flayed," *The Los Angeles Times*, March 12, 1942.

"Mapping L.A. Eastside. Boyle Heights," [n.d.], *The Los Angeles Times*. Retrieved from maps.latimes.com/neighborhoods/neighborhood/boyle-heights/.

Marcano, T., "Famed Riveter in War Effort, Rose Monroe Dies at 77," *The New York Times,* June 2, 1997. Retrieved from www.nytimes.com/1997/06/02/us/famed-riveter-in-war-effort-rose-monroe-dies-at-77.html.

"Martial Law Possible in Alien Ouster," *The Los Angeles Times*, February 9, 1942.

"Martial Rule in Effect on Coast," *Santa Ana Register*, August 22, 1942.

Martone, E., editor. *Italian Americans: The History and Culture of a People* (ABC-CLIO, 2016).

Massock, R., "Collapse in Italy Seems Unlikely," *The San Bernardino Daily Sun*, May 17, 1942.

"May Affect Immigration: House Committee on Foreign Affairs Seeks Light Regarding Laws and Practices," *The Los Angeles Herald*, July 10, 1906, p. 1.

McGrath, C., "Rosie the Riveter, a Reluctant Symbol of Patriarchy: The Evolution of an American Icon," 2012. Retrieved from msu.edu/~mcgrat71/Writing/Rosie%20the%20Riveter,%20a%20Reluctant%20Symbol%20of%20Patriarchy.pdf.

"Mexico Clears Sonora of All Enemy Aliens," *The Long Beach Independent*, March 10, 1942.

"Milestones of the Italian American Experience," The National Italian American Foundation. Retrieved from milestones.niaf.org/year_1945.asp.

"Military Control of Aliens Advocated," *The Los Angeles Times,* February 12, 1942.

"Militia No Place for Aliens," *The Philadelphia Inquirer*, March 15, 1938.

Mission 47—Bremen, Germany, [n.d.], 388th Bomb Group. Retrieved from www.388bg.info/servlet/Controller?pageType=detail&id=388-M047&dataType=Mission.

"Mob Violence in State is Feared," *La Grande Observer*, March 2, 1942, p. 1.

Neufield, W., *Slingshot Warbirds: World War II U.S. Navy Scout-Observation Airmen* (McFarland & Company, 2003).

"New Guinea Campaign: Aitape and the Driniumor River," [n.d.], The 32nd "Red Arrow" Veteran Association. Retrieved from www.32nd-division.org/history/ww2/32ww2-7.html.

"New Jap Bans Expected Today," *The Los Angeles Times,* January 31, 1942, p. 1.

"News on Defense: Gleaned from Bulletins of San Bernardino County Defense Council," *Chino Champion*, January 30, 1942.

Niotta, G., personal interview, August 28, 2016.

Niotta, J., personal interviews, ongoing beginning in 2016.

Niotta, J., personal interview, October 11, 2016.

Niotta, J. M., "American Women Los Citizenship After Marrying Aliens," July 18, 2017. Retrieved from www.jmichaelniotta.com/single-post/2017/07/18/"American-Women-Los-Citizenship-After-Marying-Aliens"; *Jack Dragna: Beneath the Hollywood Mafia Mask* (Unfinished manuscript, 2019); "Rosie the Ethnic Riveter," April 11, 2017. Retrieved from www.jmichaelniotta.com/single-post/2017/04/11/Rosie-the-ethnic-Riveter; *The Los Angeles Sugar Ring: Inside the World of Old Money, Bootleggers, & Gambling Barons* (South Carolina: The History Press, 2017).

Niotta-LaRussa, F., personal interviews, ongoing beginning June 22, 2016.

Niotta, S. G., Flight Book, 1943–1944.

"No Change on Coast," *The San Bernardino Sun*, October 13, 1942.

"No Eggs, No Butter, Little Meat Served Japanese at Manzanar, OWI States," *The Long Beach Independent*, January 29, 1943.

"No Output Now in Me109 Plant at Regensburg," *The Stars and Stripes*, February, 1944.

Northern Solomons Campaign, [n.d.], U.S. Army Divisions in World War II, *History Shots Info Art*. Retrieved from www.historyshotsinfoart.com/usarmy/DisplayCampaign.cfm?inCID=7.

"Northrop Workers Show 35,000 Visitors How Planes Are Built," *The Los Angeles Times*, December 28, 1942.

"N.Y. to Out Aliens from Guard Units," *Oakland Tribune*, March 14, 1938.

"Oppose Removal of Japs to Kern Areas," *The Bakersfield Californian*, February 20, 1942.

Palmer, R., Wiley, B., and Keast, W., *United States Army in World War II: The Army Ground Forces - The Procurement and Training of Ground Combat Troops* (Center of Military History, 1991). Retrieved from www.history.army.mil/html/books/002/2-2/CMH_Pub_2-2.pdf.

Peenemunde, [n.d.], Weapons of Mass Destruction. Retrieved from www.globalsecurity.org/wmd/ops/peenemunde.htm.

Phillips, R., "Tempo: Rosie the Riveter Won a War, Started a Revolt," *Chicago Tribune*, February 21, 1982.

"Pittsburg Italians Hard Hit by Alien Rule," *Oakland Tribune*, February 5, 1942, p. 4-D.

"Placards Placed Barring Aliens in Marin," *Mill Valley Record*, February 13, 1942.

"Plans Made to Assist Aliens in Evacuation," *The Los Angeles Times*, February 12, 1942, p. 8.

Poli-Quinn, F., personal interview, October 19, 2016.

Poli, T., personal interview, 2016.

Potter, G., and Getz, L., "Oschersleben, 11 January 1944," March 17, 2015. Retrieved from www.ideals.illinois.edu/handle/2142/73399.

"President Signs Repatriation Bill: Citizenship Restored to Wives of Aliens," *The Los Angeles Times*, July 4, 1940, p. 3.

Presidential Proclamation. No. 2525. Alien Enemies—Japanese. December 7, 1941. Retrieved from www.foitimes.com/internment/Proc2525.html.

Presidential Proclamation. No. 2526. Alien Enemies—German. December 8, 1941. Retrieved from www.foitimes.com/internment/Proc2526.html.

Presidential Proclamation. No. 2527. Alien Enemies—Italian. December 8, 1941. Retrieved from www.foitimes.com/internment/Proc2527.html.

"Prisoner Among Us: Italian American Identity & World War II," Teacher's Guide, 2005, The National Italian-American Foundation. Retrieved from prisonersamongus. com/StudyGuide.pdf.

"Proceedings Against Jack Dragna for Contempt of the Senate," 82nd Congress, 1st Session, Report No. 32, January 22, 1951.

"Protection for Rosie," *Santa Cruz Sentinel*, May 5, 1943, p. 1.

"Pt. Reyes Alien Is Suicide; Shoots Self In Head," *San Anselmo Herald*, February 5, 1942, p. 2.

Puleo, S., *The Boston Italians: A Story of Pride, Perseverance, and Paesani, from the Years of the Great Immigration to the Present Day* (Beacon Press, 2007)

"Rationing Cards Prove Problem," *The Los Angeles Times*, March 6, 1942.

Ray, M., "Selective Service Acts," *Encyclopedia Britannica*, September 10, 2015. Retrieved from www.britannica.com/topic/Selective-Service-Acts#Article-History.

"Regulations Stiffened for Enemy Aliens," *The San Bernardino County Sun*, January 22, 1942.

"Request Made By Roosevelt Stirs Congress," *Delphos Daily Herald* [Ohio], June 1, 1940, p. 1.

"Restrictions on Aliens Enforced," *Oakland Tribune*, February 5, 1942, p. 4.

"Rifleman 745," *Military Yearbook Project,* November 29, 2010. Retrieved from militaryyearbookproject.com/references/old-mos-codes/wwii-era/army-wwii-codes/ gunnery-and-gunnery-control/rifleman-745.

Rizzotto, M., personal interview, March 26, 2019.

"Rose Bonavita Hickey: A Real Wartime Rosie the Riveter Votes for Working Women," *Chicago Tribune*, February 21, 1982. Retrieved from archives.chicagotribune. com/1982/02/21/page/273/article/rose-bonavita-hickey.

Rosenfeld, A., "Neither Aliens Nor Enemies: The Hearings of German and Italian Internees in Wartime Hawai'I," *Social Process in Hawai'i*, vol. 44, 2013. Retrieved from uhwohum300.files.wordpress.com/2016/09/rosenfeld_proof_2.pdf.

"Rosie the Riveter," [n.d.], *American National Biography Online*. Retrieved from www. anb.org/articles/20/20-01920.html.

Rubottom Crew, [n.d.], 388th Bomb Group. Retrieved from www.388bg.info/servlet/ Controller?pageType=detail&id=388-C401&dataType=Crew.

"Ruling on Voting Status of Women Married to Aliens," *St. Louis Post-Dispatch*, September 27, 1922, p. 15.

Russell, J., *The Train to Crystal City: FDR's Secret Prisoner Exchange Program and America's Only Family Internment Camp During World War II* (Scribner, 2016).

Sandoval, S., personal interview, October 2, 2016.

"Says War Can't Be Won on Basis of 40-Hour Week," *Santa Ana Register,* March 14, 1942.

Scherini, R., "When Italian Americans Were Enemy Aliens," *Una Storia Segreta: The Secret History of Italian American Evacuation and Internment during World War* II, edited by Lawrence DiStasi, pp. 10-31 (Heyday Books, 2001).

Schwaller, S., "The Harsh Realities of Warfare," U.S. Army Heritage and Education Center, February 14, 2011. Retrieved from www.army.mil/article/51848/The_Harsh_ Realities_of_Warfare.

"Secret of WWII: Italian-Americans Forced To Move Were Branded Enemy Aliens," *CNN Interactive,* September 21, 1997. Retrieved from www.cnn.com/US/9709/21/italian.relocation/.

Shell, B., [n.d.], Interview. Retrieved from www.youtube.com/watch?v=pInWH5OORA8.

"Sheriff, City Police To Take Up Equipment," *The San Bernardino County Sun,* December 29, 1941.

Shippey, L., "The Brave New World," *The Los Angeles Times,* January 16, 1943, p. 4.

Smith, R., *The War in the Pacific: Triumph in the Philippines* (Washington, D. C.: Center of Military History, 1993). Retrieved from history.army.mil/html/books/005/5-10-1/CMH_Pub_5-10-1.pdf.

Snyder, J., "No New Cars, but that Didn't Stop U.S. Automakers: Dealers during WWII," *Automotive News,* October 31, 2011. Retrieved from www.autonews.com/article/20111031/CHEVY100/310319970?template=print.

"State's Drive on Illicit Gambling Will Be Pressed," *The Fresno Bee,* July 31, 1937, p. 1.

Strebig, J., "Alien Detention Camps to Be Expanded Three-Fold by U.S.," *Oakland Tribune,* November 18, 1941, p. 1.

"Successful Invasion of Kwajalein, 1944. We Did Learn from Tarawa," Smith, S. E., editor, *The United States Navy in World War II* (Morrow & Co., 1966). Retrieved from saltofamerica.com/contents/displayArticle.aspx?18_435.

Sundin, S., "Today in World War II History—Jan. 11, 1944," *Sarah's Blog.* Retrieved from www.sarahsundin.com/today-in-world-war-ii-history-jan-11-1944/.

Sundrin, L., [n.d.], "Veni Vedi Vici." Retrieved from franckruffino.chez.com/My-Site/B-17%2042-30661.htm.

Susan Miller Dorsey High School, Year Book, Los Angeles, 1942.

Sylvernale, G., "Alien in Texas," *Una Storia Segreta: The Secret History of Italian American Evacuation and Internment during World War* II, edited by Lawrence DiStasi, pp. 196-197 (Heyday Books, 2001).

"The Axis, The Azores, and America," *The Los Angeles Times,* March 19, 1941.

"The Old Missy (USS Mississippi BB-41): It Was Up to BB41 to Crack the Shuri Line," *Our Navy,* November 1, 1945. Retrieved from www.wartimepress.com/archive-article.asp?TID=The%20Old%20Missy%20(%20USS%20Mississippi%20BB-41%20)&MID=68&q=184&FID=752.

The Saturday Evening Post, May 29, 1943.

Time, September 10, 2007.

Tintori, G., "New Discoveries, Old Prejudices: The Internment of Italian Americans during World War II," *Una Storia Segreta: The Secret History of Italian American Evacuation and Internment during World War* II, edited by Lawrence DiStasi, pp. 236-254 (Heyday Books, 2001).

"Tires: Limit is Five," *Woodstock Daily Sentinel,* October 17, 1942.

Treanor, T., "The Home Front," *The Los Angeles Times,* December 24, 1941.

TSgt. Stevenson G. Niotta, [n.d.], 388th Bomb Group. Retrieved from www.388bg.info/servlet/Controller?pageType=detail&id=388-I-NIO01-01&dataType=Crewman.

Unbroken. Directed by Angelina Jolie, 2014.

United States Army, *The Capture of Makin: 20–24 November 1943* (Washington, D.C.: Center of Military History, 1990). Retrieved from www.history.army.mil/html/books/100/100-2/CMH_Pub_100-2.pdf.

United States, Congress, House, Select Committee Investigating National Defense Migration. Hearings on National Defense Migration, 77th Congress, 1st session, pp. 1-360 (Government Printing Office, February 21 and 23, 1942). Retrieved from archive.org/stream/nationaldefensem29unit/nationaldefensem29unit_djvu.txt.

"U.S. Army Aliens Removed From Ban," *The New York Times*, February 24, 1942.

U.S. Department of Justice, *Report to the Congress of the United States: A Review of the Restrictions on Persons of Italian Ancestry during World War II* (2001). Retrieved from www.schino.com/pdf/italian.pdf.

"U.S. District Attorney Starts Hearings Tomorrow for 445 Enemy Aliens," *The Long Beach Independent*, December 21, 1941.

"U.S. Italians Make Plea to Roosevelt," *The New York Times*, January 11, 1942.

"U.S.S. Honolulu (CL-48)," [n.d.], Pacific Wrecks, Inc. Retrieved from www.pacificwrecks.com/ships/usn/CL-48.html.

"U.S.S. West Virginia (BB-48)," *Dictionary of American Naval Fighting Ships*. Retrieved from www.usswestvirginia.org/uss_west_virginia_history.htm.

"Veni Vidi Vici," [n.d.], *Wings Palette*. Retrieved from wp.scn.ru/en/ww2/b/439/5255/0.

"Violators of Curfew Regulations Rounded Up," *Santa Ana Register*, August 22, 1942.

"Wages Hiked for Almost Two Million," *The Ogden Standard Examiner*, December 24, 1942.

Watkins, J., "Expatriation of Thousands of Truant Americans," *The Evening Star* (Washington), November 30, 1907.

"Weather, Morale Dog 388th Efforts during Winter Months," *Fortress For Freedom*, vol. 58, no. 4, Winter 2003, pp. 14-19. Retrieved from www.388bg.info/sources/newsletters/2003Winter.pdf.

"West Coast Is Warned To Be On Alert For Holiday Attack," *Santa Ana Register*, December 30, 1941, p. 1.

Whitehead, D., "Men From Hawaii Fight in Italy," *St. Cloud Times* (Minnesota), December 29, 1943, p. 7.

Williams, R., personal interviews, ongoing beginning June 24, 2016.

Wilson, B., "Carl Maggio Octogenarian," *Discover*, April 12, 2016. Retrieved from www.discovertheregion.com/carl-paul-maggio-octogenarian/.

"Woman's Equality in Citizenship," *The Philadelphia Inquirer*, October 12, 1922.

"World War II 8th AAF Combat Chronology: January 1944 through June 1944," [n.d.], Eighth Air Force Historical Society. Retrieved from 8thafhs.org/combat1944a.htm.

"World War II Enemy Alien Control Program Overview," [n.d.], *National Archives*. Retrieved from www.archives.gov/research/immigration/enemy-aliens-overview.html.

"World War II: Italian Americans," Senate Concurrent Resolution No. 95, August 27, 2010. Retrieved from leginfo.legislature.ca.gov/faces/billTextClient.xhtml?bill_id=200920100SCR95.

"World War II Rationing," [n.d.], United States History. Retrieved from www.u-s-history.com/pages/h1674.html.

Wright, G., [n.d.], WWII Secret: Italian-Americans Internment as Alien Enemies. Retrieved from www.ejournalncrp.org/wwii-secret-italian-americans-internment-as-alien-enemies/.

Yakushik, J., *Aboard the U.S.S. Mississippi BB41. January 2, 1944 to May 1946. A Day by Day Account of the Following Battles as Recorded by John Yakushik, EM 2/C* (Unpublished Manuscript)

Yollin, P., "A Secret History: The Harassment of Italians during World War II has Particular Relevance Today and Serves as a Warning of What Could Happen," *SF Gate,* October 21, 2001. Retrieved from www.sfgate.com/magazine/article/A-SECRET-HISTORY-The-harassment-of-Italians-2866287.php.

Young, C., "Kamikaze-The Divine Tempest Was a Devil on Wings off Okinawa," *Our Navy,* November 1, 1945.

Zimmer, J., *The History of the 43rd Infantry Division, 1941–1945* (Merriam Press, 2005).

Index

About the Author

Dr. J. Michael Niotta, author of *The Los Angeles Sugar Ring*, is an Iraqi Freedom veteran with over eighteen years of military service. The San Diego native was among the first cohort of the Rosie Network's Service 2 C.E.O. program for military entrepreneurs, and lectured on empowerment at the 2018 Service Member of the Year Awards (SMOY) in Anaheim, California. In 2019, he co-developed and instructed curriculum for the Air National Guard's statewide military leadership program, the California Force Development Course (C.F.D.C.).

As the eldest great-grandson of Los Angeles Godfather Jack I. Dragna, the realm of true crime has long been an area of interest. For Niotta, delving into SoCal's sordid past to clear up the conjecture has become a near obsession. Years of research and interview spill heavily into his work as an author, crime journalist, and even as a mixed-media artist. In 2018, he lectured at the Las Vegas Mob & Law Enforcement Museum, and headlined a panel at the Las Vegas MobWorld Summit. He has also appeared on the Travel Channel show *Mission Declassified* as a Southern California organized crime S.M.E. Niotta pens the column "The Early Days of Los Angeles" for the *National Crime Syndicate* website, and is currently engaged in several non-fiction projects. This includes a Jack Dragna biography, an inside look at the narcotics trade between Mexico and San Diego during the 1980s, and an early history of organized crime in Southern California, which he is co-authoring with longtime mafia researcher Richard N. Warner. www.jmichaelniotta.com

Dr. J. Michael Niotta, Los Angeles, Belgium Lion Photography.